ABOUT THIS PUBLICATION

FOR SERVICE ASSISTANCE

Customer Service Department
704.898.0770

North Carolina General Statues is published by The Muliti-Media Group of Greater Charlotte in Charlotte, North Carolina. Copyright 2015 by the Multi-Media Group of Greater Charlotte. This book or parts thereof may not be reproduced in any form, stored in a retrieval system, or transmitted in any form by any means—electronic, mechanical, photocopy, recording or otherwise—without prior written permission of the publisher, except as provided by United States of America copyright law.

The records required by U.S. Code 2257(a) through (c) and the pertinent regulations 28 C.F.R. Cli. 1, Part 75 with respect to this publication and all materials associated with such records are maintained by The Multi-Media Group of Greater Charlotte, Publisher and available for review by Attorney General.

www.visionbooks.org

Copyright © 2015 by MMGGC
All rights reserved!

TID: 4989514
ISBN (10) digit: 1502305984
ISBN (13) digit: 978-1502305985

123-4-56789-01240-Paperback
123-4-56789-01240-Hardback

First Edition

090520140547

Printed in the United States of America

2015 EDITION

North Carolina Criminal Law And Procedure-Pamphlet # 7

Printed In conjunction with the Administration of the Courts

North Carolina Criminal Law and Procedure
Pamphlet Reference Guide

Chapters	Pamphlet
Chapter 1 Civil Procedure	1
Chapter 1 Civil Procedure (Continue)	2
Chapter 1A Rules of Civil Procedure	2
Chapter 1B Contribution.	2
Chapter 1C Enforcement of Judgments.	2
Chapter 1D Punitive Damages.	2
Chapter 1E Eastern Band of Cherokee Indians.	2
Chapter 1F North Carolina Uniform Interstate Depositions and Discovery Act.	2
Chapter 2 - Clerk of Superior Court [Repealed and Transferred.]	3
Chapter 3 - Commissioners of Affidavits and Deeds [Repealed.]	3
Chapter 4 - Common Law	3
Chapter 5 - Contempt [Repealed.]	3
Chapter 5A - Contempt	3
Chapter 6 - Liability for Court Costs	3
Chapter 7 - Courts [Repealed and Transferred.]	3
Chapter 7A – Judicial Department	3
Chapter 7A – Continuation (Judicial Department)	4
Chapter 7A – Continuation (Judicial Department)	5
Chapter 7B - Juvenile Code	5
Chapter 8 - Evidence	6
Chapter 8A - Interpreters for Deaf Persons [Recodified.]	6
Chapter 8B - Interpreters for Deaf Persons	6
Chapter 8C - Evidence Code	6
Chapter 9 - Jurors	6
Chapter 10 - Notaries [Repealed.]	6
Chapter 10A - Notaries [Recodified.]	6
Chapter 10B - Notaries	6
Chapter 11 - Oaths	6
Chapter 12 - Statutory Construction	6
Chapter 13 - Citizenship Restored	6
Chapter 14 - Criminal Law	7
Chapter 14 –Criminal Law (Continuation)	8
Chapter 15 - Criminal Procedure	9
Chapter 15A - Criminal Procedure Act (Continuation)	10
Chapter 15A - Criminal Procedure Act (Continuation)	11
Chapter 15B - Victims Compensation	11
Chapter 15C - Address Confidentiality Program	11
Chapter 16 - Gaming Contracts and Futures	11
Chapter 17 - Habeas Corpus	11

Chapter 17A - Law-Enforcement Officers [Recodified.]	11
Chapter 17B - North Carolina Criminal Justice Education and Training System [Recodified.] Chapter 17C - North Carolina Criminal Justice Education and Training Standards Commission	11 11
Chapter 17D - North Carolina Justice Academy	11
Chapter 17E - North Carolina Sheriffs' Education and Training Standards Commission	11
Chapter 18 - Regulation of Intoxicating Liquors [Repealed.]	12
Chapter 18A - Regulation of Intoxicating Liquors [Repealed.]	12
Chapter 18B - Regulation of Alcoholic Beverages	12
Chapter 18C - North Carolina State Lottery	12
Chapter 19 - Offenses against Public Morals	12
Chapter 19A - Protection of Animals	12
Chapter 20 - Motor Vehicles	13
Chapter 20 - Motor Vehicles (Continuation)	14
Chapter 20 - Motor Vehicles (Continuation)	15
Chapter 20 - Motor Vehicles (Continuation)	16
Chapter 21 - Bills of Lading	17
Chapter 22 - Contracts Requiring Writing	17
Chapter 22A - Signatures	17
Chapter 22B - Contracts Against Public Policy	17
Chapter 22C - Payments to Subcontractors	17
Chapter 23 - Debtor and Creditor. r 24 - Interest	17
Chapter 24 – Interest	17
Chapter 25 – Uniform Commercial Code	18
Chapter 25 – Uniform Commercial Code (Continuation)	19
Chapter 25A – Retail Installment Sales Act	20
Chapter 25B - Credit	20
Chapter 25C - Sales of Artwork	20
Chapter 26 - Suretyship	20
Chapter 27 - Warehouse Receipts [Repealed.]	20
Chapter 28 - Administration [Repealed.]	20
Chapter 28A - Administration of Decedents' Estates	20
Chapter 28B - Estates of Absentees in Military Service	20
Chapter 28C - Estates of Missing Persons	20
Chapter 29 - Intestate Succession	21
Chapter 30 - Surviving Spouses	21
Chapter 31 - Wills	21
Chapter 31A - Acts Barring Property Rights	21
Chapter 31B - Renunciation of Property and Renunciation of Fiduciary Powers Act	21
Chapter 31C - Uniform Disposition of Community Property Rights at Death Act	21
Chapter 32 - Fiduciaries	21
Chapter 32A - Powers of Attorney	21
Chapter 33 - Guardian and Ward [Repealed and Recodified.]	21

Chapter 33A - North Carolina Uniform Transfers to Minors Act	21
Chapter 33B - North Carolina Uniform Custodial Trust Act	21
Chapter 34 - Veterans' Guardianship Act	22
Chapter 35 - Sterilization Procedures	22
Chapter 35A - Incompetency and Guardianship	22
Chapter 36 - Trusts and Trustees [Repealed.]	22
Chapter 36A - Trusts and Trustees	22
Chapter 36B - Uniform Management of Institutional Funds Act [Repealed.]	22
Chapter 36C - North Carolina Uniform Trust Code	22
Chapter 36D - North Carolina Community Third Party Trusts, Pooled Trusts	23
Chapter 36E - Uniform Prudent Management of Institutional Funds Act	23
Chapter 37 - Allocation of Principal and Income [Repealed.]	23
Chapter 37A - Uniform Principal and Income Act	23
Chapter 38 - Boundaries	23
Chapter 38A - Landowner Liability	23
Chapter 39 - Conveyances	23
Chapter 39A - Transfer Fee Covenants Prohibited	23
Chapter 40 - Eminent Domain [Repealed.]	23
Chapter 40A - Eminent Domain	23
Chapter 41 - Estates	23
Chapter 41A - State Fair Housing Act	23
Chapter 42 - Landlord and Tenant	23
Chapter 42A - Vacation Rental Act	23
Chapter 43 - Land Registration	23
Chapter 44 - Liens	24
Chapter 44A - Statutory Liens and Charges	24
Chapter 45 - Mortgages and Deeds of Trust	24
Chapter 45A - Good Funds Settlement Act	24
Chapter 46 - Partition	24
Chapter 47 - Probate and Registration	25
Chapter 47A - Unit Ownership	25
Chapter 47B - Real Property Marketable Title Act	25
Chapter 47C - North Carolina Condominium Act	25
Chapter 47D - Notice of Settlement Act [Expired.]	25
Chapter 47E - Residential Property Disclosure Act	25
Chapter 47F - North Carolina Planned Community Act	25
Chapter 47G - Option to Purchase Contracts	25
Chapter 47H - Contracts for Deed	25
Chapter 48 - Adoptions	26
Chapter 48A - Minors	26
Chapter 49 - Bastardy	26
Chapter 49A - Rights of Children	26
Chapter 50 - Divorce and Alimony	26
Chapter 50A - Uniform Child-Custody Jurisdiction and	

Enforcement Act	26
Chapter 50B - Domestic Violence	26
Chapter 50C - Civil No-Contact Orders	26
Chapter 51 - Marriage	26
Chapter 52 - Powers and Liabilities of Married Persons	27
Chapter 52A - Uniform Reciprocal Enforcement of Support Act [Repealed.]	27
Chapter 52B - Uniform Premarital Agreement Act	27
Chapter 52C - Uniform Interstate Family Support Act	27
Chapter 53 - Banks	27
Chapter 53A - Business Development Corporations and North Carolina Capital Resource Corporations	28
Chapter 53B - Financial Privacy Act	28
Chapter 54 - Cooperative Organizations	28
Chapter 54A - Capital Stock Savings and Loan Associations [Repealed.]	28
Chapter 54B - Savings and Loan Associations	29
Chapter 54C - Savings Banks	29
Chapter 55 - North Carolina Business Corporation Act	30
Chapter 55A - North Carolina Nonprofit Corporation Act	31
Chapter 55B - Professional Corporation Act	31
Chapter 55C - Foreign Trade Zones	31
Chapter 55D - Filings, Names, and Registered Agents for Corporations, Nonprofit Corporations, and Partnerships	31
Chapter 56 - Electric, Telegraph and Power Companies [Repealed.]	31
Chapter 57 - Hospital, Medical and Dental Service Corporations [Recodified.]	31
Chapter 57A - Health Maintenance Organization Act [Recodified.]	31
Chapter 57B - Health Maintenance Organization Act [Recodified.]	31
Chapter 57C - North Carolina Limited Liability Company Act.	31
Chapter 58 - Insurance.	32
Chapter 58 - Insurance (Continuation)	33
Chapter 58 - Insurance (Continuation)	34
Chapter 58 - Insurance (Continuation)	35
Chapter 58 - Insurance (Continuation)	36
Chapter 58 - Insurance (Continuation)	37
Chapter 58 - Insurance (Continuation)	38
Chapter 58A - North Carolina Health Insurance Trust Commission [Recodified.]	38
Chapter 59 - Partnership.	39
Chapter 59B - Uniform Unincorporated Nonprofit Association Act.	39
Chapter 60 - Railroads and Other Carriers [Repealed and Transferred.]	39
Chapter 61 - Religious Societies	39
Chapter 62 - Public Utilities	39

Chapter 62 - Public Utilities (Continuation)	40
Chapter 62A - Public Safety Telephone Service And Wireless Telephone Service	40
Chapter 63 - Aeronautics	40
Chapter 63A - North Carolina Global TransPark Authority	40
Chapter 64 - Aliens	40
Chapter 65 – Cemeteries	40
Chapter 66 - Commerce and Business	41
Chapter 67 - Dogs	41
Chapter 68 - Fences and Stock Law	41
Chapter 69 - Fire Protection	41
Chapter 70 - Indian Antiquities, Archaeological Resources and Unmarked Human Skeletal Remains Protection	42
Chapter 71 - Indians [Repealed.]	42
Chapter 71A - Indians	42
Chapter 72 - Inns, Hotels and Restaurants	42
Chapter 73 - Mills	42
Chapter 74 - Mines and Quarries	42
Chapter 74A - Company Police [Repealed.]	42
Chapter 74B - Private Protective Services Act [Repealed.]	42
Chapter 74C - Private Protective Services	42
Chapter 74D - Alarm Systems	42
Chapter 74E - Company Police Act	42
Chapter 74F - Locksmith Licensing Act	42
Chapter 74G - Campus Police Act	42
Chapter 75 - Monopolies, Trusts and Consumer Protection	42
Chapter 75A - Boating and Water Safety	43
Chapter 75B - Discrimination in Business	43
Chapter 75C - Motion Picture Fair Competition Act	43
Chapter 75D - Racketeer Influenced and Corrupt Organizations	43
Chapter 75E - Unlawful Activities in Connection With Certain Corporate Transactions	43
Chapter 76 - Navigation	43
Chapter 76A - Navigation and Pilotage Commissions	43
Chapter 77 - Rivers, Creeks, and Coastal Waters	43
Chapter 78 - Securities Law [Repealed.]	43
Chapter 78A - North Carolina Securities Act	43
Chapter 78B - Tender Offer Disclosure Act [Repealed.]	43
Chapter 78C - Investment Advisers	43
Chapter 78D - Commodities Act	43
Chapter 79 - Strays [Repealed.]	43
Chapter 80 - Trademarks, Brands, etc.	44
Chapter 81 - Weights and Measures [Recodified.]	44
Chapter 81A - Weights and Measures Act of 1975.	44
Chapter 82 - Wrecks [Repealed.]	44
Chapter 83 - Architects [Recodified.]	44

Chapter 83A - Architects	44
Chapter 84 - Attorneys-at-Law	44
Chapter 84A - Foreign Legal Consultants	44
Chapter 85 - Auctions and Auctioneers [Repealed.]	44
Chapter 85A - Bail Bondsmen and Runners [Recodified.]	44
Chapter 85B - Auctions and Auctioneers	44
Chapter 85C - Bail Bondsmen and Runners [Recodified.]	44
Chapter 86 - Barbers [Recodified.]	44
Chapter 86A - Barbers	44
Chapter 87 - Contractors	44
Chapter 88 - Cosmetic Art [Repealed.]	44
Chapter 88A - Electrolysis Practice Act	44
Chapter 88B - Cosmetic Art	45
Chapter 89 - Engineering and Land Surveying [Recodified.]	45
Chapter 89A - Landscape Architects	45
Chapter 89B - Foresters	45
Chapter 89C - Engineering and Land Surveying	45
Chapter 89D - Landscape Contractors	45
Chapter 89E - Geologists Licensing Act	45
Chapter 89F - North Carolina Soil Scientist Licensing Act	45
Chapter 89G - Irrigation Contractors	45
Chapter 90 - Medicine and Allied Occupations	45
Chapter 90 - Medicine and Allied Occupations (Continuation)	46
Chapter 90 - Medicine and Allied Occupations (Continuation)	47
Chapter 90 - Medicine and Allied Occupations (Continuation)	48
Chapter 90A - Sanitarians and Water and Wastewater Treatment Facility Operators	48
Chapter 90B - Social Worker Certification and Licensure Act	48
Chapter 90C - North Carolina Recreational Therapy Licensure Act	48
Chapter 90D - Interpreters and Transliterators	48
Chapter 91 - Pawnbrokers [Repealed.]	48
Chapter 91A - Pawnbrokers Modernization Act of 1989	48
Chapter 92 - Photographers [Deleted.]	48
Chapter 93 - Certified Public Accountants	48
Chapter 93A - Real Estate License Law	49
Chapter 93B - Occupational Licensing Boards	49
Chapter 93C - Watchmakers [Repealed.]	49
Chapter 93D - North Carolina State Hearing Aid Dealers and Fitters Board.	49
Chapter 93E - North Carolina Appraisers Act	49
Chapter 94 - Apprenticeship	49
Chapter 95 - Department of Labor and Labor Regulations	49
Chapter 95 - Department of Labor and Labor Regulations (Continuation)	50
Chapter 96 - Employment Security	50
Chapter 97 - Workers' Compensation Act	50
Chapter 97 - Workers' Compensation Act (Continuation)	51

Chapter 98 - Burnt and Lost Records	51
Chapter 99 - Libel and Slander	51
Chapter 99A - Civil Remedies for Criminal Actions	51
Chapter 99B - Products Liability	51
Chapter 99C - Actions Relating to Winter Sports Safety and Accidents	51
Chapter 99D - Civil Rights	51
Chapter 99E - Special Liability Provisions	51
Chapter 100 - Monuments, Memorials and Parks	51
Chapter 101 - Names of Persons	51
Chapter 102 - Official Survey Base	51
Chapter 103 - Sundays, Holidays and Special Days	51
Chapter 104 - United States Lands	51
Chapter 104A - Degrees of Kinship	51
Chapter 104B - Hurricanes or Other Acts of Nature	51
Chapter 104C - Atomic Energy, Radioactivity and Ionizing Radiation [Repealed and Recodified.]	51
Chapter 104D - Southern States Energy Compact	51
Chapter 104E - North Carolina Radiation Protection Act	51
Chapter 104F - Southeast Interstate Low-Level Radioactive Waste Management Compact [Repealed]	51
Chapter 104G - North Carolina Low-Level Radioactive Waste Management Authority Act of 1987 [Repealed]	51
Chapter 105 - Taxation	51
Chapter 105 - Taxation (Continuation)	52
Chapter 105 - Taxation (Continuation)	53
Chapter 105 - Taxation (Continuation)	54
Chapter 105A - Setoff Debt Collection Act	55
Chapter 105B - Defaulted Student Loan Recovery Act	55
Chapter 106 - Agriculture	55
Chapter 106 - Agriculture (Continue)	56
Chapter 106 - Agriculture (Continue)	57
Chapter 107 - Agricultural Development Districts [Repealed.]	57
Chapter 108 - Social Services [Repealed and Recodified.]	57
Chapter 108A - Social Services	57
Chapter 108B - Community Action Programs	58
Chapter 108C Medicaid and Health Choice Provider Requirements.	58
Chapter 108D Medicaid Managed Care for Behavioral Health Services.	58
Chapter 109 - Bonds [Recodified.]	58
Chapter 110 - Child Welfare	58
Chapter 111 - Aid to the Blind	58
Chapter 112 - Confederate Homes and Pensions [Repealed.]	58
Chapter 113 - Conservation and Development	58
Chapter 113 - Conservation and Development (Continuation)	59

Chapter 113A - Pollution Control and Environment	59
Chapter 113A - Pollution Control and Environment (Continuation)	60
Chapter 113B - North Carolina Energy Policy Act of 1975	60
Chapter 114 - Department of Justice	60
Chapter 115 - Elementary and Secondary Education [Repealed.]	60
Chapter 115A - Community Colleges, Technical Institutes, and Industrial Education Centers [Repealed.]	60
Chapter 115B - Tuition and Fee Waivers	60
Chapter 115C - Elementary and Secondary Education	60
Chapter 115C - Elementary and Secondary Education (Continuation)	61
Chapter 115C - Elementary and Secondary Education (Continuation)	62
Chapter 115C - Elementary and Secondary Education (Continuation)	63
Chapter 115D - Community Colleges	63
Chapter 115E - Private Educational Facilities Finance Act [Recodified]	63
Chapter 116 - Higher Education	63
Chapter 116 - Higher Education (Continuation)	63
Chapter 116A - Escheats and Abandoned Property [Repealed.]	64
Chapter 116B - Escheats and Abandoned Property	64
Chapter 116C - Continuum of Education Programs	64
Chapter 116D - Higher Education Bonds	64
Chapter 116E - Education Longitudinal Data System	64
Chapter 117 - Electrification	64
Chapter 118 - Firemen's and Rescue Squad Workers' Relief and Pension Funds [Recodified.]	64
Chapter 118A - Firemen's Death Benefit Act [Repealed.]	64
Chapter 118B - Members of a Rescue Squad Death Benefit Act [Repealed.]	64
Chapter 119 - Gasoline and Oil Inspection and Regulation	64
Chapter 120 - General Assembly	65
Chapter 120 - General Assembly (Continuation)	66
Chapter 120 - General Assembly (Continuation)	67
Chapter 120C - Lobbying	67
Chapter 121 - Archives and History	67
Chapter 122 - Hospitals for the Mentally Disordered [Repealed.]	67
Chapter 122A - North Carolina Housing Finance Agency	67
Chapter 122B - North Carolina Agricultural Facilities Finance Act [Repealed.]	67
Chapter 122C - Mental Health, Developmental Disabilities, and Substance Abuse Act of 1985	67
Chapter 122C - Mental Health, Developmental Disabilities, and Substance Abuse Act of 1985 (Continuation)	68

Chapter 122D - North Carolina Agricultural Finance Act	68
Chapter 122E - North Carolina Housing Trust and Oil Overcharge Act	68
Chapter 123 - Impeachment	69
Chapter 123A - Industrial Development [Repealed.]	69
Chapter 124 - Internal Improvements	69
Chapter 125 - Libraries	69
Chapter 126 - State Personnel System	69
Chapter 127 - Militia [Repealed.]	69
Chapter 127A - Militia	69
Chapter 127B - Military Affairs	69
Chapter 127C - Advisory Commission on Military Affairs	69
Chapter 128 - Offices and Public Officers	69
Chapter 128 - Offices and Public Officers (Continuation)	70
Chapter 129 - Public Buildings and Grounds	70
Chapter 130 - Public Health [Repealed.]	70
Chapter 130A - Public Health	70
Chapter 130A - Public Health (Continuation)	71
Chapter 130A - Public Health (Continuation)	72
Chapter 130B - Hazardous Waste Management Commission [Repealed.]	72
Chapter 131 - Public Hospitals [Repealed.]	72
Chapter 131A - Health Care Facilities Finance Act	72
Chapter 131B - Licensing of Ambulatory Surgical Facilities [Repealed.]	72
Chapter 131C - Charitable Solicitation Licensure Act [Repealed.]	72
Chapter 131D - Inspection and Licensing of Facilities	72
Chapter 131E - Health Care Facilities and Services	72
Chapter 131E - Health Care Facilities and Services (Continuation)	73
Chapter 131F - Solicitation of Contributions	73
Chapter 132 - Public Records	73
Chapter 133 - Public Works	74
Chapter 134 - Youth Development [Recodified.]	74
Chapter 134A - Youth Services [Repealed.]	74
Chapter 135 - Retirement System for Teachers and State Employees; Social Security; Health Insurance Program for Children	74
Chapter 135 - Retirement System for Teachers and State Employees; Social Security; Health Insurance Program for Children	75
Chapter 136 - Transportation	75
Chapter 136 - Transportation (Continuation)	76
Chapter 137 - Rural Rehabilitation [Repealed.]	76
Chapter 138 - Salaries, Fees and Allowances	76
Chapter 138A - State Government Ethics Act	76

Chapter 139 - Soil and Water Conservation Districts	76
Chapter 140 - State Art Museum; Symphony and Art Societies	76
Chapter 140A - State Awards System	76
Chapter 141 - State Boundaries	76
Chapter 142 - State Debt	76
Chapter 143 - State Departments, Institutions, and Commissions	77
Chapter 143 - State Departments, Institutions, and Commissions (Continuation)	78
Chapter 143 - State Departments, Institutions, and Commissions (Continuation)	79
Chapter 143 - State Departments, Institutions, and Commissions (Continuation)	80
Chapter 143A - State Government Reorganization	80
Chapter 143B - Executive Organization Act of 1973	80
Chapter 143B - Executive Organization Act of 1973 (Continuation)	81
Chapter 143B - Executive Organization Act of 1973 (Continuation)	82
Chapter 143C - State Budget Act	83
Chapter 143D - The State Governmental Accountability and Internal Control Act	83
Chapter 144 - State Flag, Official Governmental Flags, Motto, and Colors	83
Chapter 145 - State Symbols and Other Official Adoptions.	83
Chapter 146 - State Lands	83
Chapter 147 - State Officers	83
Chapter 148 - State Prison System	84
Chapter 149 - State Song and Toast	84
Chapter 150 - Uniform Revocation of Licenses [Repealed.]	84
Chapter 150A - Administrative Procedure Act [Recodified.]	84
Chapter 150B - Administrative Procedure Act	84
Chapter 151 - Constables [Repealed.]	84
Chapter 152 - Coroners	84
Chapter 152A - County Medical Examiner [Repealed.]	84
Chapter 152A - County Medical Examiner [Repealed.] (Continuation)	85
Chapter 153 - Counties and County Commissioners [Repealed.]	85
Chapter 153A - Counties	85
Chapter 153B - Mountain Resources Planning Act	85
Chapter 153C - Uwharrie Regional Resources Act	85
Chapter 154 - County Surveyor [Repealed.]	85
Chapter 155 - County Treasurer [Repealed.]	85
Chapter 156 - Drainage	85

Chapter 156 – Drainage (Continuation)	86
Chapter 157 - Housing Authorities and Projects	86
Chapter 157A - Historic Properties Commissions [Transferred.]	86
Chapter 158 - Local Development	86
Chapter 159 - Local Government Finance	86
Chapter 159 - Local Government Finance (Continuation)	87
Chapter 159A - Pollution Abatement and Industrial Facilities Financing Act [Unconstitutional.]	87
Chapter 159B - Joint Municipal Electric Power and Energy Act	87
Chapter 159C - Industrial and Pollution Control Facilities Financing Act	87
Chapter 159D - The North Carolina Capital Facilities Financing Act	87
Chapter 159E - Registered Public Obligations Act	87
Chapter 159F - North Carolina Energy Development Authority [Repealed.]	87
Chapter 159G - Water Infrastructure	87
Chapter 159H - [Reserved.]	87
Chapter 159I - Solid Waste Management Loan Program and Local Government Special Obligation Bonds	87
Chapter 160 - Municipal Corporations [Repealed And Transferred.]	87
Chapter 160A - Cities and Towns	88
Chapter 160A - Cities and Towns (Continuation)	89
Chapter 160B - Consolidated City-County Act	89
Chapter 160C - Baseball Park Districts [Repealed.]	90
Chapter 161 - Register of Deeds	90
Chapter 162 - Sheriff	90
Chapter 162A - Water and Sewer Systems	90
Chapter 162B Continuity of Local Government in Emergency.	90
Chapter 163 Elections and Election Laws.	90
Chapter 163 Elections and Election Laws. (Continuation)	91
Chapter 164 Concerning the General Statutes of North Carolina.	92
Chapter 165 Veterans.	92
Chapter 166 Civil Preparedness Agencies [Repealed.]	92
Chapter 166A North Carolina Emergency Management Act.	92
Chapter 167 State Civil Air Patrol [Repealed.]	92
Chapter 168 Persons with Disabilities.	92
Chapter 168A Persons With Disabilities Protection Act.	92

Chapter 14

Criminal Law.

SUBCHAPTER I. GENERAL PROVISIONS.

Article 1.

Felonies and Misdemeanors.

§ 14-1. Felonies and misdemeanors defined.

A felony is a crime which:

(1) Was a felony at common law;

(2) Is or may be punishable by death;

(3) Is or may be punishable by imprisonment in the State's prison; or

(4) Is denominated as a felony by statute.

Any other crime is a misdemeanor. (1891, c. 205, s. 1; Rev., s. 3291; C.S., s. 4171; 1967, c. 1251, s. 1.)

§ 14-1.1: Repealed by Session Laws 1993, c. 538, s. 2.

§ 14-2: Repealed by Session Laws 1993, c. 538, s. 2.1.

§ 14-2.1: Repealed by Session Laws 1993, c. 538, s. 3.

§ 14-2.2: Repealed by Session Laws 2003-0378, s. 1, effective August 1, 2003.

§ 14-2.3. Forfeiture of gain acquired through criminal activity.

(a) Except as is otherwise provided in Article 3 of Chapter 31A, in the case of any violation of Article 13A of Chapter 14, or a general statute constituting a felony other than a nonwillful homicide, any money or other property or interest in property acquired thereby shall be forfeited to the State of North Carolina, including any profits, gain, remuneration, or compensation directly or indirectly collected by or accruing to any offender.

(b) An action to recover such property shall be brought by either a District Attorney or the Attorney General pursuant to G.S. 1-532. The action must be brought within three years from the date of the conviction for the offense.

(c) Nothing in this section shall be construed to require forfeiture of any money or property recovered by law-enforcement officers pursuant to the investigation of an offense when the money or property is readily identifiable by the owner or guardian of the property or is traceable to him. (1981, c. 840, s. 1; 2008-214, s. 1.)

§ 14-2.4. Punishment for conspiracy to commit a felony.

(a) Unless a different classification is expressly stated, a person who is convicted of a conspiracy to commit a felony is guilty of a felony that is one class lower than the felony he or she conspired to commit, except that a conspiracy to commit a Class A or Class B1 felony is a Class B2 felony, a conspiracy to commit a Class B2 felony is a Class C felony, and a conspiracy to commit a Class I felony is a Class 1 misdemeanor.

(b) Unless a different classification is expressly stated, a person who is convicted of a conspiracy to commit a misdemeanor is guilty of a misdemeanor that is one class lower than the misdemeanor he or she conspired to commit, except that a conspiracy to commit a Class 3 misdemeanor is a Class 3 misdemeanor. (1983, c. 451, s. 1; 1993, c. 538, s. 5; 1994, Ex. Sess., c. 22, s. 12, c. 24, s. 14(b).)

§ 14-2.5. Punishment for attempt to commit a felony or misdemeanor.

Unless a different classification is expressly stated, an attempt to commit a misdemeanor or a felony is punishable under the next lower classification as the offense which the offender attempted to commit. An attempt to commit a Class A or Class B1 felony is a Class B2 felony, an attempt to commit a Class B2 felony is a Class C felony, an attempt to commit a Class I felony is a Class 1 misdemeanor, and an attempt to commit a Class 3 misdemeanor is a Class 3 misdemeanor. (1993, c. 538, s. 6; 1994, Ex. Sess., c. 22, s. 11, c. 24, s. 14(b).)

§ 14-2.6. Punishment for solicitation to commit a felony or misdemeanor.

(a) Unless a different classification is expressly stated, a person who solicits another person to commit a felony is guilty of a felony that is two classes lower than the felony the person solicited the other person to commit, except that a solicitation to commit a Class A or Class B1 felony is a Class C felony, a solicitation to commit a Class B2 felony is a Class D felony, a solicitation to commit a Class H felony is a Class 1 misdemeanor, and a solicitation to commit a Class I felony is a Class 2 misdemeanor.

(b) Unless a different classification is expressly stated, a person who solicits another person to commit a misdemeanor is guilty of a Class 3 misdemeanor. (1993, c. 538, s. 6.1; 1994, Ex. Sess., c. 22, s. 13, c. 24, s. 14(b).)

§ 14-3. Punishment of misdemeanors, infamous offenses, offenses committed in secrecy and malice, or with deceit and intent to defraud, or with ethnic animosity.

(a) Except as provided in subsections (b) and (c), every person who shall be convicted of any misdemeanor for which no specific classification and no specific punishment is prescribed by statute shall be punishable as a Class 1 misdemeanor. Any misdemeanor that has a specific punishment, but is not assigned a classification by the General Assembly pursuant to law is classified as follows, based on the maximum punishment allowed by law for the offense as it existed on the effective date of Article 81B of Chapter 15A of the General Statutes:

(1) If that maximum punishment is more than six months imprisonment, it is a Class 1 misdemeanor;

(2) If that maximum punishment is more than 30 days but not more than six months imprisonment, it is a Class 2 misdemeanor; and

(3) If that maximum punishment is 30 days or less imprisonment or only a fine, it is a Class 3 misdemeanor.

Misdemeanors that have punishments for one or more counties or cities pursuant to a local act of the General Assembly that are different from the generally applicable punishment are classified pursuant to this subsection if not otherwise specifically classified.

(b) If a misdemeanor offense as to which no specific punishment is prescribed be infamous, done in secrecy and malice, or with deceit and intent to defraud, the offender shall, except where the offense is a conspiracy to commit a misdemeanor, be guilty of a Class H felony.

(c) If any Class 2 or Class 3 misdemeanor is committed because of the victim's race, color, religion, nationality, or country of origin, the offender shall be guilty of a Class 1 misdemeanor. If any Class A1 or Class 1 misdemeanor offense is committed because of the victim's race, color, religion, nationality, or country of origin, the offender shall be guilty of a Class H felony. (R.C., c. 34, s. 120; Code, s. 1097; Rev., s. 3293; C.S., s. 4173; 1927, c. 1; 1967, c. 1251, s. 3; 1979, c. 760, s. 5; 1979, 2nd Sess., c. 1316, ss. 2, 47, 48; 1981, c. 63, s. 1; c. 179, s. 14; 1991, c. 702, s. 2; 1993, c. 538, s. 7; 1994, Ex. Sess., c. 14, s. 2; c. 24, s. 14(b); 1995 (Reg. Sess., 1996), c. 742, s. 6; 2008-197, s. 4.1.)

§ 14-3.1. Infraction defined; sanctions.

(a) An infraction is a noncriminal violation of law not punishable by imprisonment. Unless otherwise provided by law, the sanction for a person found responsible for an infraction is a penalty of not more than one hundred dollars ($100.00). The proceeds of penalties for infractions are payable to the county in which the infraction occurred for the use of the public schools.

(b) The procedure for disposition of infractions is as provided in Article 66 of Chapter 15A of the General Statutes. (1985, c. 764, s. 1.)

§ 14-4. Violation of local ordinances misdemeanor.

(a)   Except as provided in subsection (b), if any person shall violate an ordinance of a county, city, town, or metropolitan sewerage district created under Article 5 of Chapter 162A, he shall be guilty of a Class 3 misdemeanor and shall be fined not more than five hundred dollars ($500.00). No fine shall exceed fifty dollars ($50.00) unless the ordinance expressly states that the maximum fine is greater than fifty dollars ($50.00).

(b)   If any person shall violate an ordinance of a county, city, or town regulating the operation or parking of vehicles, he shall be responsible for an infraction and shall be required to pay a penalty of not more than fifty dollars ($50.00). (1871-2, c. 195, s. 2; Code, s. 3820; Rev., s. 3702; C.S., s. 4174; 1969, c. 36, s. 2; 1985, c. 764, s. 2; 1985 (Reg. Sess., 1986), c. 852, s. 17; 1991, c. 415, s. 1; c. 446, s. 1; 1993, c. 538, s. 8; c. 539, s. 9; 1994, Ex. Sess., c. 24, ss. 14(b), 14(c); 1995, c. 509, s. 133.1.)

Article 2.

Principals and Accessories.

§§ 14-5 through 14-5.1: Repealed by Session Laws 1981, c. 686, s. 2, effective July 1, 1981.

§ 14-5.2. Accessory before fact punishable as principal felon.

All distinctions between accessories before the fact and principals to the commission of a felony are abolished. Every person who heretofore would have been guilty as an accessory before the fact to any felony shall be guilty and punishable as a principal to that felony. However, if a person who heretofore would have been guilty and punishable as an accessory before the fact is convicted of a capital felony, and the jury finds that his conviction was based solely on the uncorroborated testimony of one or more principals, coconspirators, or accessories to the crime, he shall be guilty of a Class B2 felony. (1981, c. 686, s. 1; 1994, Ex. Sess., c. 22, s. 6.)

§ 14-6. Repealed by Session Laws 1981, c. 686, s. 2, effective July 1, 1981.

§ 14-7. Accessories after the fact; trial and punishment.

If any person shall become an accessory after the fact to any felony, whether the same be a felony at common law or by virtue of any statute made, or to be made, such person shall be guilty of a crime, and may be indicted and convicted together with the principal felon, or after the conviction of the principal felon, or may be indicted and convicted for such crime whether the principal felon shall or shall not have been previously convicted, or shall or shall not be amenable to justice. Unless a different classification is expressly stated, that person shall be punished for an offense that is two classes lower than the felony the principal felon committed, except that an accessory after the fact to a Class A or Class B1 felony is a Class C felony, an accessory after the fact to a Class B2 felony is a Class D felony, an accessory after the fact to a Class H felony is a Class 1 misdemeanor, and an accessory after the fact to a Class I felony is a Class 2 misdemeanor. The offense of such person may be inquired of, tried, determined and punished by any court which shall have jurisdiction of the principal felon, in the same manner as if the act, by reason whereof such person shall have become an accessory, had been committed at the same place as the principal felony, although such act may have been committed without the limits of the State; and in case the principal felony shall have been committed within the body of any county, and the act by reason whereof any person shall have become accessory shall have been committed within the body of any other county, the offense of such person guilty of a felony as aforesaid may be inquired of, tried, determined, and punished in either of said counties: Provided, that no person who shall be once duly tried for such felony shall be again indicted or tried for the same offense. (1797, c. 485, s. 1, P.R.; 1852, c. 58; R.C., c. 34, s. 54; Code, s. 978; Rev., s. 3289; C.S., s. 4177; 1979, c. 760, s. 5; 1979, 2nd Sess., c. 1316, s. 47; 1981, c. 63, s. 1; c. 179, s. 14; 1997-443, s. 19.25(p).)

Article 2A.

Habitual Felons.

§ 14-7.1. Persons defined as habitual felons.

Any person who has been convicted of or pled guilty to three felony offenses in any federal court or state court in the United States or combination thereof is declared to be an habitual felon and may be charged as a status offender pursuant to this Article. For the purpose of this Article, a felony offense is defined as an offense which is a felony under the laws of the State or other sovereign wherein a plea of guilty was entered or a conviction was returned regardless of the sentence actually imposed. Provided, however, that federal offenses relating to the manufacture, possession, sale and kindred offenses involving intoxicating liquors shall not be considered felonies for the purposes of this Article. For the purposes of this Article, felonies committed before a person attains the age of 18 years shall not constitute more than one felony. The commission of a second felony shall not fall within the purview of this Article unless it is committed after the conviction of or plea of guilty to the first felony. The commission of a third felony shall not fall within the purview of this Article unless it is committed after the conviction of or plea of guilty to the second felony. Pleas of guilty to or convictions of felony offenses prior to July 6, 1967, shall not be felony offenses within the meaning of this Article. Any felony offense to which a pardon has been extended shall not for the purpose of this Article constitute a felony. The burden of proving such pardon shall rest with the defendant and the State shall not be required to disprove a pardon. (1967, c. 1241, s. 1; 1971, c. 1231, s. 1; 1979, c. 760, s. 4; 1981, c. 179, s. 10; 2011-192, s. 3(b).)

§ 14-7.2. Punishment.

When any person is charged by indictment with the commission of a felony under the laws of the State of North Carolina and is also charged with being an habitual felon as defined in G.S. 14-7.1, he must, upon conviction, be sentenced and punished as an habitual felon, as in this Chapter provided, except in those cases where the death penalty or a life sentence is imposed. (1967, c. 1241, s. 2; 1981, c. 179, s. 11.)

§ 14-7.3. Charge of habitual felon.

The district attorney, in his or her discretion, may charge a person as an habitual felon pursuant to this Article. An indictment which charges a person who is an habitual felon within the meaning of G.S. 14-7.1 with the commission of any felony under the laws of the State of North Carolina must, in order to sustain a conviction of habitual felon, also charge that said person is an habitual felon. The indictment charging the defendant as an habitual felon shall be separate from the indictment charging him with the principal felony. An indictment which charges a person with being an habitual felon must set forth the date that prior felony offenses were committed, the name of the state or other sovereign against whom said felony offenses were committed, the dates that pleas of guilty were entered to or convictions returned in said felony offenses, and the identity of the court wherein said pleas or convictions took place. No defendant charged with being an habitual felon in a bill of indictment shall be required to go to trial on said charge within 20 days of the finding of a true bill by the grand jury; provided, the defendant may waive this 20-day period. (1967, c. 1241, s. 3; 2011-192, s. 3(c).)

§ 14-7.4. Evidence of prior convictions of felony offenses.

In all cases where a person is charged under the provisions of this Article with being an habitual felon, the record or records of prior convictions of felony offenses shall be admissible in evidence, but only for the purpose of proving that said person has been convicted of former felony offenses. A prior conviction may be proved by stipulation of the parties or by the original or a certified copy of the court record of the prior conviction. The original or certified copy of the court record, bearing the same name as that by which the defendant is charged, shall be prima facie evidence that the defendant named therein is the same as the defendant before the court, and shall be prima facie evidence of the facts set out therein. (1967, c. 1241, s. 4; 1981, c. 179, s. 12.)

§ 14-7.5. Verdict and judgment.

When an indictment charges an habitual felon with a felony as above provided and an indictment also charges that said person is an habitual felon as provided herein, the defendant shall be tried for the principal felony as provided by law. The indictment that the person is an habitual felon shall not be revealed to the jury unless the jury shall find that the defendant is guilty of the principal felony or other felony with which he is charged. If the jury finds the defendant guilty of a felony, the bill of indictment charging the defendant as an habitual felon may be presented to the same jury. Except that the same jury may be used, the proceedings shall be as if the issue of habitual felon were a principal charge. If the jury finds that the defendant is an habitual felon, the trial judge shall enter judgment according to the provisions of this Article. If the jury finds that the defendant is not an habitual felon, the trial judge shall pronounce judgment on the principal felony or felonies as provided by law. (1967, c. 1241, s. 5.)

§ 14-7.6. Sentencing of habitual felons.

When an habitual felon as defined in this Article commits any felony under the laws of the State of North Carolina, the felon must, upon conviction or plea of guilty under indictment as provided in this Article (except where the felon has been sentenced as a Class A, B1, or B2 felon) be sentenced at a felony class level that is four classes higher than the principal felony for which the person was convicted; but under no circumstances shall an habitual felon be sentenced at a level higher than a Class C felony. In determining the prior record level, convictions used to establish a person's status as an habitual felon shall not be used. Sentences imposed under this Article shall run consecutively with and shall commence at the expiration of any sentence being served by the person sentenced under this section. (1967, c. 1241, s. 6; 1981, c. 179, s. 13; 1993, c. 538, s. 9; 1994, Ex. Sess., c. 22, ss. 15, 16; c. 24, s. 14(b); 1993 (Reg. Sess., 1994), c. 767, s. 16; 2011-192, s. 3(d).)

ARTICLE 2B.

Violent Habitual Felons.

§ 14-7.7. Persons defined as violent habitual felons.

(a)   Any person who has been convicted of two violent felonies in any federal court, in a court of this or any other state of the United States, or in a combination of these courts is declared to be a violent habitual felon. For purposes of this Article, "convicted" means the person has been adjudged guilty of or has entered a plea of guilty or no contest to the violent felony charge, and judgment has been entered thereon when such action occurred on or after July 6, 1967. This Article does not apply to a second violent felony unless it is committed after the conviction or plea of guilty or no contest to the first violent felony. Any felony to which a pardon has been extended shall not, for the purposes of this Article, constitute a felony. The burden of proving a pardon shall rest with the defendant, and this State shall not be required to disprove a pardon. Conviction as an habitual felon shall not, for purposes of this Article, constitute a violent felony.

(b) For purposes of this Article, "violent felony" includes the following offenses:

(1) All Class A through E felonies.

(2) Any repealed or superseded offense substantially equivalent to the offenses listed in subdivision (1).

(3) Any offense committed in another jurisdiction substantially similar to the offenses set forth in subdivision (1) or (2). (1994, Ex. Sess., c. 22, ss. 31, 32; 2000-155, s. 14.)

§ 14-7.8. Punishment.

When a person is charged by indictment with the commission of a violent felony and is also charged with being a violent habitual felon as defined in G.S. 14-7.7, the person must, upon conviction, be sentenced in accordance with this Article, except in those cases where the death penalty is imposed. (1994, Ex. Sess., c. 22, s. 31.)

§ 14-7.9. Charge of violent habitual felon.

An indictment that charges a person who is a violent habitual felon within the meaning of G.S. 14-7.7 with the commission of any violent felony must, in order to sustain a conviction of violent habitual felon, also charge that the person is a violent habitual felon. The indictment charging the defendant as a violent habitual felon shall be separate from the indictment charging the defendant with the principal violent felony. An indictment that charges a person with being a violent habitual felon must set forth the date that prior violent felonies were committed, the name of the state or other sovereign against whom the violent felonies were committed, the dates of convictions of the violent felonies, and the identity of the court in which the convictions took place. A defendant charged with being a violent habitual felon in a bill of indictment shall not be required to go to trial on that charge within 20 days after the finding of a true bill by the grand jury unless the defendant waives this 20-day period. (1994, Ex. Sess., c. 22, s. 31.)

§ 14-7.10. Evidence of prior convictions of violent felonies.

In all cases where a person is charged under this Article with being a violent habitual felon, the records of prior convictions of violent felonies shall be admissible in evidence, but only for the purpose of proving that the person has been convicted of former violent felonies. A prior conviction may be proved by stipulation of the parties or by the original or a certified copy of the court record of the prior conviction. The original or certified copy of the court record, bearing the same name as that by which the defendant is charged, shall be prima facie evidence that the defendant named therein is the same as the defendant before the court, and shall be prima facie evidence of the facts set out therein. (1994, Ex. Sess., c. 22, s. 31.)

§ 14-7.11. Verdict and judgment.

When an indictment charges a violent habitual felon with a violent felony as provided in this Article and an indictment also charges that the person is a violent habitual felon as provided in this Article, the defendant shall be tried for the principal violent felony as provided by law. The indictment that the person is a violent habitual felon shall not be revealed to the jury unless the jury finds that the defendant is guilty of the principal violent felony or another violent felony with which the defendant is charged. If the jury finds the defendant guilty of a violent felony, the bill of indictment charging the defendant as a violent habitual felon may be presented to the same jury. Except that the same jury may be used, the proceedings shall be as if the issue of violent habitual felon were a principal charge. If the jury finds that the defendant is a violent habitual felon, the trial judge shall enter judgment according to the provisions of this Article. If the jury finds that the defendant is not a violent habitual felon, the trial judge shall pronounce judgment on the principal violent felony or felonies as provided by law. (1994, Ex. Sess., c. 22, s. 31.)

§ 14-7.12. Sentencing of violent habitual felons.

A person who is convicted of a violent felony and of being a violent habitual felon must, upon conviction (except where the death penalty is imposed), be sentenced to life imprisonment without parole. Life imprisonment without parole means that the person will spend the remainder of the person's natural life in prison. The sentencing judge may not suspend the sentence and may not place the person sentenced on probation. Sentences for violent habitual felons imposed under this Article shall run consecutively with and shall commence at the expiration of any other sentence being served by the person. (1994, Ex. Sess., c. 22, s. 31.)

§ 14-7.13: Reserved for future codification purposes.

§ 14-7.14: Reserved for future codification purposes.

§ 14-7.15: Reserved for future codification purposes.

§ 14-7.16: Reserved for future codification purposes.

§ 14-7.17: Reserved for future codification purposes.

§ 14-7.18: Reserved for future codification purposes.

§ 14-7.19: Reserved for future codification purposes.

Article 2C.

Continuing Criminal Enterprise.

§ 14-7.20. Continuing criminal enterprise.

(a)   Except as otherwise provided in subsection (a1) of this section, any person who engages in a continuing criminal enterprise shall be punished as a Class H felon and in addition shall be subject to the forfeiture prescribed in subsection (b) of this section.

(a1)   Any person who engages in a continuing criminal enterprise where the felony violation required by subdivision (c)(1) of this section is a violation of G.S. 14-10.1 shall be punished as a Class D felon and, in addition, shall be subject to the forfeiture prescribed in subsection (b) of this section.

(b)   Any person who is convicted under subsection (a) or (a1) of this section of engaging in a continuing criminal enterprise shall forfeit to the State of North Carolina:

(1)   The profits obtained by the person in the enterprise, and

(2)   Any of the person's interest in, claim against, or property or contractual rights of any kind affording a source of influence over, such enterprise.

(c)   For purposes of this section, a person is engaged in a continuing criminal enterprise if:

(1)   The person violates any provision of this Chapter, the punishment of which is a felony; and

(2)   The violation is a part of a continuing series of violations of this Chapter:

a.   Which are undertaken by the person in concert with five or more other persons with respect to whom the person occupies a position of organizer, a supervisory position, or any other position of management; and

b.   From which the person obtains substantial income or resources. (1995, c. 378, s. 1; 2012-38, s. 2.)

§ 14-7.21: Reserved for future codification purposes.

§ 14-7.22: Reserved for future codification purposes.

§ 14-7.23: Reserved for future codification purposes.

§ 14-7.24: Reserved for future codification purposes.

Article 2D.

Habitual Breaking and Entering Status Offense.

§ 14-7.25. Definitions.

The following definitions apply in this Article:

(1) "Breaking and entering." - The term means any of the following felony offenses:

a. First degree burglary (G.S. 14-51).

b. Second degree burglary (G.S. 14-51).

c. Breaking out of dwelling house burglary (G.S. 14-53).

d. Breaking or entering buildings generally (G.S. 14-54(a)).

e. Breaking or entering a building that is a place of religious worship (G.S. 14-54.1).

f. Any repealed or superseded offense substantially equivalent to any of the offenses in sub-subdivision a., b., c., d., or e. of this subdivision.

g. Any offense committed in another jurisdiction substantially similar to any of the offenses in sub-subdivision a., b., c., d., or e. of this subdivision.

(2) "Convicted." - The person has been adjudged guilty of or has entered a plea of guilty or no contest to the offense of breaking and entering.

(3) "Status offender." - A person who is a habitual breaking and entering status offender as described in G.S. 14-7.26. (2011-192, s. 3(a).)

§ 14-7.26. Habitual breaking and entering status offender.

Any person who has been convicted of or pled guilty to one or more prior felony offenses of breaking and entering in any federal court or state court in the United States, or combination thereof, is guilty of the status offense of habitual breaking and entering and may be charged with that status offense pursuant to this Article.

This Article does not apply to a second felony offense of breaking and entering unless it is committed after the conviction of the first felony offense of breaking and entering. For purposes of this Article, felony offenses of breaking and entering committed before the person is 18 years of age shall not constitute more than one felony of breaking and entering. Any felony to which a pardon has been extended shall not, for the purposes of this Article, constitute a felony offense of breaking and entering. (2011-192, s. 3(a).)

§ 14-7.27. Punishment.

When any person is charged with a felony offense of breaking and entering and is also charged with being a status offender as defined in G.S. 14-7.26, the person must, upon conviction, be sentenced and punished as a status offender as provided by this Article. (2011-192, s. 3(a).)

§ 14-7.28. Charge of habitual breaking and entering status offender.

(a) The district attorney, in his or her discretion, may charge a person with the status offense of habitual breaking and entering pursuant to this Article. To sustain a conviction of a person as a status offender, the person must be charged separately for the felony offense of breaking and entering and for the habitual breaking and entering status offense. The indictment charging the defendant as a status offender shall be separate from the indictment charging the person with the principal felony offense of breaking and entering.

(b) An indictment that charges a person with being a status offender must set forth the date that the prior felony offense of breaking and entering was committed, the name of the state or other sovereign against whom the felony offense of breaking and entering was committed, the dates that the plea of guilty was entered into or conviction returned in the felony offense of breaking and entering, and the identity of the court in which the plea or conviction took place. No defendant charged with being a status offender in a bill of indictment shall be required to go to trial on the charge within 20 days of the finding of a true bill by the grand jury; provided, the defendant may waive this 20-day period. (2011-192, s. 3(a).)

§ 14-7.29. Evidence of prior convictions of breaking and entering.

In all cases in which a person is charged under the provisions of this Article with being a status offender, the record of prior conviction of the felony offense of breaking and entering shall be admissible in evidence, but only for the purpose of proving that the person has been convicted of a former felony offense of breaking and entering. A prior conviction may be proved by stipulation of the parties or by the original or a certified copy of the court record of the prior conviction. The original or certified copy of the court record, bearing the same name as that by which the defendant is charged, shall be prima facie evidence that the defendant named therein is the same as the defendant before the court and shall be prima facie evidence of the facts set out therein. (2011-192, s. 3(a).)

§ 14-7.30. Verdict and judgment.

(a) When an indictment charges a person with a felony offense of breaking and entering as provided by this Article and an indictment also charges that the person is a status offender, the defendant shall be tried for the principal offense of breaking and entering as provided by law. The indictment that the person is a status offender shall not be revealed to the jury unless the jury shall find that the defendant is guilty of the principal felony offense of breaking and entering with which the defendant is charged.

(b) If the jury finds the defendant guilty of the felony offense of breaking and entering, the bill of indictment charging the defendant as a status offender may be presented to the same jury. Except that the same jury may be used, the proceedings shall be as if the issue of status offender were a principal charge.

(c) If the jury finds that the defendant is a status offender, the trial judge shall enter judgment according to the provisions of this Article. If the jury finds that the defendant is not a status offender, the trial judge shall pronounce judgment on the principal felony offense of breaking and entering as provided by law. (2011-192, s. 3(a).)

§ 14-7.31. Sentencing of status offenders.

(a) When a status offender as defined in this Article commits a felony offense of breaking and entering under the laws of the State of North Carolina, the status offender must, upon conviction or plea of guilty under indictment as provided in this Article, be sentenced as a Class E felon.

(b) In determining the prior record level, any conviction used to establish a person's status as a status offender shall not be used. Sentences imposed under this Article shall run consecutively with and shall commence at the expiration of any sentence being served by the person sentenced under this section.

(c) A conviction as a status offender under this Article shall not constitute commission of a felony for the purpose of either Article 2A or Article 2B of Chapter 14 of the General Statutes. (2011-192, s. 3(a).)

§ 14-7.32: Reserved for future codification purposes.

§ 14-7.33: Reserved for future codification purposes.

§ 14-7.34: Reserved for future codification purposes.

Article 2E.

Armed Habitual Felon.

§ 14-7.35. Definitions.

The following definitions apply in this Article:

(1) "Convicted." - The person has been adjudged guilty of or has entered a plea of guilty or no contest to the firearm-related felony.

(2) "Firearm-related felony." - Any felony committed by a person in which the person used or displayed a firearm while committing the felony.

(3) "Status offender." - A person who is an armed habitual felon as described in G.S. 14-7.36. (2013-369, s. 26.)

§ 14-7.36. Armed habitual felon.

Any person who has been convicted of or pled guilty to one or more prior firearm-related felony offenses in any federal court or state court in the United States, or combination thereof, is guilty of the status offense of armed habitual felon and may be charged with that status offense pursuant to this Article.

This Article does not apply to a second firearm-related felony unless it is committed after the conviction of a firearm-related felony in which evidence of the person's use, display, or threatened use or display of a firearm was needed to prove an element of the felony or was needed to establish the requirement for an enhanced or aggravated sentence. For purposes of this Article, firearm-related felonies committed before the person is 18 years of age shall not constitute more than one firearm-related felony. Any firearm-related felony to which a pardon has been extended shall not, for the purposes of this Article, constitute a firearm-related felony. (2013-369, s. 26.)

§ 14-7.37. Punishment.

When any person is charged with a firearm-related felony and is also charged with being a status offender, the person must, upon conviction, be sentenced and punished as a status offender as provided by this Article. (2013-369, s. 26.)

§ 14-7.38. Charge of status offense as an armed habitual felon.

(a) The district attorney, in the district attorney's discretion, may charge a person as a status offender pursuant to this Article. To sustain a conviction of a person as a status offender, the person must be charged separately for the principal firearm-related felony and for the status offense of armed habitual felon. The indictment charging the defendant as a status offender shall be separate from the indictment charging the person with the principal firearm-related felony.

(b) An indictment that charges a person with being a status offender must set forth all of the following information regarding the prior firearm-related felony:

(1) The date the offense was committed.

(2) The name of the state or other sovereign against whom the offense was committed.

(3) The dates that the plea of guilty was entered into or conviction returned in the offense.

(4) The identity of the court in which the plea or conviction took place.

(c) No defendant charged with being a status offender in a bill of indictment shall be required to go to trial on the charge within 20 days of the finding of a true bill by the grand jury; provided, the defendant may waive this 20-day period. (2013-369, s. 26.)

§ 14-7.39. Evidence of prior convictions of firearm-related felonies.

In all cases in which a person is charged under the provisions of this Article with being a status offender, the record of prior conviction of the firearm-related felony shall be admissible in evidence, but only for the purpose of proving that the person has been convicted of a former firearm-related felony. A prior conviction may be proved by stipulation of the parties or by the original or a certified copy of the court record of the prior conviction. The original or certified copy of the court record, bearing the same name as that by which the defendant is charged, shall be prima facie evidence that the defendant named therein is the same as the defendant before the court and shall be prima facie evidence of the facts set out therein. (2013-369, s. 26.)

§ 14-7.40. Verdict and judgment.

(a) When an indictment charges a person with a firearm-related felony as provided by this Article and an indictment also charges that the person is a status offender, the defendant shall be tried for the principal firearm-related felony as provided by law. The indictment that the person is a status offender shall not be revealed to the jury unless the jury shall find that the defendant is guilty of the principal firearm-related felony with which the defendant is charged.

(b) If the jury finds the defendant guilty of the principal firearm-related felony, and it is found as provided in this section that (i) the person committed the felony by using, displaying, or threatening the use or display of a firearm or deadly weapon and (ii) the person actually possessed the firearm or deadly weapon about his or her person, the bill of indictment charging the defendant as a status offender may be presented to the same jury. Except that the same jury may be used, the proceedings shall be as if the issue of status offender were a principal charge.

(c) If the jury finds that the defendant is a status offender, the trial judge shall enter judgment according to the provisions of this Article. If the jury finds that the defendant is not a status offender, the trial judge shall pronounce judgment on the principal firearm-related felony offense as provided by law. (2013-369, s. 26.)

§ 14-7.41. Sentencing of armed habitual felon.

(a) A person who is convicted of a firearm-related felony and is also convicted of the status offense must, upon conviction or plea of guilty under indictment as provided in this Article, be sentenced as a Class C felon (except where the felon has been sentenced as a Class A, B1, or B2 felon). However, in no case shall the person receive a minimum term of imprisonment of less than 120 months. The court may not suspend the sentence and may not place the person sentenced on probation.

(b) In determining the prior record level, any conviction used to establish a person's status as an armed habitual felon shall not be used. Sentences imposed under this Article shall run consecutively with and shall commence at the expiration of any sentence being served by the person sentenced under this section.

(c) A conviction as a status offender under this Article shall not constitute commission of a felony for the purpose of either Article 2A or Article 2B of Chapter 14 of the General Statutes.

(d) A sentence imposed under this Article may not be enhanced pursuant to G.S. 15A-1340.16A. (2013-369, s. 26.)

SUBCHAPTER II. OFFENSES AGAINST THE STATE.

Article 3.

Rebellion.

§ 14-8. Rebellion against the State.

If any person shall incite, set on foot, assist or engage in a rebellion or insurrection against the authority of the State of North Carolina or the laws thereof, or shall give aid or comfort thereto, every person so offending in any of the ways aforesaid shall be guilty of a felony, and shall be punished as a Class F felon. (Const., art. 4, s. 5; 1861, c. 18; 1866, c. 64; 1868, c. 60, s. 2; Code, s. 1106; Rev., s. 3437; C.S., s. 4178; 1979, c. 760, s. 5; 1979, 2nd Sess., c. 1316, s. 47; 1981, c. 63, s. 1, c. 179, s. 14; 1993, c. 539, s. 1122; 1994, Ex. Sess., c. 24, s. 14(c).)

§ 14-9: Repealed by Session Laws 1994, Ex. Sess., c. 14, s. 71(1).

§ 14-10. Secret political and military organizations forbidden.

If any person, for the purpose of compassing or furthering any political object, or aiding the success of any political party or organization, or resisting the laws, shall join or in any way connect or unite himself with any oath-bound secret political or military organization, society or association of whatsoever name or character; or shall form or organize or combine and agree with any other person or persons to form or organize any such organization; or as a member of any secret political or military party or organization shall use, or agree to use, any certain signs or grips or passwords, or any disguise of the person or voice, or any disguise whatsoever for the advancement of its object, and shall take or administer any extrajudicial oath or other secret, solemn pledge, or any like secret means; or if any two or more persons, for the purpose of compassing or furthering any political object, or aiding the success of any political party or organization, or circumventing the laws, shall secretly assemble, combine or agree together, and the more effectually to accomplish such purposes, or any of them, shall use any certain signs, or grips, or passwords, or any disguise of the person or voice, or other disguise whatsoever, or shall take or administer any extrajudicial oath or other secret, solemn pledge; or if any persons shall band together and assemble to muster, drill or practice any military evolutions except by virtue of the authority of an officer recognized by law, or of an instructor in institutions or schools in which such evolutions form a part of the course of instruction; or if any person shall knowingly permit any of the acts and things herein forbidden to be had, done or performed on his premises, or on any premises under his control; or if any person being a member of any such secret political or military organization shall not at once abandon the same and separate himself entirely therefrom, every person so offending shall be guilty of a Class 1 misdemeanor. (1868-9, c. 267; 1870-1, c. 133; 1871-2, c. 143; Code, s. 1095; Rev., s. 3439; C.S., s. 4180; 1993, c. 539, s. 10; 1994, Ex. Sess., c. 24, s. 14(c).)

Article 3A.

Terrorism.

§ 14-10.1. Terrorism.

(a) As used in this section, the term "act of violence" means a violation of G.S. 14-17; a felony punishable pursuant to G.S. 14-18; any felony offense in this Chapter that includes an assault, or use of violence or force against a person; any felony offense that includes either the threat or use of any explosive or incendiary device; or any offense that includes the threat or use of a nuclear, biological, or chemical weapon of mass destruction.

(b) A person is guilty of the separate offense of terrorism if the person commits an act of violence with the intent to do either of the following:

(1) Intimidate the civilian population at large, or an identifiable group of the civilian population.

(2) Influence, through intimidation, the conduct or activities of the government of the United States, a state, or any unit of local government.

(c) A violation of this section is a felony that is one class higher than the offense which is the underlying act of violence, except that a violation is a Class B1 felony if the underlying act of violence is a Class A or Class B1 felony offense. A violation of this section is a separate offense from the underlying offense and shall not merge with other offenses.

(d)   All real and personal property of every kind used or intended for use in the course of, derived from, or realized through an offense punishable pursuant to this Article shall be subject to lawful seizure and forfeiture to the State as set forth in G.S. 14-2.3 and G.S. 14-7.20. However, the forfeiture of any real or personal property shall be subordinate to any security interest in the property taken by a lender in good faith as collateral for the extension of credit and recorded as provided by law, and no real or personal property shall be forfeited under this section against an owner who made a bona fide purchase of the property, or a person with rightful possession of the property, without knowledge of a violation of this Article. (2012-38, s. 1.)

Article 4.

Subversive Activities.

§ 14-11. Activities aimed at overthrow of government; use of public buildings.

It shall be unlawful for any person, by word of mouth or writing, willfully and deliberately to advocate, advise or teach a doctrine that the government of the United States, the State of North Carolina or any political subdivision thereof shall be overthrown or overturned by force or violence or by any other unlawful means. It shall be unlawful for any public building in the State, owned by the State of North Carolina, any political subdivision thereof, or by any department or agency of the State or any institution supported in whole or in part by State funds, to be used by any person for the purpose of advocating, advising or teaching a doctrine that the government of the United States, the State of North Carolina or any political subdivision thereof should be overthrown by force, violence or any other unlawful means. (1941, c. 37, s. 1.)

§ 14-12. Punishment for violations.

Any person or persons violating any of the provisions of this Article shall, for the first offense, be guilty of a Class 1 misdemeanor and be punished accordingly, and for the second offense shall be punished as a Class H felon. (1941, c. 37, s. 2; 1979, c. 760, s. 5; 1979, 2nd Sess., c. 1316, s. 47; 1981, c. 63, s. 1, c. 179, s. 14; 1993, c. 539, s. 11; 1994, Ex. Sess., c. 24, s. 14(c).)

§ 14-12.1. Certain subversive activities made unlawful.

It shall be unlawful for any person to:

(1) By word of mouth or writing advocate, advise or teach the duty, necessity or propriety of overthrowing or overturning the government of the United States or a political subdivision of the United States by force or violence; or,

(2) Print, publish, edit, issue or knowingly circulate, sell, distribute or publicly display any book, paper, document, or written or printed matter in any form, containing or advocating, advising or teaching the doctrine that the government of the United States or a political subdivision of the United States should be overthrown by force, violence or any unlawful means; or,

(3) Organize or help to organize or become a member of or voluntarily assemble with any society, group or assembly of persons formed to teach or advocate the doctrine that the government of the United States or a political subdivision of the United States should be overthrown by force, violence or any unlawful means.

Any person violating the provisions of this section shall be punished as a Class H felon.

Whenever two or more persons assemble for the purpose of advocating or teaching the doctrine that the government of the United States or a political subdivision of the United States should be overthrown by force, violence or any unlawful means, such an assembly is unlawful, and every person voluntarily participating therein by his presence, aid or instigation, shall be punished as a Class H felon.

Every editor or proprietor of a book, newspaper or serial and every manager of a partnership or incorporated association by which a book, newspaper or serial is issued, is chargeable with the publication of any matter contained in such book, newspaper or serial. But in every prosecution therefor, the defendant may show in his defense that the matter complained of was published without his knowledge or fault and against his wishes, by another who had no authority from him to make the publication and whose act was disavowed by him as soon as known.

No person shall be employed by any department, bureau, institution or agency of the State of North Carolina who has participated in any of the activities described in this section, and any person now employed by any department, bureau, institution or agency and who has been or is engaged in any of the activities described in this section shall be forthwith discharged. Evidence satisfactory to the head of such department, bureau, institution or agency of the State shall be sufficient for refusal to employ any person or cause for discharge of any employee for the reasons set forth in this paragraph. (1947, c. 1028; 1953, c. 675, s. 2; 1979, c. 760, s. 5; 1979. 2nd Sess., c. 1316, s. 47; 1981, c. 63, s. 1; c. 179, s. 14.)

Article 4A.

Prohibited Secret Societies and Activities.

§ 14-12.2. Definitions.

The terms used in this Article are defined as follows:

(1)   The term "secret society" shall mean any two or more persons organized, associated together, combined or united for any common purpose whatsoever, who shall use among themselves any certain grips, signs or password, or who shall use for the advancement of any of their purposes or as a part of their ritual any disguise of the person, face or voice or any disguise whatsoever, or who shall take any extrajudicial oath or secret solemn pledge or administer such oath or pledge to those associated with them, or who shall transact business and advance their purposes at secret meeting or meetings which are tiled and guarded against intrusion by persons not associated with them.

(2)   The term "secret political society" shall mean any secret society, as hereinbefore defined, which shall at any time have for a purpose the hindering

or aiding the success of any candidate for public office, or the hindering or aiding the success of any political party or organization, or violating any lawfully declared policy of the government of the State or any of the laws and constitutional provisions of the State.

(3) The term "secret military society" shall mean any secret society, as hereinbefore defined, which shall at any time meet, assemble or engage in a venture when members thereof are illegally armed, or which shall at any time have for a purpose the engaging in any venture by members thereof which shall require illegal armed force or in which illegal armed force is to be used, or which shall at any time muster, drill or practice any military evolutions while illegally armed. (1953, c. 1193, s. 1.)

§ 14-12.3. Certain secret societies prohibited.

It shall be unlawful for any person to join, unite himself with, become a member of, apply for membership in, form, organize, solicit members for, combine and agree with any person or persons to form or organize, or to encourage, aid or assist in any way any secret political society or any secret military society or any secret society having for a purpose the violating or circumventing the laws of the State. (1953, c. 1193, s. 2.)

§ 14-12.4. Use of signs, grips, passwords or disguises or taking or administering oath for illegal purposes.

It shall be unlawful for any person to use, agree to use, or to encourage, aid or assist in the using of any signs, grips, passwords, disguise of the face, person or voice, or any disguise whatsoever in the furtherance of any illegal secret political purpose, any illegal secret military purpose, or any purpose of violating or circumventing the laws of the State; and it shall be unlawful for any person to take or administer, or agree to take or administer, any extrajudicial oath or secret solemn pledge to further any illegal secret political purpose, any illegal secret military purpose, or any purpose of violating or circumventing the laws of the State. (1953, c. 1193, s. 3.)

§ 14-12.5. Permitting, etc., meetings or demonstrations of prohibited secret societies.

It shall be unlawful for any person to permit or agree to permit any members of a secret political society or a secret military society or a secret society having for a purpose the violating or circumventing the laws of the State to meet or to hold any demonstration in or upon any property owned or controlled by him. (1953, c. 1193, s. 4.)

§ 14-12.6. Meeting places and meetings of secret societies regulated.

Every secret society which has been or is now being formed and organized within the State, and which has members within the State shall forthwith provide or cause to be provided for each unit, lodge, council, group of members, grand lodge or general supervising unit a regular meeting place in some building or structure, and shall forthwith place and thereafter regularly keep a plainly visible sign or placard on the immediate exterior of such building or structure or on the immediate exterior of the meeting room or hall within such building or structure, if the entire building or structure is not controlled by such secret society, bearing upon said sign or placard the name of the secret society, the name of the particular unit, lodge, council, group of members, grand lodge or general supervising unit thereof and the name of the secretary, officer, organizer or member thereof who knows the purposes of the secret society and who knows or has a list of the names and addresses of the members thereof, and as such secretary, officer, organizer or member dies, removes, resigns or is replaced, his or her successor's name shall be placed upon such sign or placard; any person or persons who shall hereafter undertake to form and organize any secret society or solicit membership for a secret society within the State shall fully comply with the foregoing provisions of this section before forming and organizing such secret society and before soliciting memberships therein; all units, lodges, councils, groups of members, grand lodge and general supervising units of all secret societies within the State shall hold all of their secret meetings at the regular meeting place of their respective units, lodges, councils, group of members, grand lodge or general supervising units or at the regular meeting place of some other unit, lodge, council, group of members, grand lodge or general supervising unit of the same secret society, and at no other place unless notice is given of the time and place of the meeting and the name of the secret society holding the meeting in some newspaper having circulation in the locality where the meeting is to be held at least two days before the meeting. (1953, c. 1193, s. 5.)

§ 14-12.7. Wearing of masks, hoods, etc., on public ways.

No person or persons at least 16 years of age shall, while wearing any mask, hood or device whereby the person, face or voice is disguised so as to conceal the identity of the wearer, enter, be or appear upon any lane, walkway, alley, street, road, highway or other public way in this State. (1953, c. 1193, s. 6; 1983, c. 175, ss. 1, 10; c. 720, s. 4.)

§ 14-12.8. Wearing of masks, hoods, etc., on public property.

No person or persons shall in this State, while wearing any mask, hood or device whereby the person, face or voice is disguised so as to conceal the identity of the wearer, enter, or appear upon or within the public property of any municipality or county of the State, or of the State of North Carolina. (1953, c. 1193, s. 7.)

§ 14-12.9. Entry, etc., upon premises of another while wearing mask, hood or other disguise.

No person or persons at least 16 years of age shall, while wearing a mask, hood or device whereby the person, face or voice is disguised so as to conceal the identity of the wearer, demand entrance or admission, enter or come upon or into, or be upon or in the premises, enclosure or house of any other person in any municipality or county of this State. (1953, c. 1193, s. 8; 1983, c. 175, ss. 2, 10; c. 720, s. 4.)

§ 14-12.10. Holding meetings or demonstrations while wearing masks, hoods, etc.

No person or persons at least 16 years of age shall while wearing a mask, hood or device whereby the person, face or voice is disguised so as to conceal the identity of the wearer, hold any manner of meeting, or make any demonstration upon the private property of another unless such person or persons shall first obtain from the owner or occupier of the property his or her written permission to do so, which said written permission shall be recorded in the office of the register of deeds of the county in which said property is located before the beginning of such meeting or demonstration. (1953, c. 1193, s. 9; 1983, c. 175, ss. 3, 10; c. 720, s. 4.)

§ 14-12.11. Exemptions from provisions of Article.

The following are exempted from the provisions of G.S. 14-12.7, 14-12.8, 14-12.9, 14-12.10 and 14-12.14:

(1)   Any person or persons wearing traditional holiday costumes in season;

(2)   Any person or persons engaged in trades and employment where a mask is worn for the purpose of ensuring the physical safety of the wearer, or because of the nature of the occupation, trade or profession;

(3)   Any person or persons using masks in theatrical productions including use in Mardi Gras celebrations and masquerade balls;

(4)   Persons wearing gas masks prescribed in civil defense drills and exercises or emergencies; and

(5)   Any person or persons, as members or members elect of a society, order or organization, engaged in any parade, ritual, initiation, ceremony, celebration or requirement of such society, order or organization, and wearing or using any manner of costume, paraphernalia, disguise, facial makeup, hood, implement or device, whether the identity of such person or persons is concealed or not, on any public or private street, road, way or property, or in any public or private building, provided permission shall have been first obtained therefor by a representative of such society, order or organization from the governing body of the municipality in which the same takes place, or, if not in a municipality, from the board of county commissioners of the county in which the same takes place.

Provided, that the provisions of this Article shall not apply to any preliminary meetings held in good faith for the purpose of organizing, promoting or forming a labor union or a local organization or subdivision of any labor union nor shall the provisions of this Article apply to any meetings held by a labor union or organization already organized, operating and functioning and holding meetings for the purpose of transacting and carrying out functions, pursuits and affairs expressly pertaining to such labor union. (1953, c. 1193, s. 10.)

§ 14-12.12. Placing burning or flaming cross on property of another or on public street or highway or on any public place.

(a) It shall be unlawful for any person or persons to place or cause to be placed on the property of another in this State a burning or flaming cross or any manner of exhibit in which a burning or flaming cross, real or simulated, is a whole or a part, without first obtaining written permission of the owner or occupier of the premises so to do.

(b) It shall be unlawful for any person or persons to place or cause to be placed on the property of another in this State or on a public street or highway, or on any public place a burning or flaming cross or any manner of exhibit in which a burning or flaming cross real or simulated, is a whole or a part, with the intention of intimidating any person or persons or of preventing them from doing any act which is lawful, or causing them to do any act which is unlawful. (1953, c. 1193, s. 11; 1967, c. 522, ss. 1, 2; 2008-197, s. 1.)

§ 14-12.13. Placing exhibit with intention of intimidating, etc., another.

It shall be unlawful for any person or persons to place or cause to be placed anywhere in this State any exhibit of any kind whatsoever, while masked or unmasked, with the intention of intimidating any person or persons, or of preventing them from doing any act which is lawful, or of causing them to do any act which is unlawful. For the purposes of this section, the term "exhibit" includes items such as a noose. (1953, c. 1193, s. 12; 2008-197, s. 2.)

§ 14-12.14. Placing exhibit while wearing mask, hood, or other disguise.

It shall be unlawful for any person or persons, while wearing a mask, hood or device whereby the person, face or voice is disguised so as to conceal the identity of the wearer, to place or cause to be placed at or in any place in the State any exhibit of any kind whatsoever, with the intention of intimidating any person or persons, or of preventing them from doing any act which is lawful, or of causing them to do any act which is unlawful. For the purposes of this section, the term "exhibit" includes items such as a noose. (1953, c. 1193, s. 13; 1967, c. 522, s. 3; 2008-197, s. 3.)

§ 14-12.15. Punishment for violation of Article.

All persons violating any of the provisions of this Article, except for G.S. 14-12.12(b), 14-12.13, and 14-12.14, shall be guilty of a Class 1 misdemeanor. All persons violating the provisions of G.S. 14-12.12(b), 14-12.13, and 14-12.14 shall be punished as a Class H felon. (1953, c. 1193, s. 14; 1967, c. 602; 1979, c. 760, s. 5; 1979, 2nd Sess., c. 1316, s. 47; 1981, c. 63, s. 1; c. 179, s. 14; 1993, c. 539, s. 12; 1994, Ex. Sess., c. 24, s. 14(c); 2008-197, s. 4.)

Article 5.

Counterferfeiting and Issuing Monetary Substitutes.

§ 14-13. Counterfeiting coin and uttering coin that is counterfeit.

If any person shall falsely make, forge or counterfeit, or cause or procure to be falsely made, forged or counterfeited, or willingly aid or assist in falsely making, forging or counterfeiting the resemblance or similitude or likeness of any coin of gold or silver which is in common use and received in the discharge of contracts by the citizens of the State; or shall pass, utter, publish or sell, or attempt to pass, utter, publish or sell, or bring into the State from any other place with intent to pass, utter, publish or sell as true, any such false, forged or counterfeited coin, knowing the same to be false, forged or counterfeited, with intent to defraud any person whatsoever, every person so offending shall be punished as a Class I felon. (1811, c. 814, s. 3, P.R.; R.C., c. 34, s. 64; Code, s. 1035; Rev., s. 3422; C.S., s. 4181; 1979, c. 760, s. 5; 1979, 2nd Sess., c. 1316, s. 47; 1981, c. 63, s. 1; c. 179, s. 14; 1993, c. 539, s. 1123; 1994, Ex. Sess., c. 24, s. 14(c); 1995, c. 379, s. 1(a).)

§ 14-14. Possessing tools for counterfeiting.

If any person shall have in his possession any instrument for the purpose of making any counterfeit similitude or likeness of any coin made of gold or silver which is in common use and received in discharge of contracts by the citizens of the State, and shall be duly convicted thereof, the person so offending shall be punished as a Class I felon. (1811, c. 814, s. 4, P.R.; R.C., c. 34, s. 65; Code, s. 1036; Rev., s. 3423; C.S., s. 4182; 1979, c. 760, s. 5; 1979, 2nd Sess., c. 1316, s. 47; 1981, c. 63, s. 1; c. 179, s. 14; 1993, c. 539, s. 1124; 1994, Ex. Sess., c. 24, s. 14(c); 1995, c. 379, s. 1(b).)

§ 14-15. Issuing substitutes for money without authority.

If any person or corporation, unless the same be expressly allowed by law, shall issue any bill, due bill, order, ticket, certificate of deposit, promissory note or obligation, or any other kind of security, whatever may be its form or name, with the intent that the same shall circulate or pass as the representative of, or as a substitute for, money, he shall be guilty of a Class 3 misdemeanor and only punishable by a fine not to exceed the sum of fifty dollars ($50.00); and if the offender be a corporation, it shall in addition forfeit its charter. Every person or corporation offending against this section, or aiding or assisting therein, shall be guilty of a Class 3 misdemeanor and only punishable by a fine not to exceed fifty dollars ($50.00). (R.C., c. 36, s. 5; Code, s. 2493; 1895, c. 127; Rev., s. 3711; C.S., s. 4183; 1993, c. 539, s. 13; 1994, Ex. Sess., c. 24, s. 14(c).)

§ 14-16. Receiving or passing unauthorized substitutes for money.

If any person or corporation shall pass or receive, as the representative of, or as the substitute for, money, any bill, check, certificate, promissory note, or other security of the kind mentioned in G.S. 14-15, whether the same be issued within or without the State, such person or corporation, and the officers and agents of such corporation aiding therein, who shall offend against this section shall be guilty of a Class 3 misdemeanor and only punishable by a fine not to exceed five dollars ($5.00). (R.C., c. 36, s. 6; Code, s. 2494; 1895, c. 127; Rev., s. 3712; C.S., s. 4184; 1993, c. 539, s. 14; 1994, Ex. Sess., c. 24, s. 14(c).)

§ 14-16.1: Reserved for future codification purposes.

§ 14-16.2: Reserved for future codification purposes.

§ 14-16.3: Reserved for future codification purposes.

§ 14-16.4: Reserved for future codification purposes.

§ 14-16.5: Reserved for future codification purposes.

Article 5A.

Endangering Executive and Legislative, and Court Officers.

§ 14-16.6. Assault on executive, legislative, or court officer.

(a) Any person who assaults any legislative officer, executive officer, or court officer, or any person who makes a violent attack upon the residence, office, temporary accommodation or means of transport of any one of those officers in a manner likely to endanger the officer, shall be guilty of a felony and shall be punished as a Class I felon.

(b) Any person who commits an offense under subsection (a) and uses a deadly weapon in the commission of that offense shall be punished as a Class F felon.

(c) Any person who commits an offense under subsection (a) and inflicts serious bodily injury to any legislative officer, executive officer, or court officer, shall be punished as a Class F felon. (1981, c. 822, s. 1; 1993, c. 539, s. 1125; 1994, Ex. Sess., c. 24, s. 14(c); 1999-398, s. 1.)

§ 14-16.7. Threats against executive, legislative, or court officers.

(a) Any person who knowingly and willfully makes any threat to inflict serious bodily injury upon or to kill any legislative officer, executive officer, or court officer, shall be guilty of a felony and shall be punished as a Class I felon.

(b) Any person who knowingly and willfully deposits for conveyance in the mail any letter, writing, or other document containing a threat to inflict serious bodily injury upon or to kill any legislative officer, executive officer, or court officer, shall be guilty of a felony and shall be punished as a Class I felon. (1981, c. 822, s. 1; 1993, c. 539, s. 1126; 1994, Ex. Sess., c. 24, s. 14(c); 1999-398, s. 1.)

§ 14-16.8. No requirement of receipt of the threat.

In prosecutions under G.S. 14-16.7 of this Article it shall not be necessary to prove that any legislative officer, executive officer, or court officer actually received the threatening communication or actually believed the threat. (1981, c. 822, s. 1; 1999-398, s. 1.)

§ 14-16.9. Officers-elect to be covered.

Any person who has been elected to any office covered by this Article but has not yet taken the oath of office shall be considered to hold the office for the purpose of this Article and G.S. 114-15. (1981, c. 822, s. 1; 2011-145, s. 19.1(dd1); 2011-391, s. 43(l).)

§ 14-16.10. Definitions.

The following definitions apply in this Article:

(1) Court officer. - Magistrate, clerk of superior court, acting clerk, assistant or deputy clerk, judge, or justice of the General Court of Justice; district attorney, assistant district attorney, or any other attorney designated by the district attorney to act for the State or on behalf of the district attorney; public defender or assistant defender; court reporter; juvenile court counselor as defined in G.S. 7B-1501(18a); any attorney or other individual employed by or acting on behalf of the department of social services in proceedings pursuant to Subchapter I of Chapter 7B of the General Statutes; any attorney or other individual appointed pursuant to G.S. 7B-601 or G.S. 7B-1108 or employed by

the Guardian ad Litem Services Division of the Administrative Office of the Courts.

(2) Executive officer. - A person named in G.S. 147-3(c).

(3) Legislative officer. - A person named in G.S. 147-2(1), (2), or (3). (1999-398, s. 1; 2001-490, s. 2.35; 2003-140, s. 10.)

SUBCHAPTER III. OFFENSES AGAINST THE PERSON.

Article 6.

Homicide.

§ 14-17. Murder in the first and second degree defined; punishment.

(a) A murder which shall be perpetrated by means of a nuclear, biological, or chemical weapon of mass destruction as defined in G.S. 14-288.21, poison, lying in wait, imprisonment, starving, torture, or by any other kind of willful, deliberate, and premeditated killing, or which shall be committed in the perpetration or attempted perpetration of any arson, rape or a sex offense, robbery, kidnapping, burglary, or other felony committed or attempted with the use of a deadly weapon shall be deemed to be murder in the first degree, a Class A felony, and any person who commits such murder shall be punished with death or imprisonment in the State's prison for life without parole as the court shall determine pursuant to G.S. 15A-2000, except that any such person who was under 18 years of age at the time of the murder shall be punished in accordance with Part 2A of Article 81B of Chapter 15A of the General Statutes.

(b) A murder other than described in subsection (a) of this section or in G.S. 14-23.2 shall be deemed second degree murder. Any person who commits second degree murder shall be punished as a Class B1 felon, except that a person who commits second degree murder shall be punished as a Class B2 felon in either of the following circumstances:

(1) The malice necessary to prove second degree murder is based on an inherently dangerous act or omission, done in such a reckless and wanton manner as to manifest a mind utterly without regard for human life and social duty and deliberately bent on mischief.

(2) The murder is one that was proximately caused by the unlawful distribution of opium or any synthetic or natural salt, compound, derivative, or preparation of opium, or cocaine or other substance described in G.S. 90-90(1)d., or methamphetamine, and the ingestion of such substance caused the death of the user.

(c) For the purposes of this section, it shall constitute murder where a child is born alive but dies as a result of injuries inflicted prior to the child being born alive. The degree of murder shall be determined as described in subsections (a) and (b) of this section. (1893, cc. 85, 281; Rev., s. 3631; C.S., s. 4200; 1949, c. 299, s. 1; 1973, c. 1201, s. 1; 1977, c. 406, s. 1; 1979, c. 682, s. 6; 1979, c. 760, s. 5; 1979, 2nd Sess., c. 1251, ss. 1, 2; c. 1316, s. 47; 1981, c. 63, s. 1; c. 179, s. 14; c. 662, s. 1; 1987, c. 693; 1989, c. 694; 1993, c. 539, s. 112; 1994, Ex. Sess., c. 21, s. 1; c. 22, s. 4; c. 24, s. 14(c); 2001-470, s. 2; 2004-178, s. 1; 2007-81, s. 1; 2012-165, s. 1; 2013-47, s. 2; 2013-410, s. 3(a).)

§ 14-17.1. Crime of suicide abolished.

The common-law crime of suicide is hereby abolished as an offense. (1973, c. 1205.)

§ 14-18. Punishment for manslaughter.

Voluntary manslaughter shall be punishable as a Class D felony, and involuntary manslaughter shall be punishable as a Class F felony. (4 Hen. VII, s. 13; 1816, c. 918, P.R.; R.C., c. 34, s. 24; 1879, c. 255; Code, s. 1055; Rev., s. 3632; C.S., s. 4201; 1933, c. 249; 1979, c. 760, s. 5; 1979, 2nd Sess., c. 1316, s. 47; 1981, c. 63, s. 1; c. 179, s. 14; 1993, c. 539, s. 112; 1994, Ex. Sess., c. 24, s. 14(c); 1997-443, s. 19.25(q).)

§ 14-18.1: Repealed by Session Laws 1994, Extra Session, c. 14, s. 73.

§ 14-18.2: Repealed by Session Laws 2011-60, s. 3, effective December 1, 2011, and applicable to offenses committed on or after that date.

§ 14-19. Repealed by Session Laws 1979, c. 760, s. 5, effective July 1, 1981.

§ 14-20: Repealed by Session Laws 1993 (Reg. Sess., 1994), c. 767, s. 29(1).

§§ 14-21 through 14-23. Repealed by Session Laws 1979, c. 682, s. 7, effective January 1, 1980.

Article 6A.

Unborn Victims.

§ 14-23.1. Definition.

As used in this Article only, "unborn child" means a member of the species homo sapiens, at any stage of development, who is carried in the womb. (2011-60, s. 2.)

§ 14-23.2. Murder of an unborn child; penalty.

(a) A person who unlawfully causes the death of an unborn child is guilty of the separate offense of murder of an unborn child if the person does any one of the following:

(1) Willfully and maliciously commits an act with the intent to cause the death of the unborn child.

(2) Causes the death of the unborn child in perpetration or attempted perpetration of any of the criminal offenses set forth under G.S. 14-17.

(3) Commits an act causing the death of the unborn child that is inherently dangerous to human life and is done so recklessly and wantonly that it reflects disregard of life.

(b) Penalty. - An offense under:

(1) Subdivision (a)(1) or (a)(2) of this section shall be a Class A felony, and any person who commits such offense shall be punished with imprisonment in the State's prison for life without parole.

(2) Subdivision (a)(3) of this section shall be subject to the same sentence as if the person had been convicted of second degree murder pursuant to G.S. 14-17. (2011-60, s. 2.)

§ 14-23.3. Voluntary manslaughter of an unborn child; penalty.

(a) A person is guilty of the separate offense of voluntary manslaughter of an unborn child if the person unlawfully causes the death of an unborn child by an act that would be voluntary manslaughter if it resulted in the death of the mother.

(b) Penalty. - Any person who commits an offense under this section shall be guilty of a Class D felony. (2011-60, s. 2.)

§ 14-23.4. Involuntary manslaughter of an unborn child; penalty.

(a) A person is guilty of the separate offense of involuntary manslaughter of an unborn child if the person unlawfully causes the death of an unborn child by an act that would be involuntary manslaughter if it resulted in the death of the mother.

(b) Penalty. - Any person who commits an offense under this section shall be guilty of a Class F felony. (2011-60, s. 2.)

§ 14-23.5. Assault inflicting serious bodily injury on an unborn child; penalty.

(a) A person is guilty of the separate offense of assault inflicting serious bodily injury on an unborn child if the person commits a battery on the mother of the unborn child and the child is subsequently born alive and suffered serious bodily harm as a result of the battery.

(b) For purposes of this section, "serious bodily harm" is defined as bodily injury that creates a substantial risk of death, or that causes serious permanent disfigurement, coma, a permanent or protracted condition that causes extreme pain, or permanent or protracted loss or impairment of the function of any bodily member or organ, or that results in prolonged hospitalization, or causes the birth of the unborn child prior to 37-weeks gestation, if the child weighs 2,500 grams or less at the time of birth.

(c)   Penalty. - Any person who commits an offense under this section shall be guilty of a Class F felony. (2011-60, s. 2.)

§ 14-23.6. Battery on an unborn child.

(a)   A person is guilty of the separate offense of battery on an unborn child if the person commits a battery on a pregnant woman. This offense is a lesser-included offense of G.S. 14-23.5.

(b)   Penalty. - Any person who commits an offense under this section is guilty of a Class A1 misdemeanor. (2011-60, s. 2.)

§ 14-23.7. Exceptions.

Nothing in this Article shall be construed to permit the prosecution under this Article of any of the following:

(1)   Acts which cause the death of an unborn child if those acts were lawful, pursuant to the provisions of G.S. 14-45.1.

(2)   Acts which are committed pursuant to usual and customary standards of medical practice during diagnostic testing or therapeutic treatment.

(3)   Acts committed by a pregnant woman with respect to her own unborn child, including, but not limited to, acts which result in miscarriage or stillbirth by the woman. The following definitions shall apply in this section:

a.   Miscarriage. - The interruption of the normal development of an unborn child, other than by a live birth, and which is not an induced abortion permitted under G.S. 14-45.1, resulting in the complete expulsion or extraction from a pregnant woman of the unborn child.

b. Stillbirth. - The death of an unborn child prior to the complete expulsion or extraction from a woman, irrespective of the duration of pregnancy and which is not an induced abortion permitted under G.S. 14-45.1. (2011-60, s. 2.)

§ 14-23.8. Knowledge not required.

Except for an offense under G.S. 14-23.2(a)(1), an offense under this Article does not require proof of either of the following:

(1) The person engaging in the conduct had knowledge or should have had knowledge that the victim of the underlying offense was pregnant.

(2) The defendant intended to cause the death of, or bodily injury to, the unborn child. (2011-60, s. 2.)

Article 7.

Rape and Kindred Offenses.

§§ 14-24 through 14-25. Repealed by Session Laws, 1975, c. 402.

§§ 14-26 through 14-27. Repealed by Session Laws 1979, c. 682, s. 7, effective January 1, 1980.

Article 7A.

Rape and Other Sex Offenses.

§ 14-27.1. Definitions.

As used in this Article, unless the context requires otherwise:

(1) "Mentally disabled" means (i) a victim who suffers from mental retardation, or (ii) a victim who suffers from a mental disorder, either of which temporarily or permanently renders the victim substantially incapable of appraising the nature of his or her conduct, or of resisting the act of vaginal intercourse or a sexual act, or of communicating unwillingness to submit to the act of vaginal intercourse or a sexual act.

(2) "Mentally incapacitated" means a victim who due to any act committed upon the victim is rendered substantially incapable of either appraising the nature of his or her conduct, or resisting the act of vaginal intercourse or a sexual act.

(3) "Physically helpless" means (i) a victim who is unconscious; or (ii) a victim who is physically unable to resist an act of vaginal intercourse or a sexual act or communicate unwillingness to submit to an act of vaginal intercourse or a sexual act.

(4) "Sexual act" means cunnilingus, fellatio, analingus, or anal intercourse, but does not include vaginal intercourse. Sexual act also means the penetration, however slight, by any object into the genital or anal opening of another person's body: provided, that it shall be an affirmative defense that the penetration was for accepted medical purposes.

(5) "Sexual contact" means (i) touching the sexual organ, anus, breast, groin, or buttocks of any person, (ii) a person touching another person with their own sexual organ, anus, breast, groin, or buttocks, or (iii) a person ejaculating, emitting, or placing semen, urine, or feces upon any part of another person.

(6) "Touching" as used in subdivision (5) of this section, means physical contact with another person, whether accomplished directly, through the clothing of the person committing the offense, or through the clothing of the victim. (1979, c. 682, s. 1; 2002-159, s. 2(a); 2003-252, s. 1; 2006-247, s. 12(a).)

§ 14-27.2. First-degree rape.

(a) A person is guilty of rape in the first degree if the person engages in vaginal intercourse:

(1) With a victim who is a child under the age of 13 years and the defendant is at least 12 years old and is at least four years older than the victim; or

(2) With another person by force and against the will of the other person, and:

a. Employs or displays a dangerous or deadly weapon or an article which the other person reasonably believes to be a dangerous or deadly weapon; or

b. Inflicts serious personal injury upon the victim or another person; or

c. The person commits the offense aided and abetted by one or more other persons.

(b) Any person who commits an offense defined in this section is guilty of a Class B1 felony.

(c) Upon conviction, a person convicted under this section has no rights to custody of or rights of inheritance from any child born as a result of the commission of the rape, nor shall the person have any rights related to the child under Chapter 48 or Subchapter 1 of Chapter 7B of the General Statutes. (1979, c. 682, s. 1; 1979, 2nd Sess., c. 1316, s. 4; 1981, c. 63; c. 106, ss. 1, 2; c. 179, s. 14; 1983, c. 175, ss. 4, 10; c. 720, s. 4; 1994, Ex. Sess., c. 22, s. 2; 2004-128, s. 7.)

§ 14-27.2A. Rape of a child; adult offender.

(a) A person is guilty of rape of a child if the person is at least 18 years of age and engages in vaginal intercourse with a victim who is a child under the age of 13 years.

(b) A person convicted of violating this section is guilty of a Class B1 felony and shall be sentenced pursuant to Article 81B of Chapter 15A of the General Statutes, except that in no case shall the person receive an active punishment of less than 300 months, and except as provided in subsection (c) of this section. Following the termination of active punishment, the person shall be enrolled in satellite-based monitoring for life pursuant to Part 5 of Article 27A of Chapter 14 of the General Statutes.

(c) Notwithstanding the provisions of Article 81B of Chapter 15A of the General Statutes, the court may sentence the defendant to active punishment for a term of months greater than that authorized pursuant to G.S. 15A-1340.17, up to and including life imprisonment without parole, if the court finds that the nature of the offense and the harm inflicted are of such brutality, duration, severity, degree, or scope beyond that normally committed in such crimes, or considered in basic aggravation of these crimes, so as to require a sentence to active punishment in excess of that authorized pursuant to G.S. 15A-1340.17. If the court sentences the defendant pursuant to this subsection, it shall make findings of fact supporting its decision, to include matters it considered as egregious aggravation. Egregious aggravation can include further consideration of existing aggravating factors where the conduct of the defendant falls outside the heartland of cases even the aggravating factors were designed to cover. Egregious aggravation may also be considered based on the extraordinarily young age of the victim, or the depraved torture or mutilation of the victim, or extraordinary physical pain inflicted on the victim.

(d) Upon conviction, a person convicted under this section has no rights to custody of or rights of inheritance from any child born as a result of the commission of the rape, nor shall the person have any rights related to the child under Chapter 48 or Subchapter 1 of Chapter 7B of the General Statutes.

(e) The offense under G.S. 14-27.2(a)(1) is a lesser included offense of the offense in this section. (2008-117, s. 1.)

§ 14-27.3. Second-degree rape.

(a) A person is guilty of rape in the second degree if the person engages in vaginal intercourse with another person:

(1) By force and against the will of the other person; or

(2) Who is mentally disabled, mentally incapacitated, or physically helpless, and the person performing the act knows or should reasonably know the other person is mentally disabled, mentally incapacitated, or physically helpless.

(b) Any person who commits the offense defined in this section is guilty of a Class C felony.

(c) Upon conviction, a person convicted under this section has no rights to custody of or rights of inheritance from any child conceived during the commission of the rape, nor shall the person have any rights related to the child under Chapter 48 or Subchapter 1 of Chapter 7B of the General Statutes. (1979, c. 682, s. 1; 1979, 2nd Sess., c. 1316, s. 5; 1981, cc. 63, 179; 1993, c. 539, s. 1130; 1994, Ex. Sess., c. 24, s. 14(c); 2002-159, s. 2(b); 2004-128, s. 8.)

§ 14-27.4. First-degree sexual offense.

(a) A person is guilty of a sexual offense in the first degree if the person engages in a sexual act:

(1) With a victim who is a child under the age of 13 years and the defendant is at least 12 years old and is at least four years older than the victim; or

(2) With another person by force and against the will of the other person, and:

a. Employs or displays a dangerous or deadly weapon or an article which the other person reasonably believes to be a dangerous or deadly weapon; or

b. Inflicts serious personal injury upon the victim or another person; or

c. The person commits the offense aided and abetted by one or more other persons.

(b) Any person who commits an offense defined in this section is guilty of a Class B1 felony. (1979, c. 682, s. 1; 1979, 2nd Sess., c. 1316, s. 6; 1981, c. 106, ss. 3, 4; 1983, c. 175, ss. 5, 10; c. 720, s. 4; 1994, Ex. Sess., c. 22, s. 3.)

§ 14-27.4A. Sexual offense with a child; adult offender.

(a) A person is guilty of sexual offense with a child if the person is at least 18 years of age and engages in a sexual act with a victim who is a child under the age of 13 years.

(b)   A person convicted of violating this section is guilty of a Class B1 felony and shall be sentenced pursuant to Article 81B of Chapter 15A of the General Statutes, except that in no case shall the person receive an active punishment of less than 300 months, and except as provided in subsection (c) of this section. Following the termination of active punishment, the person shall be enrolled in satellite-based monitoring for life pursuant to Part 5 of Article 27A of Chapter 14 of the General Statutes.

(c)   Notwithstanding the provisions of Article 81B of Chapter 15A of the General Statutes, the court may sentence the defendant to active punishment for a term of months greater than that authorized pursuant to G.S. 15A-1340.17, up to and including life imprisonment without parole, if the court finds that the nature of the offense and the harm inflicted are of such brutality, duration, severity, degree, or scope beyond that normally committed in such crimes, or considered in basic aggravation of these crimes, so as to require a sentence to active punishment in excess of that authorized pursuant to G.S. 15A-1340.17. If the court sentences the defendant pursuant to this subsection, it shall make findings of fact supporting its decision, to include matters it considered as egregious aggravation. Egregious aggravation can include further consideration of existing aggravating factors where the conduct of the defendant falls outside the heartland of cases even the aggravating factors were designed to cover. Egregious aggravation may also be considered based on the extraordinarily young age of the victim, or the depraved torture or mutilation of the victim, or extraordinary physical pain inflicted on the victim.

(d)   The offense under G.S. 14-27.4(a)(1) is a lesser included offense of the offense in this section. (2008-117, s. 2.)

§ 14-27.5. Second-degree sexual offense.

(a)   A person is guilty of a sexual offense in the second degree if the person engages in a sexual act with another person:

(1)   By force and against the will of the other person; or

(2)   Who is mentally disabled, mentally incapacitated, or physically helpless, and the person performing the act knows or should reasonably know that the other person is mentally disabled, mentally incapacitated, or physically helpless.

(b) Any person who commits the offense defined in this section is guilty of a Class C felony. (1979, c. 682, s. 1; 1979, 2nd Sess., c. 1316, s. 7; 1981, c. 63; c. 179, s. 14; 1993, c. 539, s. 1131; 1994, Ex. Sess., c. 24, s. 14(c); 2002-159, s. 2(c).)

§ 14-27.5A. Sexual battery.

(a) A person is guilty of sexual battery if the person, for the purpose of sexual arousal, sexual gratification, or sexual abuse, engages in sexual contact with another person:

(1) By force and against the will of the other person; or

(2) Who is mentally disabled, mentally incapacitated, or physically helpless, and the person performing the act knows or should reasonably know that the other person is mentally disabled, mentally incapacitated, or physically helpless.

(b) Any person who commits the offense defined in this section is guilty of a Class A1 misdemeanor. (2003-252, s. 2.)

§ 14-27.6: Repealed by Session Laws 1994, Ex. Sess., c. 14, s. 71(3).

§ 14-27.7. Intercourse and sexual offenses with certain victims; consent no defense.

(a) If a defendant who has assumed the position of a parent in the home of a minor victim engages in vaginal intercourse or a sexual act with a victim who is a minor residing in the home, or if a person having custody of a victim of any age or a person who is an agent or employee of any person, or institution, whether such institution is private, charitable, or governmental, having custody of a victim of any age engages in vaginal intercourse or a sexual act with such victim, the defendant is guilty of a Class E felony. Consent is not a defense to a charge under this section.

(b) If a defendant, who is a teacher, school administrator, student teacher, school safety officer, or coach, at any age, or who is other school personnel, and who is at least four years older than the victim engages in vaginal intercourse or a sexual act with a victim who is a student, at any time during or after the time the defendant and victim were present together in the same school, but before the victim ceases to be a student, the defendant is guilty of a Class G felony, except when the defendant is lawfully married to the student. The term "same school" means a school at which the student is enrolled and the defendant is employed, assigned, or volunteers. A defendant who is school personnel, other than a teacher, school administrator, student teacher, school safety officer, or coach, and is less than four years older than the victim and engages in vaginal intercourse or a sexual act with a victim who is a student, is guilty of a Class A1 misdemeanor. This subsection shall apply unless the conduct is covered under some other provision of law providing for greater punishment. Consent is not a defense to a charge under this section. For purposes of this subsection, the terms "school", "school personnel", and "student" shall have the same meaning as in G.S. 14-202.4(d). For purposes of this subsection, the term "school safety officer" shall include a school resource officer or any other person who is regularly present in a school for the purpose of promoting and maintaining safe and orderly schools. (1979, c. 682, s. 1; 1979, 2nd Sess., c. 1316, s. 9; 1981, c. 63; c. 179, s. 14; 1993, c. 539, s. 1132; 1994, Ex. Sess., c. 24, s. 14(c); 1999-300, s. 2; 2003-98, s. 1.)

§ 14-27.7A. Statutory rape or sexual offense of person who is 13, 14, or 15 years old.

(a) A defendant is guilty of a Class B1 felony if the defendant engages in vaginal intercourse or a sexual act with another person who is 13, 14, or 15 years old and the defendant is at least six years older than the person, except when the defendant is lawfully married to the person.

(b) A defendant is guilty of a Class C felony if the defendant engages in vaginal intercourse or a sexual act with another person who is 13, 14, or 15 years old and the defendant is more than four but less than six years older than the person, except when the defendant is lawfully married to the person. (1995, c. 281, s. 1.)

§ 14-27.8. No defense that victim is spouse of person committing act.

A person may be prosecuted under this Article whether or not the victim is the person's legal spouse at the time of the commission of the alleged rape or sexual offense. (1979, c. 682, s. 1; 1987, c. 742; 1993, c. 274.)

§ 14-27.9. No presumption as to incapacity.

In prosecutions under this Article, there shall be no presumption that any person under the age of 14 years is physically incapable of committing a sex offense of any degree or physically incapable of committing rape, or that a male child under the age of 14 years is incapable of engaging in sexual intercourse. (1979, c. 682, s. 1.)

§ 14-27.10. Evidence required in prosecutions under this Article.

It shall not be necessary upon the trial of any indictment for an offense under this Article where the sex act alleged is vaginal intercourse or anal intercourse to prove the actual emission of semen in order to constitute the offense; but the offense shall be completed upon proof of penetration only. Penetration, however slight, is vaginal intercourse or anal intercourse. (1979, c. 682, s. 1.)

Article 8.

Assaults.

§ 14-28. Malicious castration.

If any person, of malice aforethought, shall unlawfully castrate any other person, or cut off, maim or disfigure any of the privy members of any person, with intent to murder, maim, disfigure, disable or render impotent such person, the person so offending shall be punished as a Class C felon. (1831, c. 40, s. 1; R.C., c. 34, s. 4; 1868-9, c. 167, s. 6; Code, s. 999; Rev., s. 3627; C.S., s. 4210; 1979, c. 760, s. 5; 1979, 2nd Sess., c. 1316, s. 47; 1981, c. 63, s. 1, c. 179, s. 14; 1993, c. 539, s. 1133; 1994, Ex. Sess., c. 24, s. 14(c).)

§ 14-29. Castration or other maiming without malice aforethought.

If any person shall, on purpose and unlawfully, but without malice aforethought, cut, or slit the nose, bite or cut off the nose, or a lip or an ear, or disable any limb or member of any other person, or castrate any other person, or cut off, maim or disfigure any of the privy members of any other person, with intent to kill, maim, disfigure, disable or render impotent such person, the person so offending shall be punished as a Class E felon. (1754, c. 56, P.R.; 1791, c. 339, ss. 2, 3, P.R.; 1831, c. 40, s. 2; R.C., c. 34, s. 47; Code, s. 1000; Rev., s. 3626; C.S., s. 4211; 1979, c. 760, s. 5; 1979, 2nd Sess., c. 1316, s. 47; 1981, c. 63, s. 1, c. 179, s. 14; 1993, c. 539, s. 1134; 1994, Ex. Sess., c. 24, s. 14(c).)

§ 14-30. Malicious maiming.

If any person shall, of malice aforethought, unlawfully cut out or disable the tongue or put out an eye of any other person, with intent to murder, maim or disfigure, the person so offending, his counselors, abettors and aiders, knowing of and privy to the offense, shall be punished as a Class C felon. (22 and 23 Car. II, c. 1 (Coventry Act); 1754, c. 56, P.R.; 1791, c. 339, s. 1, P.R.; 1831, c. 12; R.C., c. 34, s. 14; Code, s. 1080; Rev., s. 3636; C.S., s. 4212; 1979, c. 760, s. 5; 1979, 2nd Sess., c. 1316, s. 47; 1981, c. 63, s. 1, c. 179, s. 14; 1993, c. 539, s. 1135; 1994, Ex. Sess., c. 24, s. 14(c).)

§ 14-30.1. Malicious throwing of corrosive acid or alkali.

If any person shall, of malice aforethought, knowingly and willfully throw or cause to be thrown upon another person any corrosive acid or alkali with intent to murder, maim or disfigure and inflicts serious injury not resulting in death, he shall be punished as a Class E felon. (1963, c. 354; 1979, c. 760, s. 5; 1979, 2nd Sess., c. 1316, s. 47; 1981, c. 63, s. 1, c. 179, s. 14; 1993, c. 539, s. 1136; 1994, Ex. Sess., c. 24, s. 14(c).)

§ 14-31. Maliciously assaulting in a secret manner.

If any person shall in a secret manner maliciously commit an assault and battery with any deadly weapon upon another by waylaying or otherwise, with intent to kill such other person, notwithstanding the person so assaulted may have been conscious of the presence of his adversary, he shall be punished as a Class E felon. (1887, c. 32; Rev., s. 3621; 1919, c. 25; C.S., s. 4213; 1969, c. 602, s. 1; 1979, c. 760, s. 5; 1979, 2nd Sess., c. 1316, s. 47; 1981, c. 63, s. 1, c. 179, s. 14; 1993, c. 539, s. 1137; 1994, Ex. Sess., c. 24, s. 14(c).)

§ 14-32. Felonious assault with deadly weapon with intent to kill or inflicting serious injury; punishments.

(a) Any person who assaults another person with a deadly weapon with intent to kill and inflicts serious injury shall be punished as a Class C felon.

(b) Any person who assaults another person with a deadly weapon and inflicts serious injury shall be punished as a Class E felon.

(c) Any person who assaults another person with a deadly weapon with intent to kill shall be punished as a Class E felon. (1919, c. 101; C.S., s. 4214; 1931, c. 145, s. 30; 1969, c. 602, s. 2; 1971, c. 765, s. 1, c. 1093, s. 12; 1973, c. 229, ss. 1-3; 1979, c. 760, s. 5; 1979, 2nd Sess., c. 1316, s. 47; 1981, c. 63, s. 1, c. 179, s. 14; 1993, c. 539, s. 1138; 1994, Ex. Sess., c. 24, s. 14(c).)

§ 14-32.1. Assaults on handicapped persons; punishments.

(a) For purposes of this section, a "handicapped person" is a person who has:

(1) A physical or mental disability, such as decreased use of arms or legs, blindness, deafness, mental retardation or mental illness; or

(2) Infirmity

which would substantially impair that person's ability to defend himself.

(b) through (d) Repealed by Session Laws 1993 (Reg. Sess., 1994), c. 767, s. 31, effective October 1, 1994.

(e) Unless his conduct is covered under some other provision of law providing greater punishment, any person who commits any aggravated assault or assault and battery on a handicapped person is guilty of a Class F felony. A person commits an aggravated assault or assault and battery upon a handicapped person if, in the course of the assault or assault and battery, that person:

(1) Uses a deadly weapon or other means of force likely to inflict serious injury or serious damage to a handicapped person; or

(2) Inflicts serious injury or serious damage to a handicapped person; or

(3) Intends to kill a handicapped person.

(f) Any person who commits a simple assault or battery upon a handicapped person is guilty of a Class A1 misdemeanor. (1981, c. 780, s. 1; 1993, c. 539, ss. 15, 1139; 1994, Ex. Sess., c. 24, s. 14(c); 1993 (Reg. Sess., 1994), c. 767, s. 31; 2006-179, s. 1.)

§ 14-32.2. Patient abuse and neglect; punishments.

(a) It shall be unlawful for any person to physically abuse a patient of a health care facility or a resident of a residential care facility, when the abuse results in death or bodily injury.

(b) Unless the conduct is prohibited by some other provision of law providing for greater punishment:

(1) A violation of subsection (a) above is a Class C felony where intentional conduct proximately causes the death of the patient or resident;

(2) A violation of subsection (a) above is a Class E felony where culpably negligent conduct proximately causes the death of the patient or resident;

(3) A violation of subsection (a) above is a Class F felony where such conduct is willful or culpably negligent and proximately causes serious bodily injury to the patient or resident;

(4) A violation of subsection (a) is a Class H felony where such conduct evinces a pattern of conduct and the conduct is willful or culpably negligent and proximately causes bodily injury to a patient or resident.

(c) "Health Care Facility" shall include hospitals, skilled nursing facilities, intermediate care facilities, intermediate care facilities for the mentally retarded, psychiatric facilities, rehabilitation facilities, kidney disease treatment centers, home health agencies, ambulatory surgical facilities, and any other health care related facility whether publicly or privately owned.

(c1) "Residential Care Facility" shall include adult care homes and any other residential care related facility whether publicly or privately owned.

(d) "Person" shall include any natural person, association, corporation, partnership, or other individual or entity.

(e) "Culpably negligent" shall mean conduct of a willful, gross and flagrant character, evincing reckless disregard of human life.

(e1) "Abuse" means the willful or culpably negligent infliction of physical injury or the willful or culpably negligent violation of any law designed for the health or welfare of a patient or resident.

(f) Any defense which may arise under G.S. 90-321(h) or G.S. 90-322(d) pursuant to compliance with Article 23 of Chapter 90 shall be fully applicable to any prosecution initiated under this section.

(g) Criminal process for a violation of this section may be issued only upon the request of a District Attorney.

(h) The provisions of this section shall not supersede any other applicable statutory or common law offenses. (1987, c. 527, s. 1; 1993, c. 539, s. 1140; 1994, Ex. Sess., c. 24, s. 14(c); 1995, c. 535, s. 1; 1995 (Reg. Sess., 1996), c. 742, ss. 7, 8; 1999-334, s. 3.15; 1999-456, s. 61(b); 2007-188, s. 1.)

§ 14-32.3. Domestic abuse, neglect, and exploitation of disabled or elder adults.

(a) Abuse. - A person is guilty of abuse if that person is a caretaker of a disabled or elder adult who is residing in a domestic setting and, with malice aforethought, knowingly and willfully: (i) assaults, (ii) fails to provide medical or hygienic care, or (iii) confines or restrains the disabled or elder adult in a place or under a condition that is cruel or unsafe, and as a result of the act or failure to act the disabled or elder adult suffers mental or physical injury.

If the disabled or elder adult suffers serious injury from the abuse, the caretaker is guilty of a Class F felony. If the disabled or elder adult suffers injury from the abuse, the caretaker is guilty of a Class H felony.

A person is not guilty of an offense under this subsection if the act or failure to act is in accordance with G.S. 90-321 or G.S. 90-322.

(b) Neglect. - A person is guilty of neglect if that person is a caretaker of a disabled or elder adult who is residing in a domestic setting and, wantonly, recklessly, or with gross carelessness: (i) fails to provide medical or hygienic care, or (ii) confines or restrains the disabled or elder adult in a place or under a condition that is unsafe, and as a result of the act or failure to act the disabled or elder adult suffers mental or physical injury.

If the disabled or elder adult suffers serious injury from the neglect, the caretaker is guilty of a Class G felony. If the disabled or elder adult suffers injury from the neglect, the caretaker is guilty of a Class I felony.

A person is not guilty of an offense under this subsection if the act or failure to act is in accordance with G.S. 90-321 or G.S. 90-322.

(c) Repealed by Session Laws 2005-272, s. 1, effective December 1, 2005, and applicable to offenses committed on or after that date.

(d) Definitions. - The following definitions apply in this section:

(1) Caretaker. - A person who has the responsibility for the care of a disabled or elder adult as a result of family relationship or who has assumed the responsibility for the care of a disabled or elder adult voluntarily or by contract.

(2) Disabled adult. - A person 18 years of age or older or a lawfully emancipated minor who is present in the State of North Carolina and who is physically or mentally incapacitated as defined in G.S. 108A-101(d).

(3) Domestic setting. - Residence in any residential setting except for a health care facility or residential care facility as these terms are defined in G.S. 14-32.2.

(4) Elder adult. - A person 60 years of age or older who is not able to provide for the social, medical, psychiatric, psychological, financial, or legal services necessary to safeguard the person's rights and resources and to maintain the person's physical and mental well-being. (1995, c. 246, s. 1; 1995 (Reg. Sess., 1996), c. 742, s. 9; 2005-272, s. 1.)

§ 14-32.4. Assault inflicting serious bodily injury; strangulation; penalties.

(a) Unless the conduct is covered under some other provision of law providing greater punishment, any person who assaults another person and inflicts serious bodily injury is guilty of a Class F felony. "Serious bodily injury" is defined as bodily injury that creates a substantial risk of death, or that causes serious permanent disfigurement, coma, a permanent or protracted condition that causes extreme pain, or permanent or protracted loss or impairment of the function of any bodily member or organ, or that results in prolonged hospitalization.

(b) Unless the conduct is covered under some other provision of law providing greater punishment, any person who assaults another person and inflicts physical injury by strangulation is guilty of a Class H felony. (1996, 2nd Ex. Sess., c. 18, s. 20.13(a); 2004-186, s. 9.1.)

§ 14-33. Misdemeanor assaults, batteries, and affrays, simple and aggravated; punishments.

(a) Any person who commits a simple assault or a simple assault and battery or participates in a simple affray is guilty of a Class 2 misdemeanor.

(b) Unless his conduct is covered under some other provision of law providing greater punishment, any person who commits any assault, assault and battery, or affray is guilty of a Class 1 misdemeanor if, in the course of the assault, assault and battery, or affray, he:

(1) through (3) Repealed by Session Laws 1995, c. 507, s. 19.5(b);

(4) through (7) Repealed by Session Laws 1991, c. 525, s. 1;

(8) Repealed by Session Laws 1995, c. 507, s. 19.5(b);

(9) Commits an assault and battery against a sports official when the sports official is discharging or attempting to discharge official duties at a sports event, or immediately after the sports event at which the sports official discharged official duties. A "sports official" is a person at a sports event who enforces the rules of the event, such as an umpire or referee, or a person who supervises the participants, such as a coach. A "sports event" includes any interscholastic or intramural athletic activity in a primary, middle, junior high, or high school, college, or university, any organized athletic activity sponsored by a community, business, or nonprofit organization, any athletic activity that is a professional or semiprofessional event, and any other organized athletic activity in the State.

(c) Unless the conduct is covered under some other provision of law providing greater punishment, any person who commits any assault, assault and battery, or affray is guilty of a Class A1 misdemeanor if, in the course of the assault, assault and battery, or affray, he or she:

(1) Inflicts serious injury upon another person or uses a deadly weapon;

(2) Assaults a female, he being a male person at least 18 years of age;

(3) Assaults a child under the age of 12 years;

(4) Assaults an officer or employee of the State or any political subdivision of the State, when the officer or employee is discharging or attempting to discharge his official duties;

(5) Repealed by Session Laws 1999-105, s. 1, effective December 1, 1999; or

(6) Assaults a school employee or school volunteer when the employee or volunteer is discharging or attempting to discharge his or her duties as an employee or volunteer, or assaults a school employee or school volunteer as a result of the discharge or attempt to discharge that individual's duties as a school employee or school volunteer. For purposes of this subdivision, the following definitions shall apply:

a. "Duties" means:

1. All activities on school property;

2. All activities, wherever occurring, during a school authorized event or the accompanying of students to or from that event; and

3. All activities relating to the operation of school transportation.

b. "Employee" or "volunteer" means:

1. An employee of a local board of education; or a charter school authorized under G.S. 115C-238.29D, or a nonpublic school which has filed intent to operate under Part 1 or Part 2 of Article 39 of Chapter 115C of the General Statutes;

2. An independent contractor or an employee of an independent contractor of a local board of education, charter school authorized under G.S. 115C-238.29D, or a nonpublic school which has filed intent to operate under Part 1 or Part 2 of Article 39 of Chapter 115C of the General Statutes, if the independent contractor carries out duties customarily performed by employees of the school; and

3. An adult who volunteers his or her services or presence at any school activity and is under the supervision of an individual listed in sub-sub-subdivision 1. or 2. of this sub-subdivision.

(7) Assaults a public transit operator, including a public employee or a private contractor employed as a public transit operator, when the operator is discharging or attempting to discharge his or her duties.

(8) Assaults a company police officer certified pursuant to the provisions of Chapter 74E of the General Statutes or a campus police officer certified pursuant to the provisions of Chapter 74G, Chapter 17C, or Chapter 116 of the General Statutes in the performance of that person's duties.

(c1) No school personnel as defined in G.S. 14-33(c)(6) who takes reasonable actions in good faith to end a fight or altercation between students shall incur any civil or criminal liability as the result of those actions.

(d) Any person who, in the course of an assault, assault and battery, or affray, inflicts serious injury upon another person, or uses a deadly weapon, in violation of subdivision (c)(1) of this section, on a person with whom the person has a personal relationship, and in the presence of a minor, is guilty of a Class A1 misdemeanor. A person convicted under this subsection, who is sentenced to a community punishment, shall be placed on supervised probation in addition to any other punishment imposed by the court.

A person committing a second or subsequent violation of this subsection shall be sentenced to an active punishment of no less than 30 days in addition to any other punishment imposed by the court.

The following definitions apply to this subsection:

(1) "Personal relationship" is as defined in G.S. 50B-1(b).

(2) "In the presence of a minor" means that the minor was in a position to have observed the assault.

(3) "Minor" is any person under the age of 18 years who is residing with or is under the care and supervision of, and who has a personal relationship with, the person assaulted or the person committing the assault. (1870-1, c. 43, s. 2; 1873-4, c. 176, s. 6; 1879, c. 92, ss. 2, 6; Code, s. 987; Rev., s. 3620, 1911, c. 193; C.S., s. 4215; 1933, c. 189; 1949, c. 298; 1969, c. 618, s. 1; 1971, c. 765, s. 2; 1973, c. 229, s. 4; c. 1413; 1979, cc. 524, 656; 1981, c. 180; 1983, c. 175, ss. 6, 10; c. 720, s. 4; 1985, c. 321; 1991, c. 525, s. 1; 1993, c. 286, s. 1; c. 539, s. 16; 1994, Ex. Sess., c. 14, s. 3; c. 24, s. 14(c); 1993 (Reg. Sess., 1994), c. 687, s. 1; 1995, c. 352, s. 1; 1995, c. 507, s. 19.5(b); 1999-105, s. 1; 2003-409, s. 1; 2004-26, s. 1; 2004-199, s. 7; 2005-231, s. 6.2; 2012-149, s. 1.)

§ 14-33.1. Evidence of former threats upon plea of self-defense.

In any case of assault, assault and battery, or affray in which the plea of the defendant is self-defense, evidence of former threats against the defendant by the person alleged to have been assaulted by him, if such threats shall have been communicated to the defendant before the altercation, shall be competent as bearing upon the reasonableness of the claim of apprehension by the defendant of bodily harm, and also as bearing upon the amount of force which reasonably appeared necessary to the defendant, under the circumstances, to repel his assailant. (1969, c. 618, s. 2.)

§ 14-33.2. Habitual misdemeanor assault.

A person commits the offense of habitual misdemeanor assault if that person violates any of the provisions of G.S. 14-33 and causes physical injury, or G.S. 14-34, and has two or more prior convictions for either misdemeanor or felony assault, with the earlier of the two prior convictions occurring no more than 15 years prior to the date of the current violation. A conviction under this section shall not be used as a prior conviction for any other habitual offense statute. A person convicted of violating this section is guilty of a Class H felony. (1995, c. 507, s. 19.5(c); 2004-186, s. 10.1.)

§ 14-34. Assaulting by pointing gun.

If any person shall point any gun or pistol at any person, either in fun or otherwise, whether such gun or pistol be loaded or not loaded, he shall be guilty of a Class A1 misdemeanor. (1889, c. 527; Rev., s. 3622; C.S., s. 4216; 1969, c. 618, s. 2 1/2; 1993, c. 539, s. 17; 1994, Ex. Sess., c. 24, s. 14(c); 1995, c. 507, s. 19.5(d).)

§ 14-34.1. Discharging certain barreled weapons or a firearm into occupied property.

(a)   Any person who willfully or wantonly discharges or attempts to discharge any firearm or barreled weapon capable of discharging shot, bullets, pellets, or other missiles at a muzzle velocity of at least 600 feet per second into any building, structure, vehicle, aircraft, watercraft, or other conveyance, device, equipment, erection, or enclosure while it is occupied is guilty of a Class E felony.

(b)   A person who willfully or wantonly discharges a weapon described in subsection (a) of this section into an occupied dwelling or into any occupied vehicle, aircraft, watercraft, or other conveyance that is in operation is guilty of a Class D felony.

(c)   If a person violates this section and the violation results in serious bodily injury to any person, the person is guilty of a Class C felony. (1969, c. 341; c. 869, s. 7; 1979, c. 760, s. 5; 1979, 2nd Sess., c. 1316, s. 47; 1981, c. 63, s. 1; c. 179, s. 14; c. 755; 1993, c. 539, s. 1141; 1994, Ex. Sess., c. 24, s. 14(c); 2005-461, s. 1.)

§ 14-34.2. Assault with a firearm or other deadly weapon upon governmental officers or employees, company police officers, or campus police officers.

Unless a person's conduct is covered under some other provision of law providing greater punishment, any person who commits an assault with a firearm or any other deadly weapon upon an officer or employee of the State or of any political subdivision of the State, a company police officer certified pursuant to the provisions of Chapter 74E of the General Statutes, or a campus police officer certified pursuant to the provisions of Chapter 74G, Chapter 17C or Chapter 116 of the General Statutes, in the performance of his duties shall be guilty of a Class F felony. (1969, c. 1134; 1977, c. 829; 1979, c. 760, s. 5; 1979, 2nd Sess., c. 1316, s. 47; 1981, c. 63, s. 1; c. 179, s. 14; 1981, c. 535, s. 1; 1991, c. 525, s. 2; 1993, c. 539, s. 1142; 1994, Ex. Sess., c. 24, s. 14(c); 1993 (Reg. Sess., 1994), c. 687, s. 2; 1995, c. 507, s. 19.5(i); 2005-231, s. 6.1.)

§ 14-34.3. Manufacture, sale, purchase, or possession of teflon-coated types of bullets prohibited.

(a)   It is unlawful for any person to import, manufacture, possess, store, transport, sell, offer to sell, purchase, offer to purchase, deliver or give to another, or acquire any teflon-coated bullet.

(b)   This section does not apply to:

(1)   Officers and enlisted personnel of the Armed Forces of the United States when in discharge of their official duties as such and acting under orders requiring them to carry arms or weapons, civil officers of the United States while in the discharge of their official duties, officers and soldiers of the militia when

called into actual service, officers of the State, or of any county, city or town, charged with the execution of the laws of the State, when acting in the discharge of their official duties;

(2)   Importers, manufacturers, and dealers validly licensed under the laws of the United States or the State of North Carolina who possess for the purpose of sale to authorized law-enforcement agencies only;

(3)   Inventors, designers, ordinance consultants and researchers, chemists, physicists, and other persons employed by or under contract with a manufacturing company engaged in making or doing research designed to enlarge knowledge or to facilitate the creation, development, or manufacture of more effective police-type body armor.

(c)   Any person who violates any provision of this section is guilty of a Class 1 misdemeanor. (1981 (Reg. Sess., 1982), c. 1272, s. 1; 1993, c. 539, s. 18; 1994, Ex. Sess., c. 24, s. 14(c); 1999-456, s. 33(a); 2011-183, s. 8.)

§ 14-34.4. Adulterated or misbranded food, drugs, or cosmetics; intent to cause serious injury or death; intent to extort.

(a)   Any person who with the intent to cause serious injury or death manufactures, sells, delivers, offers, or holds for sale, any food, drug, or cosmetic that is adulterated or misbranded, or adulterates or misbrands any food, drug, or cosmetic, in violation of G.S. 106-122, is guilty of a Class C felony.

(b)   Any person who with the intent to wrongfully obtain, directly or indirectly, anything of value or any acquittance, advantage, or immunity communicates to another that he has violated, or intends to violate, subsection (a) of this section, is guilty of a Class C felony. (1987, c. 313.)

§ 14-34.5. Assault with a firearm on a law enforcement, probation, or parole officer or on a person employed at a State or local detention facility.

(a) Any person who commits an assault with a firearm upon a law enforcement officer, probation officer, or parole officer while the officer is in the performance of his or her duties is guilty of a Class E felony.

(b) Anyone who commits an assault with a firearm upon a person who is employed at a detention facility operated under the jurisdiction of the State or a local government while the employee is in the performance of the employee's duties is guilty of a Class E felony. (1995, c. 507, s. 19.5(j); 1995 (Reg. Sess., 1996), c. 742, s. 10; 1997-443, s. 19.25(gg).)

§ 14-34.6. Assault or affray on a firefighter, an emergency medical technician, medical responder, and emergency department personnel.

(a) A person is guilty of a Class I felony if the person commits an assault or affray causing physical injury on any of the following persons who are discharging or attempting to discharge their official duties:

(1) An emergency medical technician or other emergency health care provider.

(2) A medical responder.

(3) The following emergency department personnel: physicians, physicians assistants, nurses, and licensed nurse practitioners.

(4) Repealed by Session Laws 2011-356, s. 2, effective December 1, 2011, and applicable to offenses committed on or after that date.

(5) A firefighter.

(b) Unless a person's conduct is covered under some other provision of law providing greater punishment, a person is guilty of a Class H felony if the person violates subsection (a) of this section and (i) inflicts serious bodily injury or (ii) uses a deadly weapon other than a firearm.

(c) Unless a person's conduct is covered under some other provision of law providing greater punishment, a person is guilty of a Class F felony if the person violates subsection (a) of this section and uses a firearm. (1995, c. 507, s.

19.6(a); 1996, 2nd Ex. Sess., c. 18, s. 20.14B(b); 1997-9, s. 2; 1997-443, s. 11A.129A; 1998-217, s. 1; 2011-356, s. 2.)

§ 14-34.7. Assault inflicting serious injury on a law enforcement, probation, or parole officer or on a person employed at a State or local detention facility; penalty.

(a) Unless covered under some other provision of law providing greater punishment, a person is guilty of a Class F felony if the person assaults a law enforcement officer, probation officer, or parole officer while the officer is discharging or attempting to discharge his or her official duties and inflicts serious bodily injury on the officer.

(b) Anyone who assaults a person who is employed at a detention facility operated under the jurisdiction of the State or a local government while the employee is in the performance of the employee's duties and inflicts serious bodily injury on the employee is guilty of a Class F felony, unless the person's conduct is covered under some other provision of law providing greater punishment.

(c) Unless covered under some other provision of law providing greater punishment, a person is guilty of a Class I felony if the person does either of the following:

(1) Assaults a law enforcement officer, probation officer, or parole officer while the officer is discharging or attempting to discharge his or her official duties and inflicts physical injury on the officer.

(2) Assaults a person who is employed at a detention facility operated under the jurisdiction of the State or a local government while the employee is in the performance of the employee's duties and inflicts physical injury on the employee.

For the purposes of this subsection, "physical injury" includes cuts, scrapes, bruises, or other physical injury which does not constitute serious injury. (1996, 2nd Ex. Sess., c. 18, s. 20.14B(a); 1997-443, s. 19.25(hh); 2001-487, s. 41; 2011-356, s. 1.)

§ 14-34.8. Criminal use of laser device.

(a)   For purposes of this section, the term "laser" means light amplification by stimulated emission of radiation.

(b)   It is unlawful intentionally to point a laser device at a law enforcement officer, or at the head or face of another person, while the device is emitting a laser beam.

(c)   A violation of this section is an infraction.

(d)   This section does not apply to a law enforcement officer who uses a laser device in discharging or attempting to discharge the officer's official duties. This section does not apply to a health care professional who uses a laser device in providing services within the scope of practice of that professional nor to any other person who is licensed or authorized by law to use a laser device or uses it in the performance of the person's official duties.

(e)   This section does not apply to laser tag, paintball guns, and other similar games and devices using light emitting diode (LED) technology. (1999-401, s. 1.)

§ 14-34.9. Discharging a firearm from within an enclosure.

Unless covered under some other provision of law providing greater punishment, any person who willfully or wantonly discharges or attempts to discharge a firearm, as a part of a pattern of criminal street gang activity, from within any building, structure, motor vehicle, or other conveyance, erection, or enclosure toward a person or persons not within that enclosure shall be punished as a Class E felon. (2008-214, s. 2.)

§ 14-34.10. Discharge firearm within enclosure to incite fear.

Unless covered under some other provision of law providing greater punishment, any person who willfully or wantonly discharges or attempts to discharge a firearm within any occupied building, structure, motor vehicle, or other conveyance, erection, or enclosure with the intent to incite fear in another shall be punished as a Class F felon. (2013-144, s. 1.)

Article 9.

Hazing.

§ 14-35. Hazing; definition and punishment.

It is unlawful for any student in attendance at any university, college, or school in this State to engage in hazing, or to aid or abet any other student in the commission of this offense. For the purposes of this section hazing is defined as follows: "to subject another student to physical injury as part of an initiation, or as a prerequisite to membership, into any organized school group, including any society, athletic team, fraternity or sorority, or other similar group." Any violation of this section shall constitute a Class 2 misdemeanor. (1913, c. 169, ss. 1, 2, 3, 4; C.S., s. 4217; 1969, c. 1224, s. 1; 1993, c. 539, s. 19; 1994, Ex. Sess., c. 24, s. 14(c); 2003-299, s. 1.)

§ 14-36: Repealed by Session Laws 2003-299, § 2, effective December 1, 2003, and applicable to offenses committed on or after that date.

§ 14-37. Repealed by Session Laws 1979, c. 7, s. 1.

§ 14-38. Witnesses in hazing trials; no indictment to be founded on self-criminating testimony.

In all trials for the offense of hazing any student or other person subpoenaed as a witness in behalf of the State shall be required to testify if called upon to do so: Provided, however, that no student or other person so testifying shall be amenable or subject to indictment on account of, or by reason of, such testimony. (1913, c. 169, s. 8; C.S., s. 4220.)

Article 10.

Kidnapping and Abduction.

§ 14-39. Kidnapping.

(a) Any person who shall unlawfully confine, restrain, or remove from one place to another, any other person 16 years of age or over without the consent of such person, or any other person under the age of 16 years without the consent of a parent or legal custodian of such person, shall be guilty of kidnapping if such confinement, restraint or removal is for the purpose of:

(1) Holding such other person for a ransom or as a hostage or using such other person as a shield; or

(2) Facilitating the commission of any felony or facilitating flight of any person following the commission of a felony; or

(3) Doing serious bodily harm to or terrorizing the person so confined, restrained or removed or any other person; or

(4) Holding such other person in involuntary servitude in violation of G.S. 14-43.12.

(5) Trafficking another person with the intent that the other person be held in involuntary servitude or sexual servitude in violation of G.S. 14-43.11.

(6) Subjecting or maintaining such other person for sexual servitude in violation of G.S. 14-43.13.

(b) There shall be two degrees of kidnapping as defined by subsection (a). If the person kidnapped either was not released by the defendant in a safe place or had been seriously injured or sexually assaulted, the offense is kidnapping in the first degree and is punishable as a Class C felony. If the person kidnapped was released in a safe place by the defendant and had not been seriously injured or sexually assaulted, the offense is kidnapping in the second degree and is punishable as a Class E felony.

(c) Any firm or corporation convicted of kidnapping shall be punished by a fine of not less than five thousand dollars ($5,000) nor more than one hundred thousand dollars ($100,000), and its charter and right to do business in the

State of North Carolina shall be forfeited. (1933, c. 542; 1975, c. 843, s. 1; 1979, c. 760, s. 5; 1979, 2nd Sess., c. 1316, s. 47; 1981, c. 63, s. 1; c. 179, s. 14; 1983, c. 746, s. 2; 1993, c. 539, s. 1143; 1994, Ex. Sess., c. 24, s. 14(c); 1995, c. 509, s. 8; 2006-247, s. 20(c).)

§ 14-40. Enticing minors out of the State for the purpose of employment.

If any person shall employ and carry beyond the limits of this State any minor, or shall induce any minor to go beyond the limits of this State, for the purpose of employment without the consent in writing, duly authenticated, of the parent, guardian or other person having authority over such minor, he shall be guilty of a Class 2 misdemeanor. The fact of the employment and going out of the State of the minor, or of the going out of the State by the minor, at the solicitation of the person for the purpose of employment, shall be prima facie evidence of knowledge that the person employed or solicited to go beyond the limits of the State is a minor. (1891, c. 45; Rev., s. 3630; C.S., s. 4222; 1969, c. 1224, s. 4; 1993, c. 539, s. 21; 1994, Ex. Sess., c. 24, s. 14(c).)

§ 14-41. Abduction of children.

(a) Any person who, without legal justification or defense, abducts or induces any minor child who is at least four years younger than the person to leave any person, agency, or institution lawfully entitled to the child's custody, placement, or care shall be guilty of a Class F felony.

(b) The provisions of this section shall not apply to any public officer or employee in the performance of his or her duty. (1879, c. 81; Code, s. 973; Rev., s. 3358; C.S., s. 4223; 1979, c. 760, s. 5; 1979, 2nd Sess., c. 1316, s. 47; 1981, c. 63, s. 1; c. 179, s. 14; 1993, c. 539, s. 1144; 1994, Ex. Sess., c. 24, s. 14(c); 1995 (Reg. Sess., 1996), c. 745, s. 1.)

§ 14-42: Repealed by Session Laws 1993, c. 539, s. 1358.2.

§ 14-43: Repealed by Session Laws 1993 (Reg. Sess., 1994), c. 767, s. 29(2).

§ 14-43.1. Unlawful arrest by officers from other states.

A law-enforcement officer of a state other than North Carolina who, knowing that he is in the State of North Carolina and purporting to act by authority of his office, arrests a person in the State of North Carolina, other than as is permitted by G.S. 15A-403, is guilty of a Class 2 misdemeanor. (1973, c. 1286, s. 10; 1993, c. 539, s. 22; 1994, Ex. Sess., c. 24, s. 14(c).)

§ 14-43.2: Repealed by Session Laws 2006-247, s. 20(a), effective December 1, 2006, and applicable to offenses committed on or after that date.

§ 14-43.3. Felonious restraint.

A person commits the offense of felonious restraint if he unlawfully restrains another person without that person's consent, or the consent of the person's parent or legal custodian if the person is less than 16 years old, and moves the person from the place of the initial restraint by transporting him in a motor vehicle or other conveyance. Violation of this section is a Class F felony. Felonious restraint is considered a lesser included offense of kidnapping. (1985, c. 545, s. 1; 1993, c. 539, s. 1147; 1994, Ex. Sess., c. 24, s. 14(c).)

§ 14-43.4. Reserved for future codification purposes.

§ 14-43.5. Reserved for future codification purposes.

§ 14-43.6. Reserved for future codification purposes.

§ 14-43.7. Reserved for future codification purposes.

§ 14-43.8. Reserved for future codification purposes.

§ 14-43.9. Reserved for future codification purposes.

Article 10A.

Human Trafficking.

§ 14-43.10. Definitions.

(a) Definitions. - The following definitions apply in this Article:

(1) Coercion. - The term includes all of the following:

a. Causing or threatening to cause bodily harm to any person, physically restraining or confining any person, or threatening to physically restrain or confine any person.

b. Exposing or threatening to expose any fact or information that if revealed would tend to subject a person to criminal or immigration proceedings, hatred, contempt, or ridicule.

c. Destroying, concealing, removing, confiscating, or possessing any actual or purported passport or other immigration document, or any other actual or purported government identification document, of any person.

d. Providing a controlled substance, as defined by G.S. 90-87, to a person.

(2) Deception. - The term includes all of the following:

a. Creating or confirming another's impression of an existing fact or past event that is false and which the accused knows or believes to be false.

b. Maintaining the status or condition of a person arising from a pledge by that person of his or her personal services as security for a debt, if the value of those services as reasonably assessed is not applied toward the liquidation of the debt or the length and nature of those services are not respectively limited and defined, or preventing a person from acquiring information pertinent to the disposition of such debt.

c. Promising benefits or the performance of services that the accused does not intend to deliver or perform or knows will not be delivered or performed.

(3) Involuntary servitude. - The term includes the following:

a. The performance of labor, whether or not for compensation, or whether or not for the satisfaction of a debt; and

b. By deception, coercion, or intimidation using violence or the threat of violence or by any other means of coercion or intimidation.

(4) Minor. - A person who is less than 18 years of age.

(5) Sexual servitude. - The term includes the following:

a. Any sexual activity as defined in G.S. 14-190.13 for which anything of value is directly or indirectly given, promised to, or received by any person, which conduct is induced or obtained by coercion or deception or which conduct is induced or obtained from a person under the age of 18 years; or

b. Any sexual activity as defined in G.S. 14-190.13 that is performed or provided by any person, which conduct is induced or obtained by coercion or deception or which conduct is induced or obtained from a person under the age of 18 years. (2006-247, s. 20(b).)

§ 14-43.11. Human trafficking.

(a) A person commits the offense of human trafficking when that person (i) knowingly or in reckless disregard of the consequences of the action recruits, entices, harbors, transports, provides, or obtains by any means another person with the intent that the other person be held in involuntary servitude or sexual servitude or (ii) willfully or in reckless disregard of the consequences of the action causes a minor to be held in involuntary servitude or sexual servitude.

(b) A person who violates this section is guilty of a Class F felony if the victim of the offense is an adult. A person who violates this section is guilty of a Class C felony if the victim of the offense is a minor.

(c) Each violation of this section constitutes a separate offense and shall not merge with any other offense. Evidence of failure to deliver benefits or perform services standing alone shall not be sufficient to authorize a conviction under this section.

(c1)   Mistake of age is not a defense to prosecution under this section. Consent of a minor is not a defense to prosecution under this section.

(d)   A person who is not a legal resident of North Carolina, and would consequently be ineligible for State public benefits or services, shall be eligible for the public benefits and services of any State agency if the person is otherwise eligible for the public benefit and is a victim of an offense charged under this section. Eligibility for public benefits and services shall terminate at such time as the victim's eligibility to remain in the United States is terminated under federal law. (2006-247, s. 20(b); 2007-547, s. 1; 2013-368, s. 1.)

§ 14-43.12. Involuntary servitude.

(a)   A person commits the offense of involuntary servitude when that person knowingly and willfully or in reckless disregard of the consequences of the action holds another in involuntary servitude.

(b)   A person who violates this section is guilty of a Class F felony if the victim of the offense is an adult. A person who violates this section is guilty of a Class C felony if the victim of the offense is a minor.

(c)   Each violation of this section constitutes a separate offense and shall not merge with any other offense. Evidence of failure to deliver benefits or perform services standing alone shall not be sufficient to authorize a conviction under this section.

(c1)   Mistake of age is not a defense to prosecution under this section. Consent of a minor is not a defense to prosecution under this section.

(d)   Nothing in this section shall be construed to affect the laws governing the relationship between an unemancipated minor and his or her parents or legal guardian.

(e)   If any person reports a violation of this section, which violation arises out of any contract for labor, to any party to the contract, the party shall immediately report the violation to the sheriff of the county in which the violation is alleged to have occurred for appropriate action. A person violating this subsection shall be guilty of a Class 1 misdemeanor. (1983, ch. 746, s. 1; 1993, c. 539, ss. 23, 1146; 1994, Ex. Sess., c. 24, s. 14(c); 2006-247, s. 20(b); 2013-368, s. 2.)

§ 14-43.13. Sexual servitude.

(a) A person commits the offense of sexual servitude when that person knowingly or in reckless disregard of the consequences of the action subjects or maintains another in sexual servitude.

(b) A person who violates this section is guilty of a Class D felony if the victim of the offense is an adult. A person who violates this section is guilty of a Class C felony if the victim of the offense is a minor.

(b1) Mistake of age is not a defense to prosecution under this section. Consent of a minor is not a defense to prosecution under this section.

(c) Each violation of this section constitutes a separate offense and shall not merge with any other offense. Evidence of failure to deliver benefits or perform services standing alone shall not be sufficient to authorize a conviction under this section. (2006-247, s. 20(b); 2013-368, s. 3.)

§ 14-43.14. Unlawful sale, surrender, or purchase of a minor.

(a) A person commits the offense of unlawful sale, surrender, or purchase of a minor when that person, acting with willful or reckless disregard for the life or safety of a minor, participates in any of the following: the acceptance, solicitation, offer, payment, or transfer of any compensation, in money, property, or other thing of value, at any time, by any person in connection with the unlawful acquisition or transfer of the physical custody of a minor, except as ordered by the court. This section does not apply to actions that are ordered by a court, authorized by statute, or otherwise lawful.

(b) A person who violates this section is guilty of a Class F felony and shall pay a minimum fine of five thousand dollars ($5,000). For each subsequent violation, a person is guilty of a Class F felony and shall pay a minimum fine of ten thousand dollars ($10,000).

(c) A minor whose parent, guardian, or custodian has sold or attempted to sell a minor in violation of this Article is an abused juvenile as defined by G.S. 7B-101(1). The court may place the minor in the custody of the Department of Social Services or with such other person as is in the best interest of the minor.

(d) A violation of this section is a lesser included offense of G.S. 14-43.11.

(e) When a person is convicted of a violation of this section, the sentencing court shall consider whether the person is a danger to the community and whether requiring the person to register as a sex offender pursuant to Article 27A of this Chapter would further the purposes of that Article as stated in G.S. 14-208.5. If the sentencing court rules that the person is a danger to the community and that the person shall register, then an order shall be entered requiring the person to register. (2012-153, s. 1.)

§ 14-43.15: Reserved for future codification purposes.

§ 14-43.16: Reserved for future codification purposes.

§ 14-43.17: Reserved for future codification purposes.

§ 14-43.18: Reserved for future codification purposes.

§ 14-43.19: Reserved for future codification purposes.

§ 14-43.20. Mandatory restitution; victim services; forfeiture.

(a) Definition. - For purposes of this section, a "victim" is a person subjected to the practices set forth in G.S. 14-43.11, 14-43.12, or 14-43.13.

(b) Restitution. - Restitution for a victim is mandatory under this Article. At a minimum, the court shall order restitution in an amount equal to the value of the victim's labor as guaranteed under the Minimum Wage Law and overtime provisions of the Fair Labor Standards Act (FLSA). In addition, the judge may order any other amount of loss identified, including the gross income or value to the defendant of the victim's labor or services.

(c) Trafficking Victim Services. - Subject to the availability of funds, the Department of Health and Human Services may provide or fund emergency services and assistance to individuals who are victims of one or more offenses under G.S. 14-43.11, 14-43.12, or 14-43.13.

(d) Certification. - The Attorney General, a district attorney, or any law enforcement official shall certify in writing to the United States Department of Justice or other federal agency, such as the United States Department of Homeland Security, that an investigation or prosecution under this Article for a violation of G.S. 14-43.11, 14-43.12, or 14-43.13 has begun and the individual who is a likely victim of one of those crimes is willing to cooperate or is cooperating with the investigation to enable the individual, if eligible under federal law, to qualify for an appropriate special immigrant visa and to access available federal benefits. Cooperation with law enforcement shall not be required of victims who are under 18 years of age. This certification shall be made available to the victim and the victim's designated legal representative.

(e) A person who commits a violation of G.S. 14-43.11, 14-43.12, or 14-43.13 is subject to the property forfeiture provisions set forth in G.S. 14-2.3. (2013-368, s. 17.)

Article 11.

Abortion and Kindred Offenses.

§ 14-44. Using drugs or instruments to destroy unborn child.

If any person shall willfully administer to any woman, either pregnant or quick with child, or prescribe for any such woman, or advise or procure any such woman to take any medicine, drug or other substance whatever, or shall use or employ any instrument or other means with intent thereby to destroy such child, he shall be punished as a Class H felon. (1881, c. 351, s. 1; Code, s. 975; Rev., s. 3618; C.S., s. 4226; 1967, c. 367, s. 1; 1979, c. 760, s. 5; 1979, 2nd Sess., c. 1316, s. 47; 1981, c. 63, s. 1; c 179, s. 14.)

§ 14-45. Using drugs or instruments to produce miscarriage or injure pregnant woman.

If any person shall administer to any pregnant woman, or prescribe for any such woman, or advise and procure such woman to take any medicine, drug or anything whatsoever, with intent thereby to procure the miscarriage of such woman, or to injure or destroy such woman, or shall use any instrument or application for any of the above purposes, he shall be punished as a Class I felon. (1881, c. 351, s. 2; Code, s. 976; Rev., s. 3619; C.S., s. 4227; 1979, c. 760, s. 5; 1979, 2nd Sess., c. 1316, s. 47; 1981, c. 63, s. 1; c. 179, s. 14.)

§ 14-45.1. When abortion not unlawful.

(a) Notwithstanding any of the provisions of G.S. 14-44 and 14-45, it shall not be unlawful, during the first 20 weeks of a woman's pregnancy, to advise, procure, or cause a miscarriage or abortion when the procedure is performed by a physician licensed to practice medicine in North Carolina in a hospital or clinic certified by the Department of Health and Human Services to be a suitable facility for the performance of abortions.

(b) Notwithstanding any of the provisions of G.S. 14-44 and 14-45, it shall not be unlawful, after the twentieth week of a woman's pregnancy, to advise, procure or cause a miscarriage or abortion when the procedure is performed by a physician licensed to practice medicine in North Carolina in a hospital licensed by the Department of Health and Human Services, if there is substantial risk that continuance of the pregnancy would threaten the life or gravely impair the health of the woman.

(c) The Department of Health and Human Services shall prescribe and collect on an annual basis, from hospitals or clinics where abortions are performed, such representative samplings of statistical summary reports concerning the medical and demographic characteristics of the abortions provided for in this section as it shall deem to be in the public interest. Hospitals or clinics where abortions are performed shall be responsible for providing these statistical summary reports to the Department of Health and Human Services. The reports shall be for statistical purposes only and the confidentiality of the patient relationship shall be protected.

(d) The requirements of G.S. 130-43 are not applicable to abortions performed pursuant to this section.

(e) Nothing in this section shall require a physician licensed to practice medicine in North Carolina, any nurse, or any other health care provider who shall state an objection to abortion on moral, ethical, or religious grounds, to perform or participate in medical procedures which result in an abortion. The refusal of a physician, nurse, or health care provider to perform or participate in these medical procedures shall not be a basis for damages for the refusal, or for any disciplinary or any other recriminatory action against the physician, nurse, or health care provider. For purposes of this section, the phrase "health care provider" shall have the same meaning as defined under G.S. 90-410(1).

(f)   Nothing in this section shall require a hospital, other health care institution, or other health care provider to perform an abortion or to provide abortion services. (1967, c. 367, s. 2; 1971, c. 383, ss. 1, 11/2; 1973, c. 139; c. 476, s. 128; c. 711; 1997-443, s. 11A.118(a); 2013-366, s. 1(a), (b).)

§ 14-46. Concealing birth of child.

If any person shall, by secretly burying or otherwise disposing of the dead body of a newborn child, endeavor to conceal the birth of such child, such person shall be punished as a Class I felon. Any person aiding, counseling or abetting any other person in concealing the birth of a child in violation of this statute shall be guilty of a Class 1 misdemeanor. (21 Jac. I, c. 27; 43 Geo. III, c. 58, s. 3; 9 Geo. IV, c. 31, s. 14; 1818, c. 985, P.R.; R.C., c. 34, s. 28; 1883, c. 390; Code, s. 1004; Rev., s. 3623; C.S., s. 4228; 1977, c. 577; 1979, c. 760, s. 5; 1979, 2nd Sess., c. 1316, s. 47; 1981, c. 63, s. 1, c. 179, s. 14; 1993, c. 539, ss. 24, 1148; 1994, Ex. Sess., c. 24, s. 14(c).)

Article 12.

Libel and Slander.

§ 14-47. Communicating libelous matter to newspapers.

If any person shall state, deliver or transmit by any means whatever, to the manager, editor, publisher or reporter of any newspaper or periodical for publication therein any false and libelous statement concerning any person or corporation, and thereby secure the publication of the same, he shall be guilty of a Class 2 misdemeanor. (1901, c. 557, ss. 2, 3; Rev., s. 3635; C.S., s. 4229; 1969, c. 1224, s. 1; 1993, c. 539, s. 25; 1994, Ex. Sess., c. 24, s. 14(c).)

§ 14-48. Repealed by Session Laws 1975, c. 402.

Article 13.

Malicious Injury or Damage by Use of Explosive or Incendiary Device or Material.

§ 14-49. Malicious use of explosive or incendiary; punishment.

(a) Any person who willfully and maliciously injures another by the use of any explosive or incendiary device or material is guilty of a Class D felony.

(b) Any person who willfully and maliciously damages any real or personal property of any kind or nature belonging to another by the use of any explosive or incendiary device or material is guilty of a Class G felony.

(b1) Any person who willfully and maliciously damages, aids, counsels, or procures the damaging of any church, chapel, synagogue, mosque, masjid, or other building of worship by the use of any explosive or incendiary device or material is guilty of a Class E felony.

(b2) Any person who willfully and maliciously damages, aids, counsels, or procures the damaging of the State Capitol, the Legislative Building, the Justice Building, or any building owned or occupied by the State or any of its agencies, institutions, or subdivisions or by any county, incorporated city or town, or other governmental entity by the use of any explosive or incendiary device or material is guilty of a Class E felony.

(c) Repealed by Session Laws 1993, c. 539, s. 1149, effective October 1, 1994. (1923, c. 80, s. 1; C.S., s. 4231(a); 1951, c. 1126, s. 1; 1969, c. 869, s. 6; 1979, c. 760, s. 5; 1979, 2nd Sess., c. 1316, s. 47; 1981, c. 63, s. 1; c. 179, s. 14; 1993, c. 539, s. 1149; 1994, Ex. Sess., c. 24, s. 14(c); 1995 (Reg. Sess., 1996), c. 751, s. 1; 2003-392, s. 3(c).)

§ 14-49.1. Malicious damage of occupied property by use of explosive or incendiary; punishment.

Any person who willfully and maliciously damages any real or personal property of any kind or nature, being at the time occupied by another, by the use of any explosive or incendiary device or material is guilty of a felony punishable as a Class D felony. (1967, c. 342; 1969, c. 869, s. 6; 1979, c. 760, s. 5; 1979, 2nd.

Sess., c. 1316, s. 47; 1981, c. 63, s. 1, c. 179, s. 14; 1993, c. 539, s. 1150; 1994, Ex. Sess., c. 24, s. 14(c).)

§ 14-50: Repealed by Session Laws 1994, Ex. Sess., c. 14, s. 71(4).

§ 14-50.1. Explosive or incendiary device or material defined.

As used in this Article, "explosive or incendiary device or material" means nitroglycerine, dynamite, gunpowder, other high explosive, incendiary bomb or grenade, other destructive incendiary device, or any other destructive incendiary or explosive device, compound, or formulation; any instrument or substance capable of being used for destructive explosive or incendiary purposes against persons or property, when the circumstances indicate some probability that such instrument or substance will be so used; or any explosive or incendiary part or ingredient in any instrument or substance included above, when the circumstances indicate some probability that such part or ingredient will be so used. (1969, c. 869, s. 6.)

§ 14-50.2. Reserved for future codification purposes.

§ 14-50.3. Reserved for future codification purposes.

§ 14-50.4. Reserved for future codification purposes.

§ 14-50.5. Reserved for future codification purposes.

§ 14-50.6. Reserved for future codification purposes.

§ 14-50.7. Reserved for future codification purposes.

§ 14-50.8. Reserved for future codification purposes.

§ 14-50.9. Reserved for future codification purposes.

§ 14-50.10. Reserved for future codification purposes.

§ 14-50.11. Reserved for future codification purposes.

§ 14-50.12. Reserved for future codification purposes.

§ 14-50.13. Reserved for future codification purposes.

§ 14-50.14. Reserved for future codification purposes.

Article 13A.

North Carolina Street Gang Suppression Act.

§ 14-50.15. Short title.

This Article shall be known and may be cited as the "North Carolina Street Gang Suppression Act." (2008-214, s. 3.)

§ 14-50.16. Pattern of criminal street gang activity.

(a) It is unlawful for any person employed by or associated with a criminal street gang to do either of the following:

(1) To conduct or participate in a pattern of criminal street gang activity.

(2) To acquire or maintain any interest in or control of any real or personal property through a pattern of criminal street gang activity.

A violation of this section is a Class H felony, except that a person who violates subdivision (a)(1) of this section, and is an organizer, supervisor, or acts in any other position of management with regard to the criminal street gang, shall be guilty of a Class F felony.

(b) As used in this Article, "criminal street gang" or "street gang" means any ongoing organization, association, or group of three or more persons, whether formal or informal, that:

(1) Has as one of its primary activities the commission of one or more felony offenses, or delinquent acts that would be felonies if committed by an adult;

(2) Has three or more members individually or collectively engaged in, or who have engaged in, criminal street gang activity; and

(3) May have a common name, common identifying sign or symbol.

(c) As used in this Article, "criminal street gang activity" means to commit, to attempt to commit, or to solicit, coerce, or intimidate another person to commit an act or acts, with the specific intent that such act or acts were intended or committed for the purpose, or in furtherance, of the person's involvement in a criminal street gang or street gang. An act or acts are included if accompanied by the necessary mens rea or criminal intent and would be chargeable by indictment under the following laws of this State:

(1) Any offense under Article 5 of Chapter 90 of the General Statutes (Controlled Substances Act).

(2) Any offense under Chapter 14 of the General Statutes except Articles 9, 22A, 40, 46, 47, 59 thereof; and further excepting G.S. 14-78.1, 14-82, 14-86, 14-145, 14-179, 14-183, 14-184, 14-186, 14-190.9, 14-195, 14-197, 14-201, 14-247, 14-248, 14-313 thereof.

(d) As used in this Article, "pattern of criminal street gang activity" means engaging in, and having a conviction for, at least two prior incidents of criminal street gang activity, that have the same or similar purposes, results, accomplices, victims, or methods of commission or otherwise are interrelated by common characteristics and are not isolated and unrelated incidents, provided that at least one of these offenses occurred after December 1, 2008, and the last of the offenses occurred within three years, excluding any periods of imprisonment, of prior criminal street gang activity. Any offenses committed by a defendant prior to indictment for an offense based upon a pattern of street gang activity shall not be used as the basis for any subsequent indictments for offenses involving a pattern of street gang activity. (2008-214, s. 3.)

§ 14-50.17. Soliciting; encouraging participation.

(a) It is unlawful for any person to cause, encourage, solicit, or coerce a person 16 years of age or older to participate in criminal street gang activity.

(b) A violation of this section is a Class H felony. (2008-214, s. 3.)

§ 14-50.18. Soliciting; encouraging participation; minor.

(a) It is unlawful for any person to cause, encourage, solicit, or coerce a person under 16 years of age to participate in criminal street gang activity.

(b) A violation of this section is a Class F felony.

(c) Nothing in this section shall preclude a person who commits a violation of this section from criminal culpability for the underlying offense committed by the minor under any other provision of law. (2008-214, s. 3.)

§ 14-50.19. Threats to deter from gang withdrawal.

(a) It is unlawful for any person to communicate a threat of injury to a person, or to damage the property of another, with the intent to deter a person from assisting another to withdraw from membership in a criminal street gang.

(b) A violation of this section is a Class H felony. (2008-214, s. 3.)

§ 14-50.20. Threats of punishment or retaliation.

(a) It is unlawful for any person to communicate a threat of injury to a person, or to damage the property of another, as punishment or retaliation against a person for having withdrawn from a criminal street gang.

(b) A violation of this section is a Class H felony. (2008-214, s. 3.)

§ 14-50.21. Separate offense.

Any offense committed in violation of G.S. 14-50.16 through G.S. 14-50.20 shall be considered a separate offense. (2008-214, s. 3.)

§ 14-50.22. Enhanced offense for criminal gang activity.

A person age 15 or older who is convicted of a misdemeanor offense that is committed for the benefit of, at the direction of, or in association with, any criminal street gang is guilty of an offense that is one class higher than the offense committed. A Class A1 misdemeanor shall be enhanced to a Class I felony under this section. (2008-214, s. 3.)

§ 14-50.23. Contraband, seizure, and forfeiture.

(a) All property of every kind used or intended for use in the course of, derived from, or realized through criminal street gang activity or a pattern of criminal street gang activity is subject to the seizure and forfeiture provisions of G.S. 14-2.3.

(b) In any action under this section, the court may enter a restraining order in connection with any interest that is subject to forfeiture.

(c) Innocent Activities. - The provisions of this section shall not apply to property used for criminal street gang activity where the owner or person who has legal possession of the property does not have actual knowledge that the property is being used for criminal street gang activity. (2008-214, s. 3.)

§ 14-50.24: Repealed by Session Laws 2012-28, s. 2, effective October 1, 2012.

§ 14-50.25. Reports of disposition; criminal street gang activity.

When a defendant is found guilty of a criminal offense, other than an offense under G.S. 14-50.16 through G.S. 14-50.20, the presiding judge shall determine whether the offense involved criminal street gang activity. If the judge so determines, then the judge shall indicate on the form reflecting the judgment that the offense involved criminal street gang activity. The clerk of court shall ensure that the official record of the defendant's conviction includes a notation of the court's determination. (2008-214, s. 3.)

§ 14-50.26. Matters proved in criminal trial court.

A conviction of an offense defined as criminal gang activity shall preclude the defendant from contesting any factual matters determined in the criminal proceeding in any subsequent civil action or proceeding based on the same conduct. (2008-214, s. 3.)

§ 14-50.27. Local ordinances not preempted by State law.

Nothing in this Article shall prevent a local governing body from adopting and enforcing ordinances relating to gangs and gang violence that are consistent with this Article. Where local laws duplicate or supplement the provisions of this Article, this Article shall be construed as providing alternative remedies and not as preempting the field. (2008-214, s. 3.)

§ 14-50.27A. Dissemination of criminal intelligence information.

A law enforcement agency may disseminate an assessment of criminal intelligence information to the principal of a school when necessary to avoid imminent danger to the life of a student or employee of the school or to the public school property pursuant to 28 C.F.R. § 23.20. The notification may be made in person or by telephone. As used in this subsection, the term "school" means any public or private school in the State under Chapter 115C of the General Statutes. (2009-93, s. 1.)

§ 14-50.28. Applicability to juveniles under the age of 16.

Except as provided in G.S. 14-50.22, 14-50.29, and 14-50.30, the provisions of this Article shall not apply to juveniles under the age of 16. (2008-214, s. 3.)

§ 14-50.29. Conditional discharge for first offenders under the age of 18.

(a) Whenever any person who has not previously been convicted of any felony or misdemeanor other than a traffic violation under the laws of the United States or the laws of this State or any other state, pleads guilty to or is guilty of (i) a Class H felony under this Article or (ii) an enhanced offense under G.S. 14-50.22, and the offense was committed before the person attained the age of 18 years, the court may, without entering a judgment of guilt and with the consent of the defendant, defer further proceedings and place the defendant on probation upon such reasonable terms and conditions as the court may require.

(b) If the court, in its discretion, defers proceedings pursuant to this section, it shall place the defendant on supervised probation for not less than one year, in addition to any other conditions. Prior to taking any action to discharge and dismiss under this section, the court shall make a finding that the defendant has no previous criminal convictions. Upon fulfillment of the terms and conditions of the probation provided for in this section, the court shall discharge the defendant and dismiss the proceedings against the defendant.

(c) Discharge and dismissal under this section shall be without court adjudication of guilt and shall not be deemed a conviction for purposes of this section or for purposes of disqualifications or disabilities imposed by law upon conviction of a crime. Discharge and dismissal under this section may occur only once with respect to any person. Disposition of a case to determine discharge and dismissal under this section at the district court division of the General Court of Justice shall be final for the purpose of appeal. Upon violation of a term or condition of the probation provided for in this section, the court may enter an adjudication of guilt and proceed as otherwise provided.

(d) Upon discharge and dismissal pursuant to this section, the person may apply for an order to expunge the complete record of the proceedings resulting in the dismissal and discharge, pursuant to the procedures and requirements set forth in G.S. 15A-145.1.

(e) The clerk shall notify State and local agencies of the court's order as provided in G.S. 15A-150. (2008-214, s. 3; 2009-510, s. 2; 2009-577, s. 4.)

§ 14-50.30. Expunction of records.

Any person who has not previously been convicted of any felony or misdemeanor other than a traffic violation under the laws of the United States or the laws of this State or any other state, may, if the offense was committed before the person attained the age of 18 years, be eligible to apply for expunction of certain offenses under this Article pursuant to G.S. 15A-145.1. (2008-214, s. 3; 2009-510, s. 3; 2009-577, s. 5; 2010-174, s. 1.)

§ 14-50.31: Reserved for future codification purposes.

§ 14-50.32: Reserved for future codification purposes.

§ 14-50.33: Reserved for future codification purposes.

§ 14-50.34: Reserved for future codification purposes.

§ 14-50.35: Reserved for future codification purposes.

§ 14-50.36: Reserved for future codification purposes.

§ 14-50.37: Reserved for future codification purposes.

§ 14-50.38: Reserved for future codification purposes.

§ 14-50.39: Reserved for future codification purposes.

§ 14-50.40: Reserved for future codification purposes.

Article 13B.

North Carolina Street Gang Nuisance Abatement Act.

§ 14-50.41. Short title.

This Article shall be known and may be cited as the "North Carolina Street Gang Nuisance Abatement Act." (2012-28, s. 1.)

§ 14-50.42. Real property used by criminal street gangs declared a public nuisance: abatement.

(a) Public Nuisance. - Any real property that is erected, established, maintained, owned, leased, or used by any criminal street gang for the purpose of conducting criminal street gang activity, as defined in G.S. 14-50.16(c), shall constitute a public nuisance and may be abated as provided by and subject to the provisions of Article 1 of Chapter 19 of the General Statutes.

(b) Innocent Activities. - The provisions of this section shall not apply to real property used for criminal street gang activity where the owner or person who has legal possession of the real property does not have actual knowledge that the real property is being used for criminal street gang activity or the owner is being coerced into allowing the property to be used for criminal street gang activity. (2008-214, s. 3; 2012-28, ss. 1, 2.)

§ 14-50.43. Street gangs declared a public nuisance.

(a) A street gang, as defined in G.S. 14-50.16(b), that regularly engages in criminal street gang activities, as defined in G.S. 14-50.16(c), constitutes a public nuisance. For the purposes of this section, the term "regularly" means at least five times in a period of not more than 12 months.

(b) Any person who regularly associates with others to engage in criminal street gang activity, as defined in G.S. 14-50.16(c), may be made a defendant in a suit, brought pursuant to Chapter 19 of the General Statutes, to abate any public nuisance resulting from criminal street gang activity.

(c) If the court finds that a public nuisance exists under this section, the court may enter an order enjoining the defendant in the suit from engaging in criminal street gang activities and impose other reasonable requirements to prevent the defendant or a gang from engaging in future criminal street gang activities.

(d) An order entered under this section shall expire one year after entry; however, the order may be modified, rescinded, or vacated at any time prior to its expiration date upon the motion of any party if it appears to the court that one or more of the defendants is no longer engaging in criminal street gang activities. (2012-28, s. 1.)

SUBCHAPTER IV. OFFENSES AGAINST THE HABITATION AND OTHER BUILDINGS.

Article 14.

Burglary and Other Housebreakings.

§ 14-51. First and second degree burglary.

There shall be two degrees in the crime of burglary as defined at the common law. If the crime be committed in a dwelling house, or in a room used as a sleeping apartment in any building, and any person is in the actual occupation of any part of said dwelling house or sleeping apartment at the time of the commission of such crime, it shall be burglary in the first degree. If such crime be committed in a dwelling house or sleeping apartment not actually occupied by anyone at the time of the commission of the crime, or if it be committed in any house within the curtilage of a dwelling house or in any building not a dwelling house, but in which is a room used as a sleeping apartment and not actually occupied as such at the time of the commission of the crime, it shall be burglary in the second degree. For the purposes of defining the crime of burglary, larceny shall be deemed a felony without regard to the value of the property in question. (1889, c. 434, s. 1; Rev., s. 3331; C.S., s. 4232; 1969, c. 543, s. 1.)

§ 14-51.1: Repealed by Session Laws 2011-268, s. 2, effective December 1, 2011.

§ 14-51.2. Home, workplace, and motor vehicle protection; presumption of fear of death or serious bodily harm.

(a)   The following definitions apply in this section:

(1)   Home. - A building or conveyance of any kind, to include its curtilage, whether the building or conveyance is temporary or permanent, mobile or immobile, which has a roof over it, including a tent, and is designed as a temporary or permanent residence.

(2) Law enforcement officer. - Any person employed or appointed as a full-time, part-time, or auxiliary law enforcement officer, correctional officer, probation officer, post-release supervision officer, or parole officer.

(3) Motor vehicle. - As defined in G.S. 20-4.01(23).

(4) Workplace. - A building or conveyance of any kind, whether the building or conveyance is temporary or permanent, mobile or immobile, which has a roof over it, including a tent, which is being used for commercial purposes.

(b) The lawful occupant of a home, motor vehicle, or workplace is presumed to have held a reasonable fear of imminent death or serious bodily harm to himself or herself or another when using defensive force that is intended or likely to cause death or serious bodily harm to another if both of the following apply:

(1) The person against whom the defensive force was used was in the process of unlawfully and forcefully entering, or had unlawfully and forcibly entered, a home, motor vehicle, or workplace, or if that person had removed or was attempting to remove another against that person's will from the home, motor vehicle, or workplace.

(2) The person who uses defensive force knew or had reason to believe that an unlawful and forcible entry or unlawful and forcible act was occurring or had occurred.

(c) The presumption set forth in subsection (b) of this section shall be rebuttable and does not apply in any of the following circumstances:

(1) The person against whom the defensive force is used has the right to be in or is a lawful resident of the home, motor vehicle, or workplace, such as an owner or lessee, and there is not an injunction for protection from domestic violence or a written pretrial supervision order of no contact against that person.

(2) The person sought to be removed from the home, motor vehicle, or workplace is a child or grandchild or is otherwise in the lawful custody or under the lawful guardianship of the person against whom the defensive force is used.

(3) The person who uses defensive force is engaged in, attempting to escape from, or using the home, motor vehicle, or workplace to further any

criminal offense that involves the use or threat of physical force or violence against any individual.

(4) The person against whom the defensive force is used is a law enforcement officer or bail bondsman who enters or attempts to enter a home, motor vehicle, or workplace in the lawful performance of his or her official duties, and the officer or bail bondsman identified himself or herself in accordance with any applicable law or the person using force knew or reasonably should have known that the person entering or attempting to enter was a law enforcement officer or bail bondsman in the lawful performance of his or her official duties.

(5) The person against whom the defensive force is used (i) has discontinued all efforts to unlawfully and forcefully enter the home, motor vehicle, or workplace and (ii) has exited the home, motor vehicle, or workplace.

(d) A person who unlawfully and by force enters or attempts to enter a person's home, motor vehicle, or workplace is presumed to be doing so with the intent to commit an unlawful act involving force or violence.

(e) A person who uses force as permitted by this section is justified in using such force and is immune from civil or criminal liability for the use of such force, unless the person against whom force was used is a law enforcement officer or bail bondsman who was lawfully acting in the performance of his or her official duties and the officer or bail bondsman identified himself or herself in accordance with any applicable law or the person using force knew or reasonably should have known that the person was a law enforcement officer or bail bondsman in the lawful performance of his or her official duties.

(f) A lawful occupant within his or her home, motor vehicle, or workplace does not have a duty to retreat from an intruder in the circumstances described in this section.

(g) This section is not intended to repeal or limit any other defense that may exist under the common law. (2011-268, s. 1.)

§ 14-51.3. Use of force in defense of person; relief from criminal or civil liability.

(a) A person is justified in using force, except deadly force, against another when and to the extent that the person reasonably believes that the conduct is necessary to defend himself or herself or another against the other's imminent use of unlawful force. However, a person is justified in the use of deadly force and does not have a duty to retreat in any place he or she has the lawful right to be if either of the following applies:

(1)   He or she reasonably believes that such force is necessary to prevent imminent death or great bodily harm to himself or herself or another.

(2)   Under the circumstances permitted pursuant to G.S. 14-51.2.

(b)   A person who uses force as permitted by this section is justified in using such force and is immune from civil or criminal liability for the use of such force, unless the person against whom force was used is a law enforcement officer or bail bondsman who was lawfully acting in the performance of his or her official duties and the officer or bail bondsman identified himself or herself in accordance with any applicable law or the person using force knew or reasonably should have known that the person was a law enforcement officer or bail bondsman in the lawful performance of his or her official duties. (2011-268, s. 1.)

§ 14-51.4. Justification for defensive force not available.

The justification described in G.S. 14-51.2 and G.S. 14-51.3 is not available to a person who used defensive force and who:

(1)   Was attempting to commit, committing, or escaping after the commission of a felony.

(2)   Initially provokes the use of force against himself or herself. However, the person who initially provokes the use of force against himself or herself will be justified in using defensive force if either of the following occur:

a.   The force used by the person who was provoked is so serious that the person using defensive force reasonably believes that he or she was in imminent danger of death or serious bodily harm, the person using defensive force had no reasonable means to retreat, and the use of force which is likely to cause death or serious bodily harm to the person who was provoked was the only way to escape the danger.

b. The person who used defensive force withdraws, in good faith, from physical contact with the person who was provoked, and indicates clearly that he or she desires to withdraw and terminate the use of force, but the person who was provoked continues or resumes the use of force. (2011-268, s. 1.)

§ 14-52. Punishment for burglary.

Burglary in the first degree shall be punishable as a Class D felony, and burglary in the second degree shall be punishable as a Class G felony. (1870-1, c. 222; Code, s. 994; 1889, c. 434, s. 2; Rev., s. 3330; C.S., s. 4233; 1941, c. 215, s. 1; 1949, c. 299, s. 2; 1973, c. 1201, s. 3; 1977, c. 871, s. 2; 1979, c. 672; 1979, c. 760, s. 5; 1979, 2nd Sess., c. 1316, s. 47; 1981, c. 63, s. 1, c. 179, s. 14; 1993, c. 539, s. 1151; 1994, Ex. Sess., c. 24, s. 14(c).)

§ 14-53. Breaking out of dwelling house burglary.

If any person shall enter the dwelling house of another with intent to commit any felony or larceny therein, or being in such dwelling house, shall commit any felony or larceny therein, and shall, in either case, break out of such dwelling house in the nighttime, such person shall be punished as a Class D felon. (12 Anne, c. 7, s. 3; R.C., c. 34, s. 8; Code, s. 995; Rev., s. 3332; C.S., s. 4234; 1969, c. 543, s. 2; 1979, c. 760, s. 5; 1979, 2nd Sess., c. 1316, s. 47; 1981, c. 63, s. 1; c. 179, s. 14.)

§ 14-54. Breaking or entering buildings generally.

(a) Any person who breaks or enters any building with intent to commit any felony or larceny therein shall be punished as a Class H felon.

(a1) Any person who breaks or enters any building with intent to terrorize or injure an occupant of the building is guilty of a Class H felony.

(b) Any person who wrongfully breaks or enters any building is guilty of a Class 1 misdemeanor.

(c) As used in this section, "building" shall be construed to include any dwelling, dwelling house, uninhabited house, building under construction, building within the curtilage of a dwelling house, and any other structure designed to house or secure within it any activity or property. (1874-5, c. 166; 1879, c. 323; Code, s. 996; Rev., s. 3333; C.S., s. 4235; 1955, c. 1015; 1969, c. 543, s. 3; 1979, c. 760, s. 5; 1979, 2nd Sess., c. 1316, s. 47; 1981, c. 63, s. 1; c. 179, s. 14; 1993, c. 539, s. 26; 1994, Ex. Sess., c. 24, s. 14(c); 2013-95, s. 1.)

§ 14-54.1. Breaking or entering a building that is a place of religious worship.

(a) Any person who wrongfully breaks or enters any building that is a place of religious worship with intent to commit any felony or larceny therein is guilty of a Class G felony.

(b) As used in this section, a "building that is a place of religious worship" shall be construed to include any church, chapel, meetinghouse, synagogue, temple, longhouse, or mosque, or other building that is regularly used, and clearly identifiable, as a place for religious worship. (2005-235, s. 1.)

§ 14-55. Preparation to commit burglary or other housebreakings.

If any person shall be found armed with any dangerous or offensive weapon, with the intent to break or enter a dwelling, or other building whatsoever, and to commit any felony or larceny therein; or shall be found having in his possession, without lawful excuse, any picklock, key, bit, or other implement of housebreaking; or shall be found in any such building, with intent to commit any felony or larceny therein, such person shall be punished as a Class I felon. (Code, s. 997; Rev., s. 3334; 1907, c. 822; C.S., s. 4236; 1969, c. 543, s. 4; 1979, c. 760, s. 5; 1979, 2nd Sess., c. 1316, s. 47; 1981, c. 63, s. 1, c. 179, s. 14; 1993, c. 539, s. 1152; 1994, Ex. Sess., c. 24, s. 14(c).)

§ 14-56. Breaking or entering into or breaking out of railroad cars, motor vehicles, trailers, aircraft, boats, or other watercraft.

If any person, with intent to commit any felony or larceny therein, breaks or enters any railroad car, motor vehicle, trailer, aircraft, boat, or other watercraft of any kind, containing any goods, wares, freight, or other thing of value, or, after having committed any felony or larceny therein, breaks out of any railroad car, motor vehicle, trailer, aircraft, boat, or other watercraft of any kind containing any goods, wares, freight, or other thing of value, that person is guilty of a Class I felony. It is prima facie evidence that a person entered in violation of this section if he is found unlawfully in such a railroad car, motor vehicle, trailer, aircraft, boat, or other watercraft. (1907, c. 468; C.S., s. 4237; 1969, c. 543, s. 5; 1979, c. 437; c. 760, s. 5; 1979, 2nd Sess., c. 1316, s. 10; 1981, c. 63, s. 1; c. 179, s. 14.)

§ 14-56.1. Breaking into or forcibly opening coin-or currency-operated machines.

Any person who forcibly breaks into, or by the unauthorized use of a key or other instrument opens, any coin-or currency-operated machine with intent to steal any property or moneys therein shall be guilty of a Class 1 misdemeanor, but if such person has previously been convicted of violating this section, such person shall be punished as a Class I felon. The term "coin-or currency-operated machine" shall mean any coin-or currency-operated vending machine, pay telephone, telephone coin or currency receptacle, or other coin-or currency-activated machine or device.

There shall be posted on the machines referred to in G.S. 14-56.1 a decal stating that it is a crime to break into vending machines, and that a second offense is a felony. The absence of such a decal is not a defense to a prosecution for the crime described in this section. (1963, c. 814, s. 1; 1977, c. 723, ss. 1, 3; 1979, c. 760, s. 5; c. 767, s. 1; 1993, c. 539, ss. 27, 1153; 1994, Ex. Sess., c. 24, s. 14(c).)

§ 14-56.2. Damaging or destroying coin-or currency-operated machines.

Any person who shall willfully and maliciously damage or destroy any coin-or currency-operated machine shall be guilty of a Class 1 misdemeanor. The term "coin-or currency-operated machine" shall be defined as set out in G.S. 14-56.1.

(1963, c. 814, s. 2; 1977, c. 723, s. 2; 1993, c. 539, s. 28; 1994, Ex. Sess., c. 24, s. 14(c).)

§ 14-56.3. Breaking into paper currency machines.

Any person, who with intent to steal any moneys therein forcibly breaks into any vending or dispensing machine or device which is operated or activated by the use, deposit or insertion of United States paper currency, shall be guilty of a Class 1 misdemeanor, but if such person has previously been convicted of violating this section, such person shall be punished as a Class I felon.

There shall be posted on the machines referred to in this section a decal stating that it is a crime to break into paper currency machines. The absence of such a decal is not a defense to a prosecution for the crime described in this section. (1977, c. 853, ss. 1, 2; 1979, c. 760, s. 5; c. 767, s. 2; 1993, c. 539, ss. 29, 1154; 1994, Ex. Sess., c. 24, s. 14(c).)

§ 14-56.4. Preparation to commit breaking or entering into motor vehicles.

(a)   For purposes of this section:

(1)   "Manipulative key" means a key, device or instrument, other than a key that is designed to operate a specific lock, that can be variably positioned and manipulated in a vehicle keyway to operate a lock or cylinder or multiple locks or cylinders, including a wiggle key, jiggle key, or rocket key.

(2)   "Master key" means a key that operates all the keyed locks or cylinders in a similar type or group of locks.

(b)   It is unlawful for any person to possess any motor vehicle master key, manipulative key, or other motor vehicle lock-picking device or hot wiring device, with the intent to commit any felony, larceny, or unauthorized use of a motor propelled conveyance.

(c)   It is unlawful for a person to willfully buy, sell, or transfer a motor vehicle master key, manipulative key or device, key-cutting device, lock pick or lock-picking device, or hot wiring device, designed to open or capable of opening the door or trunk of any motor vehicle or of starting the engine of a motor vehicle for use in any manner prohibited by this section.

(d)   Violation of this section is a Class 1 misdemeanor. A second or subsequent violation of this section is a Class I felony.

(e)   This section shall not apply to any person who is a dealer of new or used motor vehicles, a car rental agent, a locksmith, an employee of a towing service, an employee of an automotive repair business, a person who is lawfully repossessing a vehicle, or a state, county, or municipal law enforcement officer, when that person is acting within the scope of the person's official duties or employment. This section shall not apply to a business which has a key-cutting device located and used on the premises for the purpose of making replacement keys for the owner or person who is in lawful custody of a vehicle. (2005-352, s. 1.)

§ 14-57. Burglary with explosives.

Any person who, with intent to commit any felony or larceny therein, breaks and enters, either by day or by night, any building, whether inhabited or not, and opens or attempts to open any vault, safe, or other secure place by use of nitroglycerine, dynamite, gunpowder, or any other explosive, or acetylene torch, shall be deemed guilty of burglary with explosives. Any person convicted under this section shall be punished as a Class D felon. (1921, c. 5; C.S., s. 4237(a); 1969, c. 543, s. 6; 1979, c. 760, s. 5; 1993, c. 539, s. 1155; 1994, Ex. Sess., c. 24, s. 14(c).)

Article 15.

Arson and Other Burnings.

§ 14-58. Punishment for arson.

There shall be two degrees of arson as defined at the common law. If the dwelling burned was occupied at the time of the burning, the offense is arson in the first degree and is punishable as a Class D felony. If the dwelling burned was unoccupied at the time of the burning, the offense is arson in the second degree and is punishable as a Class G felony. (R.C., c. 34, s. 2; 1870-1, c. 222; Code, s. 985; Rev., s. 3335; C.S., s. 4238; 1941, c. 215, s. 2; 1949, c. 299, s. 3; 1973, c. 1201, s. 4; 1979, c. 760, s. 5; 1979, 2nd Sess., c. 1316, s. 47; 1981, c. 63, s. 1, c. 179, s. 14; 1993, c. 539, s. 1156; 1994, Ex. Sess., c. 24, s. 14(c).)

§ 14-58.1. Definition of "house" and "building."

As used in this Article, the terms "house" and "building" shall be defined to include mobile and manufactured-type housing and recreational trailers. (1973, c. 1374.)

§ 14-58.2. Burning of mobile home, manufactured-type house or recreational trailer home.

If any person shall willfully and maliciously burn any mobile home or manufactured-type house or recreational trailer home which is the dwelling house of another and which is occupied at the time of the burning, the same shall constitute the crime of arson in the first degree. (1973, c. 1374; 1979, c. 760, s. 5; 1979, 2nd Sess., c. 1316, s. 47; 1981, c. 63, s. 1; c. 179, s. 14.)

§ 14-59. Burning of certain public buildings.

If any person shall wantonly and willfully set fire to or burn or cause to be burned or aid, counsel or procure the burning of, the State Capitol, the Legislative Building, the Justice Building or any building owned or occupied by the State or any of its agencies, institutions or subdivisions or by any county, incorporated city or town or other governmental or quasi-governmental entity, he shall be punished as a Class F felon. (1830, c. 41, s. 1; R.C., c. 34, s. 7; 1868-9, c. 167, s. 5; Code, s. 985, subsec. 3; Rev., s. 3344; C.S., s. 4239; 1965, c. 14; 1971, c. 816, s. 1; 1979, c. 760, s. 5; 1979, 2nd Sess., c. 1316, s. 47; 1981, c. 63, s.1, c. 179, s. 14; 1993, c. 539, s. 1157; 1994, Ex. Sess., c. 24, s. 14(c).)

§ 14-60. Burning of schoolhouses or buildings of educational institutions.

If any person shall wantonly and willfully set fire to or burn or cause to be burned or aid, counsel or procure the burning of, any schoolhouse or building owned, leased or used by any public or private school, college or educational institution, he shall be punished as a Class F felon. (1901, c. 4, s. 28; Rev., s. 3345; 1919, c. 70; C.S., s. 4240; 1965, c. 870; 1971, c. 816, s. 2; 1979, c. 760, s. 5; 1979, 2nd Sess., c. 1316, s. 47; 1981, c. 63, s. 1, c. 179, s. 14; 1993, c. 539, s. 1158; 1994, Ex. Sess., c. 24, s. 14(c).)

§ 14-61. Burning of certain bridges and buildings.

If any person shall wantonly and willfully set fire to or burn or cause to be burned, or aid, counsel or procure the burning of, any public bridge, or private toll bridge, or the bridge of any incorporated company, or any fire-engine house or rescue-squad building, or any house belonging to an incorporated company or unincorporated association and used in the business of such company or association, he shall be punished as a Class F felon. (1825, c. 1278, P.R.; R.C., c. 34, s. 30; Code, s. 985, subsec. 4; Rev., s. 3337; C.S., s. 4241; 1971, c. 816, s. 3; 1979, c. 760, s. 5; 1979, 2nd Sess., c. 1316, s. 47; 1981, c. 63, s. 1, c. 179, s. 14; 1993, c. 539, s. 1159; 1994, Ex. Sess., c. 24, s. 14(c).)

§ 14-62. Burning of certain buildings.

If any person shall wantonly and willfully set fire to or burn or cause to be burned, or aid, counsel or procure the burning of, any uninhabited house, or any stable, coach house, outhouse, warehouse, office, shop, mill, barn or granary, or any building, structure or erection used or intended to be used in carrying on any trade or manufacture, or any branch thereof, whether the same or any of them respectively shall then be in the possession of the offender, or in the possession of any other person, he shall be punished as a Class F felon. (1874-5, c. 228; Code, s. 985, subsec. 6; 1885, c. 66; 1903, c. 665, s. 2; Rev., s. 3338; C.S., s. 4242; 1927, c. 11, s. 1; 1953, c. 815; 1959, c. 1298, s. 1; 1971, c. 816, s. 4; 1979, c. 760, s. 5; 1979, 2nd Sess., c. 1316, s. 47; 1981, c. 63, s. 1; c. 179, s. 14; 1993, c. 539, s. 1160; 1994, Ex. Sess., c. 24, s. 14(c); 1995 (Reg. Sess., 1996), c. 751, s. 2.)

§ 14-62.1. Burning of building or structure in process of construction.

If any person shall wantonly and willfully set fire to or burn or cause to be burned, or aid, counsel or procure the burning of, any building or structure in the process of construction for use or intended to be used as a dwelling house or in carrying on any trade or manufacture, or otherwise, whether the same or any of them respectively shall then be in the possession of the offender, or in the possession of any other person, he shall be punished as a Class H felon. (1957, c. 792; 1971, c. 816, s. 5; 1979, c. 760, s. 5; 1979, 2nd Sess., c. 1316, s. 47, 1981, c. 63, s. 1, c. 179, s. 14; 1993, c. 539, s. 1161; 1994, Ex. Sess., c. 24, s. 14(c).)

§ 14-62.2. Burning of churches and certain other religious buildings.

If any person shall wantonly and willfully set fire to or burn or cause to be burned, or aid, counsel or procure the burning of any church, chapel, or meetinghouse, the person shall be punished as a Class E felon. (1995 (Reg. Sess., 1996), c. 751, s. 3.)

§ 14-63. Burning of boats and barges.

If any person shall wantonly and willfully set fire to or burn or cause to be burned or aid, counsel or procure the burning of, any boat, barge, ferry or float, without the consent of the owner thereof, he shall be punished as a Class H felon. In the event the consent of the owner is given for an unlawful or fraudulent purpose, however, the penalty provisions of this section shall remain in full force and effect. (1909, c. 854; C.S., s. 4243; 1971, c. 816, s. 6; 1979, c. 760, s. 5; 1979, 2nd Sess., c. 1316, s. 47; 1981, c. 63, s. 1; c. 179, s. 14.)

§ 14-64. Burning of ginhouses and tobacco houses.

If any person shall wantonly and willfully set fire to or burn or cause to be burned, or aid, counsel or procure the burning of, any ginhouse or tobacco house, or any part thereof, he shall be punished as a Class H felon. (1863, c. 17; 1868-9, c. 167, s. 5; Code, s. 985, subsec. 2; 1903, c. 665, s. 1; Rev., s.

3341; C.S., s. 4244; 1971, c. 816, s. 7; 1979, c. 760, s. 5; 1979, 2nd Sess., c. 1316, s. 47; 1981, c. 63, s. 1; c. 179, s. 14.)

§ 14-65. Fraudulently setting fire to dwelling houses.

If any person, being the occupant of any building used as a dwelling house, whether such person be the owner thereof or not, or, being the owner of any building designed or intended as a dwelling house, shall wantonly and willfully or for a fraudulent purpose set fire to or burn or cause to be burned, or aid, counsel or procure the burning of such building, he shall be punished as a Class H felon. (Code, s. 985; 1903, c. 665, s. 3; Rev., s. 3340; 1909, c. 862; C.S., s. 4245; 1927, c. 11, s. 2; 1971, c. 816, s. 8; 1979, c. 760, s. 5; 1979 2nd Sess., c. 1316, s. 47; 1981, c. 63, s. 1; c. 179, s. 14.)

§ 14-66. Burning of personal property.

If any person shall wantonly and willfully set fire to or burn, or cause to be burned, or aid, counsel or procure the burning of, any goods, wares, merchandise or other chattels or personal property of any kind, whether or not the same shall at the time be insured by any person or corporation against loss or damage by fire, with intent to injure or prejudice the insurer, the creditor or the person owning the property, or any other person, whether the property is that of such person or another, he shall be punished as a Class H felon. (1921, c. 119; C.S., s. 4245(a); 1971, c. 816, s. 9; 1979, c. 760, s. 5; 1979, 2nd Sess., c. 1316, s. 47; 1981, c. 63, s. 1; c. 179, s. 14.)

§ 14-67: Repealed by Session Laws 1993, c. 539, s. 1358.2.

§ 14-67.1. Burning other buildings.

If any person shall wantonly and willfully set fire to or burn or cause to be burned or aid, counsel or procure the burning of any building or other structure of any type not otherwise covered by the provisions of this Article, he shall be punished as a Class H felon. (1971, c. 816, s. 11; 1979, c. 760, s. 5; 1979, 2nd Sess., c. 1316, s. 47; 1981, c. 63, s. 1, c. 179, s. 14; 1993, c. 539, s. 1192.1; 1994, Ex. Sess., c. 24, s. 14(c).)

§ 14-68. Failure of owner of property to comply with orders of public authorities.

If the owner or occupant of any building or premises shall fail to comply with the duly authorized orders of the chief of the fire department, or of the Commissioner of Insurance, or of any municipal or county inspector of buildings or of particular features, facilities, or installations of buildings, he shall be guilty of a Class 3 misdemeanor, and punished only by a fine of not less than ten ($10.00) nor more than fifty dollars ($50.00) for each day's neglect, failure, or refusal to obey such orders. (1899, c. 58, s. 4; Rev., s. 3343; C.S., s. 4247; 1969, c. 1063, s. 1; 1993, c. 539, s. 30; 1994, Ex. Sess., c. 24, s. 14(c).)

§ 14-69. Failure of officers to investigate incendiary fires.

If any town or city officer shall fail, neglect or refuse to comply with any of the requirements of the law in regard to the investigation of incendiary fires, he shall be guilty of a Class 3 misdemeanor and shall only be punished by a fine not less than twenty-five ($25.00) nor more than two hundred dollars ($200.00). (1899, c. 58, s. 5; Rev., s. 3342; C.S., s. 4248; 1993, c. 539, s. 31; 1994, Ex. Sess., c. 24, s. 14(c).)

§ 14-69.1. Making a false report concerning destructive device.

(a) Except as provided in subsection (c) of this section, any person who, by any means of communication to any person or group of persons, makes a report, knowing or having reason to know the report is false, that there is located in or in sufficient proximity to cause damage to any building, house or other structure whatsoever or any vehicle, aircraft, vessel or boat any device designed to destroy or damage the building, house or structure or vehicle, aircraft, vessel or boat by explosion, blasting or burning, is guilty of a Class H felony.

(b) Repealed by S.L. 1997-443, s. 19.25(cc).

(c) Any person who, by any means of communication to any person or groups of persons, makes a report, knowing or having reason to know the report is false, that there is located in or in sufficient proximity to cause damage to any public building any device designed to destroy or damage the public building by explosion, blasting, or burning, is guilty of a Class H felony. Any person who receives a second conviction for a violation of this subsection within five years of the first conviction for violation of this subsection is guilty of a Class G felony. For purposes of this subsection, "public building" means educational property as defined in G.S. 14-269.2(a)(1), a hospital as defined in G.S. 131E-76(3), a building housing only State, federal, or local government offices, or the offices of State, federal, or local government located in a building that is not exclusively occupied by the State, federal, or local government.

(d) The court may order a person convicted under this section to pay restitution, including costs and consequential damages resulting from the disruption of the normal activity that would have otherwise occurred on the premises but for the false report, pursuant to Article 81C of Chapter 15A of the General Statutes.

(e) For purposes of this section, the term "report" shall include making accessible to another person by computer. (1959, c. 555, s. 1; 1991, c. 648, s. 1; 1993, c. 539, ss. 32, 116; 1994, Ex. Sess., c. 24, s. 14(c); 1997-443, s. 19.25(cc); 1999-257, s. 1; 2005-311, s. 1.)

§ 14-69.2. Perpetrating hoax by use of false bomb or other device.

(a) Except as provided in subsection (c) of this section, any person who, with intent to perpetrate a hoax, conceals, places, or displays any device, machine, instrument or artifact, so as to cause any person reasonably to believe the same to be a bomb or other device capable of causing injury to persons or property is guilty of a Class H felony.

(b) Repealed by S.L. 1997-443, s. 19.25(dd).

(c) Any person who, with intent to perpetrate a hoax, conceals, places, or displays in or at a public building any device, machine, instrument, or artifact, so as to cause any person reasonably to believe the same to be a bomb or other device capable of causing injury to persons or property is guilty of a Class H felony. Any person who receives a second conviction for a violation of this subsection within five years of the first conviction for violation of this subsection is guilty of a Class G felony. For purposes of this subsection "public building" means educational property as defined in G.S. 14-269.2(a)(1), a hospital as defined in G.S. 131E-76(3), a building housing only State, federal, or local government offices, or the offices of State, federal, or local government located in a building that is not exclusively occupied by the State, federal, or local government.

(d) The court may order a person convicted under this section to pay restitution, including costs and consequential damages resulting from the disruption of the normal activity that would have otherwise occurred on the premises but for the hoax, pursuant to Article 81C of Chapter 15A of the General Statutes. (1959, c. 555, s. 1; 1991, c. 648, s. 2; 1993, c. 539, s. 33; 1994, Ex. Sess., c. 24, s. 14(c); 1997-443, s. 19.25(dd); 1999-257, s. 2.)

§ 14-69.3. Arson or other unlawful burning that results in serious injury to a firefighter or emergency medical technician.

A person is guilty of a Class E felony if the person commits a felony under Article 15 of Chapter 14 of the General Statutes and a firefighter or emergency medical technician suffers serious bodily injury while discharging or attempting to discharge the firefighter's or emergency medical technician's duties on the property, or proximate to the property, that is the subject of the firefighter's or emergency medical technician's discharge or attempt to discharge his or her respective duties. As used in this section, the term "emergency medical technician" includes an emergency medical technician, an emergency medical technician-intermediate, and an emergency medical technician-paramedic, as those terms are defined in G.S. 131E-155. (2003-392, s. 3(a).)

SUBCHAPTER V. OFFENSES AGAINST PROPERTY.

Article 16.

Larceny.

§ 14-70. Distinctions between grand and petit larceny abolished; punishment; accessories to larceny.

All distinctions between petit and grand larceny are abolished. Unless otherwise provided by statute, larceny is a Class H felony and is subject to the same rules of criminal procedure and principles of law as to accessories before and after the fact as other felonies. (R.C., c. 34, s. 26; Code, s. 1075; Rev., s. 3500; C.S., s. 4249; 1969, c. 522, s. 1; 1993, c. 539, s. 1163; 1994, Ex. Sess., c. 24, s. 14(c).)

§ 14-71. Receiving stolen goods; receiving or possessing goods represented as stolen.

(a)   If any person shall receive any chattel, property, money, valuable security or other thing whatsoever, the stealing or taking whereof amounts to larceny or a felony, either at common law or by virtue of any statute made or hereafter to be made, such person knowing or having reasonable grounds to believe the same to have been feloniously stolen or taken, he shall be guilty of a Class H felony, and may be indicted and convicted, whether the felon stealing and taking such chattels, property, money, valuable security or other thing, shall or shall not have been previously convicted, or shall or shall not be amenable to justice; and any such receiver may be dealt with, indicted, tried and punished in any county in which he shall have, or shall have had, any such property in his possession or in any county in which the thief may be tried, in the same manner as such receiver may be dealt with, indicted, tried and punished in the county where he actually received such chattel, money, security, or other thing; and such receiver shall be punished as one convicted of larceny.

(b)   If a person knowingly receives or possesses property in the custody of a law enforcement agency that was explicitly represented to the person by an agent of the law enforcement agency or a person authorized to act on behalf of a law enforcement agency as stolen, the person is guilty of a Class H felony and may be indicted, tried, and punished in any county in which the person received or possessed the property. (1797, c. 485, s. 2; R.C., c. 34, s. 56; Code, s. 1074; Rev., s. 3507; C.S., s. 4250; 1949, c. 145, s. 1; 1975, c. 163, s. 1; 1993, c. 539, s. 1164; 1994, Ex. Sess., c. 24, s. 14(c); 2007-373, s. 1; 2008-187, s. 34(a).)

§ 14-71.1. Possessing stolen goods.

If any person shall possess any chattel, property, money, valuable security or other thing whatsoever, the stealing or taking whereof amounts to larceny or a felony, either at common law or by virtue of any statute made or hereafter to be made, such person knowing or having reasonable grounds to believe the same to have been feloniously stolen or taken, he shall be guilty of a Class H felony, and may be indicted and convicted, whether the felon stealing and taking such chattels, property, money, valuable security or other thing shall or shall not have been previously convicted, or shall or shall not be amenable to justice; and any such possessor may be dealt with, indicted, tried and punished in any county in which he shall have, or shall have had, any such property in his possession or in any county in which the thief may be tried, in the same manner as such possessor may be dealt with, indicted, tried and punished in the county where he actually possessed such chattel, money, security, or other thing; and such possessor shall be punished as one convicted of larceny. (1977, c. 978, s. 1; 1993, c. 539, s. 1165; 1994, Ex. Sess., c. 24, s. 14(c).)

§ 14-72. Larceny of property; receiving stolen goods or possessing stolen goods.

(a) Larceny of goods of the value of more than one thousand dollars ($1,000) is a Class H felony. The receiving or possessing of stolen goods of the value of more than one thousand dollars ($1,000) while knowing or having reasonable grounds to believe that the goods are stolen is a Class H felony. Larceny as provided in subsection (b) of this section is a Class H felony. Receiving or possession of stolen goods as provided in subsection (c) of this section is a Class H felony. Except as provided in subsections (b) and (c) of this section, larceny of property, or the receiving or possession of stolen goods knowing or having reasonable grounds to believe them to be stolen, where the value of the property or goods is not more than one thousand dollars ($1,000), is a Class 1 misdemeanor. In all cases of doubt, the jury shall, in the verdict, fix the value of the property stolen.

(b) The crime of larceny is a felony, without regard to the value of the property in question, if the larceny is any of the following:

(1) From the person.

(2) Committed pursuant to a violation of G.S. 14-51, 14-53, 14-54, 14-54.1, or 14-57.

(3)   Of any explosive or incendiary device or substance. As used in this section, the phrase "explosive or incendiary device or substance" shall include any explosive or incendiary grenade or bomb; any dynamite, blasting powder, nitroglycerin, TNT, or other high explosive; or any device, ingredient for such device, or type or quantity of substance primarily useful for large-scale destruction of property by explosive or incendiary action or lethal injury to persons by explosive or incendiary action. This definition shall not include fireworks; or any form, type, or quantity of gasoline, butane gas, natural gas, or any other substance having explosive or incendiary properties but serving a legitimate nondestructive or nonlethal use in the form, type, or quantity stolen.

(4)   Of any firearm. As used in this section, the term "firearm" shall include any instrument used in the propulsion of a shot, shell or bullet by the action of gunpowder or any other explosive substance within it. A "firearm," which at the time of theft is not capable of being fired, shall be included within this definition if it can be made to work. This definition shall not include air rifles or air pistols.

(5)   Of any record or paper in the custody of the North Carolina State Archives as defined by G.S. 121-2(7) and G.S. 121-2(8).

(6)   Committed after the defendant has been convicted in this State or in another jurisdiction for any offense of larceny under this section, or any offense deemed or punishable as larceny under this section, or of any substantially similar offense in any other jurisdiction, regardless of whether the prior convictions were misdemeanors, felonies, or a combination thereof, at least four times. A conviction shall not be included in the four prior convictions required under this subdivision unless the defendant was represented by counsel or waived counsel at first appearance or otherwise prior to trial or plea. If a person is convicted of more than one offense of misdemeanor larceny in a single session of district court, or in a single week of superior court or of a court in another jurisdiction, only one of the convictions may be used as a prior conviction under this subdivision; except that convictions based upon offenses which occurred in separate counties shall each count as a separate prior conviction under this subdivision.

(c)   The crime of possessing stolen goods knowing or having reasonable grounds to believe them to be stolen in the circumstances described in subsection (b) is a felony or the crime of receiving stolen goods knowing or having reasonable grounds to believe them to be stolen in the circumstances described in subsection (b) is a felony, without regard to the value of the property in question.

(d)   Where the larceny or receiving or possession of stolen goods as described in subsection (a) of this section involves the merchandise of any store, a merchant, a merchant's agent, a merchant's employee, or a peace officer who detains or causes the arrest of any person shall not be held civilly liable for detention, malicious prosecution, false imprisonment, or false arrest of the person detained or arrested, when such detention is upon the premises of the store or in a reasonable proximity thereto, is in a reasonable manner for a reasonable length of time, and, if in detaining or in causing the arrest of such person, the merchant, the merchant's agent, the merchant's employee, or the peace officer had, at the time of the detention or arrest, probable cause to believe that the person committed an offense under subsection (a) of this section. If the person being detained by the merchant, the merchant's agent, or the merchant's employee, is a minor under the age of 18 years, the merchant, the merchant's agent, or the merchant's employee, shall call or notify, or make a reasonable effort to call or notify the parent or guardian of the minor, during the period of detention. A merchant, a merchant's agent, or a merchant's employee, who makes a reasonable effort to call or notify the parent or guardian of the minor shall not be held civilly liable for failing to notify the parent or guardian of the minor. (1895, c. 285; Rev., s. 3506; 1913, c. 118, s. 1; C.S., s. 4251; 1941, c. 178, s. 1; 1949, c. 145, s. 2; 1959, c. 1285; 1961, c. 39, s. 1; 1965, c. 621, s. 5; 1969, c. 522, s. 2; 1973, c. 238, ss. 1, 2; 1975, c. 163, s. 2; c. 696, s. 4; 1977, c. 978, ss. 2, 3; 1979, c. 408, s. 1; c. 760, s. 5; 1979, 2nd Sess., c. 1316, ss. 11, 47; 1981, c. 63, s. 1; c. 179, s. 14; 1991, c. 523, s. 2; 1993, c. 539, s. 34; 1994, Ex. Sess., c. 24, s. 14(c); 1995, c. 185, s. 2; 2006-259, s. 4(a); 2012-154, s. 1.)

§ 14-72.1. Concealment of merchandise in mercantile establishments.

(a)   Whoever, without authority, willfully conceals the goods or merchandise of any store, not theretofore purchased by such person, while still upon the premises of such store, shall be guilty of a misdemeanor and, upon conviction, shall be punished as provided in subsection (e). Such goods or merchandise found concealed upon or about the person and which have not theretofore been purchased by such person shall be prima facie evidence of a willful concealment.

(b)   Repealed by Session Laws 1985 (Regular Session, 1986), c. 841, s. 2.

(c)   A merchant, or the merchant's agent or employee, or a peace officer who detains or causes the arrest of any person shall not be held civilly liable for detention, malicious prosecution, false imprisonment, or false arrest of the person detained or arrested, where such detention is upon the premises of the store or in a reasonable proximity thereto, is in a reasonable manner for a reasonable length of time, and, if in detaining or in causing the arrest of such person, the merchant, or the merchant's agent or employee, or the peace officer had at the time of the detention or arrest probable cause to believe that the person committed the offense created by this section. If the person being detained by the merchant, or the merchant's agent or employee, is a minor under the age of 18 years, the merchant or the merchant's agent or employee, shall call or notify, or make a reasonable effort to call or notify the parent or guardian of the minor, during the period of detention. A merchant, or the merchant's agent or employee, who makes a reasonable effort to call or notify the parent or guardian of the minor shall not be held civilly liable for failing to notify the parent or guardian of the minor.

(d)   Whoever, without authority, willfully transfers any price tag from goods or merchandise to other goods or merchandise having a higher selling price or marks said goods at a lower price or substitutes or superimposes thereon a false price tag and then presents said goods or merchandise for purchase shall be guilty of a misdemeanor and, upon conviction, shall be punished as provided in subsection (e).

Nothing herein shall be construed to provide that the mere possession of goods or the production by shoppers of improperly priced merchandise for checkout shall constitute prima facie evidence of guilt.

(d1)   Notwithstanding subsection (e) of this section, any person who violates subsection (a) of this section by using a lead-lined or aluminum-lined bag, a lead-lined or aluminum-lined article of clothing, or a similar device to prevent the activation of any antishoplifting or inventory control device is guilty of a Class H felony.

(e)   Punishment. - For a first conviction under subsection (a) or (d), or for a subsequent conviction for which the punishment is not specified by this subsection, the defendant shall be guilty of a Class 3 misdemeanor. The term of imprisonment may be suspended only on condition that the defendant perform community service for a term of at least 24 hours. For a second offense committed within three years after the date the defendant was convicted of an offense under this section, the defendant shall be guilty of a Class 2 misdemeanor. The term of imprisonment may be suspended only on condition that the defendant be imprisoned for a term of at least 72 hours as a condition of special probation, perform community service for a term of at least 72 hours, or both. For a third or subsequent offense committed within five years after the date the defendant was convicted of two other offenses under this section, the defendant shall be guilty of a Class 1 misdemeanor. The term of imprisonment may be suspended only if a condition of special probation is imposed to require the defendant to serve a term of imprisonment of at least 11 days. However, if the sentencing judge finds that the defendant is unable, by reason of mental or physical infirmity, to perform the service required under this section, and the reasons for such findings are set forth in the judgment, the judge may pronounce such other sentence as the judge finds appropriate.

(f)   Repealed by Session Laws 2009-372, s. 12, effective December 1, 2009, and applicable to offenses committed on or after that date.

(g)   Limitations. - For active terms of imprisonment imposed under this section:

(1)   The judge may not give credit to the defendant for the first 24 hours of time spent in incarceration pending trial;

(2)   The defendant must serve the mandatory minimum period of imprisonment and good or gain time credit may not be used to reduce that mandatory minimum period; and

(3)   The defendant may not be released or paroled unless he is otherwise eligible and has served the mandatory minimum period of imprisonment. (1957, c. 301; 1971, c. 238; 1973, c. 457, ss. 1, 2; 1985 (Reg. Sess., 1986), c. 841, ss. 1-3; 1987, c. 660; 1993, c. 539, s. 35; 1994, Ex. Sess., c. 24, s. 14(c); c. 28, s. 1; 1995, c. 185, s. 3; c. 509, s. 9; 1997-80, s. 1; 1997-443, s. 19.25(ff); 2009-372, s. 12.)

§ 14-72.2. Unauthorized use of a motor-propelled conveyance.

(a)   A person is guilty of an offense under this section if, without the express or implied consent of the owner or person in lawful possession, he takes or operates an aircraft, motorboat, motor vehicle, or other motor-propelled conveyance of another.

(b) Unauthorized use of an aircraft is a Class H felony. All other unauthorized use of a motor-propelled conveyance is a Class 1 misdemeanor.

(c) Unauthorized use of a motor-propelled conveyance shall be a lesser-included offense of unauthorized use of an aircraft.

(d) As used in this section, "owner" means any person with a property interest in the motor-propelled conveyance. (1973, c. 1330, s. 38; 1977, c. 919; 1979, c. 760, s. 5; 1979, 2nd Sess., c. 1316, s. 47; 1981, c. 63, s. 1, c. 179, s. 14; 1993, c. 539, ss. 36, 1166; 1994, Ex. Sess., c. 24, s. 14(c).)

§ 14-72.3. Removal of shopping cart from shopping premises.

(a) As used in this section:

(1) "Shopping cart" means the type of push cart commonly provided by grocery stores, drugstores, and other retail stores for customers to transport commodities within the store and from the store to their motor vehicles outside the store.

(2) "Premises" includes the motor vehicle parking area set aside for customers of the store.

(b) It is unlawful for any person to remove a shopping cart from the premises of a store without the consent, given at the time of the removal, of the store owner, manager, agent or employee.

(c) Violation of this section is a Class 3 misdemeanor. (1983, c. 705, s. 1; 1994, Ex. Sess., c. 14, s. 3.1.)

§ 14-72.4. Unauthorized taking or sale of labeled dairy milk cases or milk crates bearing the name or label of owner.

(a) A person is guilty of the unauthorized taking or sale of a dairy milk case or milk crate on or after January 1, 1990, if he:

(1) Takes, buys, sells or disposes of any dairy milk case or milk crate, bearing the name or label of the owner, without the express or implied consent of the owner or his designated agent; or

(2) Refuses upon demand of the owner or his designated agent to return to the owner or his designated agent any dairy milk case or milk crate, bearing the name or label of the owner; or

(3) Defaces, obliterates, erases, covers up, or otherwise removes or conceals any name, label, registered trademark, insignia, or other business identification of an owner of a dairy milk case or milk crate, for the purpose of destroying or removing from the milk case or milk crate evidence of its ownership.

(b) For purposes of this section dairy milk cases or milk crates shall be deemed to bear a name or label of an owner when there is imprinted or attached on the case or crate a name, insignia, mark, business identification or label showing ownership or sufficient information to ascertain ownership. For purposes of this section, the term "dairy case" shall be defined as a wire or plastic container which holds 16 quarts or more of beverage and is used by distributors or retailers, or their agents, as a means to transport, store, or carry dairy products.

(c) A violation of this section is a Class 2 misdemeanor.

(d) Nothing in this section shall preclude the prosecution of any misdemeanor or felony offense that is applicable under any other statute or common law. (1989, c. 303; 1994, Ex. Sess., c. 14, s. 3.2.)

§ 14-72.5. Larceny of motor fuel.

(a) If any person shall take and carry away motor fuel valued at less than one thousand dollars ($1,000) from an establishment where motor fuel is offered for retail sale with the intent to steal the motor fuel, that person shall be guilty of a Class 1 misdemeanor.

(b) The term "motor fuel" as used in this section shall have the same meaning as found in G.S. 105-449.60(20).

(c) Conviction Report Sent to Division of Motor Vehicles. - The court shall report final convictions of violations of this section to the Division of Motor Vehicles. The Division of Motor Vehicles shall revoke a person's drivers license for a second or subsequent conviction under this section in accordance with G.S. 20-17(a)(16). (2001-352, s. 1.)

§ 14-72.6. Felonious larceny, possession, or receiving of stolen goods from a permitted construction site.

(a) A person is guilty of a Class I felony if he commits any of the following offenses, where the goods are valued in excess of three hundred dollars ($300.00) but less than one thousand dollars ($1,000):

(1) Larceny of goods from a permitted construction site.

(2) Possessing or receiving of stolen goods, with actual knowledge or having reasonable grounds to believe that the goods were stolen from a permitted construction site.

(b) As used in this section, a "permitted construction site" is a site where a permit, license, or other authorization has been issued by the State or a local governmental entity for the placement of new construction or improvements to real property. (2005-208, s. 1.)

§ 14-72.7. Chop shop activity.

(a) A person is guilty of a Class G felony if that person engages in any of the following activities, without regard to the value of the property in question:

(1) Altering, destroying, disassembling, dismantling, reassembling, or storing any motor vehicle or motor vehicle part the person knows or has reasonable grounds to believe has been illegally obtained by theft, fraud, or other illegal means.

(2) Permitting a place to be used for any activity prohibited by this section, where the person either owns or has legal possession of the place, and knows

or has reasonable grounds to believe that the place is being used for any activity prohibited by this section.

(3)   Purchasing, disposing of, selling, transferring, receiving, or possessing a motor vehicle or motor vehicle part either knowing or having reasonable grounds to believe that the vehicle identification number of the motor vehicle, or vehicle part identification number of the vehicle part, has been altered, counterfeited, defaced, destroyed, disguised, falsified, forged, obliterated, or removed.

(4)   Purchasing, disposing of, selling, transferring, receiving, or possessing a motor vehicle or motor vehicle part to or from a person engaged in any activity prohibited by this section, knowing or having reasonable grounds to believe that the person is engaging in that activity.

(b)   Innocent Activities. - The provisions of this section shall not apply to either of the following:

(1)   Purchasing, disposing of, selling, transferring, receiving, possessing, crushing, or compacting a motor vehicle or motor vehicle part in good faith and without knowledge of previous illegal activity in regard to that vehicle or part, as long as the person engaging in the activity does not remove a vehicle identification number or vehicle part identification number before or during the activity.

(2)   Purchasing, disposing of, selling, transferring, receiving, possessing, crushing, or compacting a motor vehicle or motor vehicle part after law enforcement proceedings are completed or as a part of law enforcement proceedings, as long as the activity is not in conflict with law enforcement proceedings.

(c)   Civil Penalty. - Any court with jurisdiction of a criminal prosecution under this section may also assess a civil penalty. The clear proceeds of the civil penalties shall be remitted to the Civil Penalty and Forfeiture Fund in accordance with G.S. 115C-457.2. The civil penalty shall not exceed three times the assets obtained by the defendant as a result of violations of this section.

(d)   Private Actions. - Any person aggrieved by a violation of this section may, in a civil action in any court of competent jurisdiction, obtain appropriate relief, including preliminary and other equitable or declaratory relief, compensatory and punitive damages, reasonable investigation expenses, costs of suit, and any attorneys' fees as may be provided by law.

(e) Seizure and Forfeiture. - Any instrumentality possessed or used to engage in the activities prohibited by this section are subject to the seizure and forfeiture provisions of G.S. 14-86.1. The real property of a place used to engage in the activities prohibited by this section is subject to the abatement and forfeiture provisions of Chapter 19 of the General Statutes.

(f) Definitions. - For the purposes of this section, the following definitions apply:

(1) Instrumentality. - Motor vehicle, motor vehicle part, other conveyance, tool, implement, or equipment possessed or used in the activities prohibited under this section.

(2) Vehicle identification number. - A number, a letter, a character, a datum, a derivative, or a combination thereof, used by the manufacturer or the Division of Motor Vehicles for the purpose of uniquely identifying a motor vehicle.

(3) Vehicle part identification number. - A number, a letter, a character, a datum, a derivative, or a combination thereof, used by the manufacturer for the purpose of uniquely identifying a motor vehicle part. (2007-178, s. 1; 2013-323, s. 1.)

§ 14-72.8. Felony larceny of motor vehicle parts.

Unless the conduct is covered under some other provision of law providing greater punishment, larceny of a motor vehicle part is a Class I felony if the cost of repairing the motor vehicle is one thousand dollars ($1,000) or more.

For purposes of this section, the cost of repairing a motor vehicle means the cost of any replacement part and any additional costs necessary to install the replacement part in the motor vehicle. (2009-379, s. 1.)

§ 14-72.9. Reserved for future codification purposes.

§ 14-72.10. Reserved for future codification purposes.

§ 14-72.11. Larceny from a merchant.

A person is guilty of a Class H felony if the person commits larceny against a merchant under any of the following circumstances:

(1)   If the property taken has a value of more than two hundred dollars ($200.00), by using an exit door erected and maintained to comply with the requirements of 29 C.F.R. § 1910.36 and 29 C.F.R. § 1910.37 upon which door has been placed a notice, sign, or poster providing information about the felony offense and punishment provided under this subsection, to exit the premises of a store.

(2)   By removing, destroying, or deactivating a component of an antishoplifting or inventory control device to prevent the activation of any antishoplifting or inventory control device.

(3)   By affixing a product code created for the purpose of fraudulently obtaining goods or merchandise from a merchant at less than its actual sale price.

(4)   When the property is infant formula valued in excess of one hundred dollars ($100.00). As used in this subsection, the term "infant formula," has the same meaning as found in 21 U.S.C. § 321(z). (2007-373, s. 2; 2008-187, s. 34(b).)

§ 14-73. Jurisdiction of the superior courts in cases of larceny and receiving stolen goods.

The superior courts shall have exclusive jurisdiction of the trial of all cases of the larceny of property, or the receiving of stolen goods knowing them to be stolen, of the value of more than one thousand dollars ($1,000). (1913, c. 118, s. 2; C.S., s. 4252; 1941, c. 178, s. 2; 1949, c. 145, s. 3; 1961, c. 39, s. 2; 1979, c. 408, s. 2; 1991, c. 523, s. 3.)

§ 14-73.1. Petty misdemeanors.

The offenses of larceny and the receiving of stolen goods knowing the same to have been stolen, which are made misdemeanors by Article 16, Subchapter V,

Chapter 14 of the General Statutes, as amended, are hereby declared to be petty misdemeanors. (1949, c. 145, s. 4; 1973, c. 108, s. 1.)

§ 14-74. Larceny by servants and other employees.

If any servant or other employee, to whom any money, goods or other chattels, or any of the articles, securities or choses in action mentioned in G.S. 14-75, by his master shall be delivered safely to be kept to the use of his master, shall withdraw himself from his master and go away with such money, goods or other chattels, or any of the articles, securities or choses in action mentioned as aforesaid, or any part thereof, with intent to steal the same and defraud his master thereof, contrary to the trust and confidence in him reposed by his said master; or if any servant, being in the service of his master, without the assent of his master, shall embezzle such money, goods or other chattels, or any of the articles, securities or choses in action mentioned as aforesaid, or any part thereof, or otherwise convert the same to his own use, with like purpose to steal them, or to defraud his master thereof, the servant so offending shall be guilty of a felony: Provided, that nothing contained in this section shall extend to apprentices or servants within the age of 16 years. If the value of the money, goods, or other chattels, or any of the articles, securities, or choses in action mentioned in G.S. 14-75, is one hundred thousand dollars ($100,000) or more, the person is guilty of a Class C felony. If the value of the money, goods, or other chattels, or any of the articles, securities, or choses in action mentioned in G.S. 14-75, is less than one hundred thousand dollars ($100,000), the person is guilty of a Class H felony. (21 Hen. VIII, c. 7, ss. 1, 2; R.C., c. 34, s. 18; Code, s. 1065; Rev., s. 3499; C.S., s. 4253; 1979, c. 760, s. 5; 1979, 2nd Sess., c. 1316, s. 47; 1981, c. 63, s. 1; c. 179, s. 14; 1997-443, s. 19.25(c); 1998-217, s. 4(a).)

§ 14-75. Larceny of chose in action.

If any person shall feloniously steal, take and carry away, or take by robbery, any bank note, check or other order for the payment of money issued by or drawn on any bank or other society or corporation within this State or within any of the United States, or any treasury warrant, debenture, certificate of stock or other public security, or certificate of stock in any corporation, or any order, bill of exchange, bond, promissory note or other obligation, either for the payment of money or for the delivery of specific articles, being the property of any other person, or of any corporation (notwithstanding any of the said particulars may be termed in law a chose in action), that person is guilty of a Class H felony. (1811, c. 814, s. 1; R.C., c. 34, s. 20; Code, s. 1064; Rev., s. 3498; C.S., s. 4254; 1945, c. 635; 1993, c. 539, s. 1167; 1994, Ex. Sess., c. 24, s. 14(c).)

§ 14-75.1. Larceny of secret technical processes.

Any person who steals property consisting of a sample, culture, microorganism, specimen, record, recording, document, drawing, or any other article, material, device, or substance which constitutes, represents, evidences, reflects, or records a secret scientific or technical process, invention, formula, or any phase or part thereof shall be punished as a Class H felon. A process, invention, or formula is "secret" when it is not, and is not intended to be, available to anyone other than the owner thereof or selected persons having access thereto for limited purposes with his consent, and when it accords or may accord the owner an advantage over competitors or other persons who do not have knowledge or the benefit thereof. (1967, c. 1175; 1979, c. 760, s. 5; 1979, 2nd Sess., c. 1316, s. 47; 1981, c. 63, s. 1; c. 179, s. 14.)

§ 14-76. Larceny, mutilation, or destruction of public records and papers.

If any person shall steal, or for any fraudulent purpose shall take from its place of deposit for the time being, or from any person having the lawful custody thereof, or shall unlawfully and maliciously obliterate, injure or destroy any record, writ, return, panel, process, interrogatory, deposition, affidavit, rule, order or warrant of attorney or any original document whatsoever, of or belonging to any court of record, or relating to any matter, civil or criminal, begun, pending or terminated in any such court, or any bill, answer, interrogatory, deposition, affidavit, order or decree or any original document whatsoever, of or belonging to any court or relating to any cause or matter begun, pending or terminated in any such court, every such offender shall be guilty of a Class 1 misdemeanor; and in any indictment for such offense it shall not be necessary to allege that the article, in respect to which the offense is committed, is the property of any person or that the same is of any value. If any person shall steal or for any fraudulent purpose shall take from the register's office, or from any person having the lawful custody thereof, or shall unlawfully and willfully obliterate, injure or destroy any book wherein deeds or other instruments of writing are registered, or any other book of registration or record required to be kept by the register of deeds or shall unlawfully destroy, obliterate, deface or remove any records of proceedings of the board of county commissioners, or unlawfully and fraudulently abstract any record, receipt, order or voucher or other paper writing required to be kept by the clerk of the board of commissioners of any county, he shall be guilty of a Class 1 misdemeanor. (8 Hen. VI, c. 12, s. 3; R.C., c. 34, s. 31; 1881, c. 17; Code, s. 1071; Rev., s. 3508; C.S., s. 4255; 1993, c. 539, s. 37; 1994, Ex. Sess., c. 24, s. 14(c).)

§ 14-76.1. Mutilation or defacement of records and papers in the North Carolina State Archives.

If any person shall willfully or maliciously obliterate, injure, deface, or alter any record or paper in the custody of the North Carolina State Archives as defined by G.S. 121-2(7) and 121-2(8), he shall be guilty of a Class 1 misdemeanor. The provisions of this section do not apply to employees of the Department of Cultural Resources who may destroy any accessioned records or papers that are approved for destruction by the North Carolina Historical Commission pursuant to the authority contained in G.S. 121-4(12). (1975, c. 696, s. 3; 1993, c. 539, s. 38; 1994, Ex. Sess., c. 24, s. 14(c).)

§ 14-77. Larceny, concealment or destruction of wills.

If any person, either during the life of the testator or after his death, shall steal or, for any fraudulent purpose, shall destroy or conceal any will, codicil or other testamentary instrument, he shall be guilty of a Class 1 misdemeanor. (R.C., c. 34, s. 32; Code, s. 1072; Rev., s. 3510; C.S., s. 4256; 1993, c. 539, s. 39; 1994, Ex. Sess., c. 24, s. 14(c).)

§ 14-78. Larceny of ungathered crops.

If any person shall steal or feloniously take and carry away any maize, corn, wheat, rice or other grain, or any cotton, tobacco, potatoes, peanuts, pulse, fruit, vegetable or other product cultivated for food or market, growing, standing or remaining ungathered in any field or ground, that person is guilty of a Class H felony. (1811, c. 816, P.R.; R.C., c. 34, s. 21; 1868-9, c. 251; Code, s. 1069; Rev., s. 3503; C.S., s. 4257; 1975, c. 697; 1993, c. 539, s. 1168; 1994, Ex. Sess., c. 24, s. 14(c).)

§ 14-78.1: Repealed by Session Laws 1994, Ex. Sess., c. 14, s. 72(1).

§ 14-79. Larceny of ginseng.

If any person shall take and carry away, or shall aid in taking or carrying away, any ginseng growing upon the lands of another person, with intent to steal the same, he shall be punished as a Class H felon. (1905, c. 211; Rev., s. 3502; C.S., s. 4258; 1979, c. 760, s. 5; 1979, 2nd Sess., c. 1316, s. 47; 1981, c. 63, s. 1; c. 179, s. 14; 1993, c. 539, s. 1169; 1994, Ex. Sess., c. 24, s. 14(c); 1999-107, s. 1.)

§ 14-79.1. Larceny of pine needles or pine straw.

If any person shall take and carry away, or shall aid in taking or carrying away, any pine needles or pine straw being produced on the land of another person upon which land notices, signs, or posters prohibiting the raking or removal of pine needles or pine straw have been placed in accordance with the provisions of G.S. 14-159.7, or upon which posted notices have been placed in accordance with the provisions of G.S. 14-159.7, with the intent to steal the pine needles or pine straw, that person shall be guilty of a Class H felony. (1997-443, s. 19.25(aa).)

§ 14-79.2. Waste kitchen grease; unlawful acts and penalties.

(a)   It shall be unlawful for any person to do any of the following:

(1)   Take and carry away, or aid in taking or carrying away, any waste kitchen grease container or the waste kitchen grease contained therein, which container bears a notice that unauthorized removal is prohibited without written consent of the owner of the container.

(2) Intentionally contaminate or purposely damage any waste kitchen grease container or grease therein.

(3) Place a label on a waste kitchen grease container knowing that it is owned by another person in order to claim ownership of the container.

(b) Any person who violates subsection (a) of this section shall be penalized as follows:

(1) If the value of the waste kitchen grease container, or the container and the waste kitchen grease contained therein, is one thousand dollars ($1,000) or less, it shall be a Class 1 misdemeanor.

(2) If the value of the waste kitchen grease container, or the container and the waste kitchen grease contained therein, is more than one thousand dollars ($1,000), it shall be a Class H felony.

(c) A container in which waste kitchen grease is deposited that bears a name on the container shall be presumed to be owned by that person named on the container.

(d) As used in this section, "waste kitchen grease" has the same meaning as in G.S. 106-168.1. (2012-127, s. 6.)

§ 14-80: Repealed by Session Laws 1994, Ex. Sess., c. 14, s. 72(2).

§ 14-81. Larceny of horses, mules, swine, cattle, or dogs.

(a) Larceny of horses, mules, swine, or cattle is a Class H felony.

(a1) Larceny of a dog is a Class I felony.

(b) In sentencing a person convicted of violating this section, the judge shall, as a minimum punishment, place a person on probation subject to the following conditions:

(1) A person must make restitution for the damage or loss caused by the larceny of the livestock or dogs, and

(2) A person must pay a fine of not less than the amount of the damages or loss caused by the larceny of the livestock or dogs.

(c) No provision in this section shall limit the authority of the judge to sentence the person convicted of violating this section to an active sentence. (1866-7, c. 62; 1868, c. 37, s. 1; 1879, c. 234, s. 2; Code, s. 1066; Rev., s. 3505; 1917, c. 162, s. 2; C.S., s. 4260; 1965, c. 621, s. 6; 1981, c. 664, s. 2; 1989, c. 773, s. 2; 1993, c. 539, s. 1171; 1994, Ex. Sess., c. 24, s. 14(c).)

§ 14-82. Taking horses, mules, or dogs for temporary purposes.

If any person shall unlawfully take and carry away any horse, gelding, mare, mule, or dog, the property of another person, secretly and against the will of the owner of such property, with intent to deprive the owner of the special or temporary use of the same, or with the intent to use such property for a special or temporary purpose, the person so offending shall be guilty of a Class 2 misdemeanor. (1879, c. 234, s. 1; Code, s. 1067; Rev., s. 3509; 1913, c. 11; C.S., s. 4261; 1969, c. 1224, s. 3; 1989, c. 773, s. 3; 1994, Ex. Sess., c. 14, s. 3.3.)

§ 14-83. Repealed by Session Laws 1943, c. 543.

§ 14-83.1. Fixtures subject to larceny.

All common law distinctions providing that personal property that has become affixed to real property is not subject to a charge of larceny are abolished. Any person who shall remove or take and carry away, or shall aid another in removing, taking or carrying away, any property that is affixed to real property, with the intent to steal the property, shall be guilty of larceny and shall be punished as provided by statute. (2008-128, s. 2.)

§ 14-84. Animals subject to larceny.

All common-law distinctions among animals with respect to their being subject to larceny are abolished. Any animal that is in a person's possession is the subject of larceny. (1919, c. 116, s. 9; C.S., s. 4263; 1955, c. 804; 1983, c. 35, s. 1.)

§ 14-85. Pursuing or injuring livestock with intent to steal.

If any person shall pursue, kill or wound any horse, mule, ass, jennet, cattle, hog, sheep or goat, the property of another, with the intent unlawfully and feloniously to convert the same to his own use, he shall be guilty of a Class H felony, and shall be punishable, in all respects, as if convicted of larceny, though such animal may not have come into the actual possession of the person so offending. (1866, c. 57; Code, s. 1068; Rev., s. 3504; C.S., s. 4264; 1993, c. 539, s. 1172; 1994, Ex. Sess., c. 24, s. 14(c).)

§ 14-86: Repealed by Session Laws 1994, Ex. Sess., c. 14, s. 72(3).

§ 14-86.1. Seizure and forfeiture of conveyances used in committing larceny and similar crimes.

(a)   All conveyances, including vehicles, watercraft or aircraft, used to unlawfully conceal, convey or transport property in violation of G.S. 14-71, 14-71.1, or 20-106, or used by any person in the commission of armed or common-law robbery, or used in violation of G.S. 14-72.7, or used by any person in the commission of any larceny when the value of the property taken is more than two thousand dollars ($2,000) shall be subject to forfeiture as provided herein, except that:

(1)   No conveyance used by any person as a common carrier in the transaction of the business of the common carrier shall be forfeited under the provisions of this section unless it shall appear that the owner or other person in custody or control of such conveyance was a consenting party or privy to a violation that may subject the conveyance to forfeiture under this section;

(2) No conveyance shall be forfeited under the provisions of this section by reason of any act or omission committed or omitted while such conveyance was unlawfully in the possession of a person other than the owner in violation of the criminal laws of the United States, or any state;

(3) No conveyance shall be forfeited pursuant to this section unless the violation involved is a felony;

(4) A forfeiture of a conveyance encumbered by a bona fide security interest is subject to the interest of the secured party who neither had knowledge of nor consented to the act or omission;

(5) No conveyance shall be forfeited under the provisions of this section unless the owner knew or had reason to believe the vehicle was being used in the commission of any violation that may subject the conveyance to forfeiture under this section;

(6) The trial judge in the criminal proceeding which may subject the conveyance to forfeiture may order the seized conveyance returned to the owner if he finds forfeiture inappropriate. If the conveyance is not returned to the owner the procedures provided in subsection (e) shall apply.

As used in this section concerning a violation of G.S. 14-72.7, the term "conveyance" includes any "instrumentality" as defined in that section.

(b) Any conveyance subject to forfeiture under this section may be seized by any law-enforcement officer upon process issued by any district or superior court having original jurisdiction over the offense except that seizure without such process may be made when:

(1) The seizure is incident to an arrest or subject to a search under a search warrant; or

(2) The property subject to seizure has been the subject of a prior judgment in favor of the State in a criminal injunction or forfeiture proceeding under this section.

(c) The conveyance shall be deemed to be in custody of the law-enforcement agency seizing it. The law-enforcement agency may remove the property to a place designated by it or request that the North Carolina Department of Justice or Department of Public Safety take custody of the property and remove it to an appropriate location for disposition in accordance with law; provided, the conveyance shall be returned to the owner upon execution by him of a good and valid bond, with sufficient sureties, in a sum double the value of the property, which said bond shall be approved by an officer of the agency seizing the conveyance and shall be conditioned upon the return of said property to the custody of said officer on the day of trial to abide the judgment of the court.

(d)   Whenever a conveyance is forfeited under this section, the law-enforcement agency having custody of it may:

(1)   Retain the conveyance for official use; or

(2)   Transfer the conveyance which was forfeited under the provisions of this section to the North Carolina Department of Justice or to the North Carolina Department of Public Safety when, in the discretion of the presiding judge and upon application of the North Carolina Department of Justice or the North Carolina Department of Public Safety, said conveyance may be of official use to the North Carolina Department of Justice or the North Carolina Department of Public Safety; or

(3)   Upon determination by the director of any law-enforcement agency that a conveyance transferred pursuant to the provisions of this section is of no further use to said agency, such conveyance may be sold as surplus property in the same manner as other conveyances owned by the law-enforcement agency. The proceeds from such sale, after deducting the cost thereof, shall be paid to the school fund of the county in which said conveyance was seized. Any conveyance transferred to any law-enforcement agency under the provisions of this section which has been modified or especially equipped from its original manufactured condition so as to increase its speed shall be used in the performance of official duties only. Such conveyance shall not be resold, transferred or disposed of other than as junk unless the special equipment or modification has been removed and destroyed, and the vehicle restored to its original manufactured condition.

(e)   All conveyances subject to forfeiture under the provisions of this section shall be forfeited pursuant to the procedures for forfeiture of conveyances used to conceal, convey, or transport intoxicating beverages found in G.S. 18B-504. Provided, nothing in this section or G.S. 18B-504 shall be construed to require a conveyance to be sold when it can be used in the performance of official duties of the law-enforcement agency. (1979, c. 592; 1983, c. 74; c. 768, s. 2; 1991, c. 523, s. 4; 2007-178, s. 2; 2011-145, s. 19.1(g).)

§ 14-86.2. Larceny, destruction, defacement, or vandalism of portable toilets or pumper trucks.

Unless the conduct is covered under some other provision of law providing greater punishment, if any person steals, takes from its temporary location or from any person having the lawful custody thereof, or willfully destroys, defaces, or vandalizes a chemical or portable toilet as defined in G.S. 130A-290 or a pumper truck that is operated by a septage management firm that is permitted by the Department of Environment and Natural Resources under G.S. 130A-291.1, the person is guilty of a Class 1 misdemeanor. (2009-37, s. 1.)

§ 14-86.3. Reserved for future codification purposes.

§ 14-86.4. Reserved for future codification purposes.

Article 16A.

Organized Retail Theft.

§ 14-86.5. Definitions.

The following definitions apply in this Article:

(1)   "Retail property." - Any new article, product, commodity, item, or component intended to be sold in retail commerce.

(2)   "Retail property fence." - A person or business that buys retail property knowing or believing that retail property is stolen.

(3)   "Theft." - To take possession of, carry away, transfer, or cause to be carried away the retail property of another with the intent to steal the retail property.

(4)   "Value." - The retail value of an item as advertised by the affected retail establishment, to include all applicable taxes. (2007-373, s. 3.)

§ 14-86.6. Organized retail theft.

(a)   A person is guilty of a Class H felony if the person:

(1)   Conspires with another person to commit theft of retail property from retail establishments, with a value exceeding one thousand five hundred dollars ($1,500) aggregated over a 90-day period, with the intent to sell that retail property for monetary or other gain, and who takes or causes that retail property to be placed in the control of a retail property fence or other person in exchange for consideration.

(2)   Receives or possesses any retail property that has been taken or stolen in violation of subdivision (1) of this subsection while knowing or having reasonable grounds to believe the property is stolen.

(b)   Any interest a person has acquired or maintained in violation of this section shall be subject to forfeiture pursuant to the procedures for forfeiture set out in G.S. 18B-504. (2007-373, s. 3; 2008-187, s. 34(c).)

Article 17.

Robbery.

§ 14-87. Robbery with firearms or other dangerous weapons.

(a)   Any person or persons who, having in possession or with the use or threatened use of any firearms or other dangerous weapon, implement or means, whereby the life of a person is endangered or threatened, unlawfully takes or attempts to take personal property from another or from any place of business, residence or banking institution or any other place where there is a person or persons in attendance, at any time, either day or night, or who aids or abets any such person or persons in the commission of such crime, shall be guilty of a Class D felony.

(b), (c) Repealed by Session Laws 1979, c. 760, s. 5.

(d)   Repealed by Session Laws 1993, c. 539, s. 1173. (1929, c. 187, s. 1; 1975, cc. 543, 846; 1977, c. 871, ss. 1, 6; 1979, c. 760, s. 5; 1979, 2nd Sess., c. 1316, ss. 12, 47; 1981, c. 63, s. 1, c. 179, s. 14; 1993, c. 539, s. 1173; 1994, Ex. Sess., c. 24, s. 14(c).)

§ 14-87.1. Punishment for common-law robbery.

Robbery as defined at common law, other than robbery with a firearm or other dangerous weapon as defined by G.S. 14-87, shall be punishable as a Class G felony. (1979, c. 760, s. 5; 1993, c. 539, s. 1174; 1994, Ex. Sess., c. 24, s. 14(c).)

§ 14-88. Train robbery.

If any person shall enter upon any locomotive engine or car on any railroad in this State, and by threats, the exhibition of deadly weapons or the discharge of any pistol or gun, in or near any such engine or car, shall induce or compel any person on such engine or car to submit and deliver up, or allow to be taken therefrom, or from him, anything of value, he shall be guilty of train robbery, and on conviction thereof shall be punished as a Class D felon. (1895, c. 204, s. 2; Rev., s. 3765; C.S., s. 4266; 1979, c. 760, s. 5; 1979, 2nd Sess., c. 1316, s. 47; 1981, c. 63, s. 1, c. 179, s. 14; 1993, c. 539, s. 1175; 1994, Ex. Sess., c. 24, s. 14(c).)

§ 14-89: Repealed by Session Laws 1994, Ex. Sess., c. 14, s. 71(5).

§ 14-89.1. Safecracking.

(a)   A person is guilty of safecracking if he unlawfully opens, enters, or attempts to open or enter a safe or vault :

(1) By the use of explosives, drills, or tools; or

(2) Through the use of a stolen combination, key, electronic device, or other fraudulently acquired implement or means; or

(3) Through the use of a master key, duplicate key or device made or obtained in an unauthorized manner, stethoscope or other listening device, electronic device used for unauthorized entry in a safe or vault, or other surreptitious means; or

(4) By the use of any other safecracking implement or means.

(b) A person is also guilty of safecracking if he unlawfully removes from its premises a safe or vault for the purpose of stealing, tampering with, or ascertaining its contents.

(c) Safecracking shall be punishable as a Class I felony. (1961, c. 653; 1973, c. 235, s. 1; 1977, c. 1106; 1979, c. 760, s. 5; 1979, 2nd Sess., c. 1316, s. 47; 1981, c. 63, s. 1, c. 179, s. 14; 1993, c. 539, s. 1176; 1994, Ex. Sess., c. 24, s. 14(c).)

Article 18.

Embezzlement.

§ 14-90. Embezzlement of property received by virtue of office or employment.

(a) This section shall apply to any person:

(1) Exercising a public trust.

(2) Holding a public office.

(3) Who is a guardian, administrator, executor, trustee, or any receiver, or any other fiduciary, including, but not limited to, a settlement agent, as defined in G.S. 45A-3.

(4) Who is an officer or agent of a corporation, or any agent, consignee, clerk, bailee or servant, except persons under the age of 16 years, of any person.

(b) Any person who shall:

(1) Embezzle or fraudulently or knowingly and willfully misapply or convert to his own use, or

(2) Take, make away with or secrete, with intent to embezzle or fraudulently or knowingly and willfully misapply or convert to his own use,

any money, goods or other chattels, bank note, check or order for the payment of money issued by or drawn on any bank or other corporation, or any treasury warrant, treasury note, bond or obligation for the payment of money issued by the United States or by any state, or any other valuable security whatsoever that (i) belongs to any other person or corporation, unincorporated association or organization or (ii) are closing funds as defined in G.S. 45A-3, which shall have come into his possession or under his care, shall be guilty of a felony.

(c) If the value of the property described in subsection (b) of this section is one hundred thousand dollars ($100,000) or more, the person is guilty of a Class C felony. If the value of the property is less than one hundred thousand dollars ($100,000), the person is guilty of a Class H felony. (21 Hen. VII, c. 7; 1871-2, c. 145, s. 2; Code, s. 1014; 1889, c. 226; 1891, c. 188; 1897, c. 31; Rev., s. 3406; 1919, c. 97, s. 25; C.S., s. 4268; 1931, c. 158; 1939, c. 1; 1941, c. 31; 1967, c. 819; 1979, c. 760, s. 5; 1979, 2nd Sess., c. 1316, s. 47; 1981, c. 63, s. 1; c. 179, s. 14; 1997-443, s. 19.25(d); 2009-348, s. 1; 2009-570, s. 31.)

§ 14-91. Embezzlement of State property by public officers and employees.

If any officer, agent, or employee of the State, or other person having or holding in trust for the same any bonds issued by the State, or any security, or other property and effects of the same, shall embezzle or knowingly and willfully misapply or convert the same to his own use, or otherwise willfully or corruptly abuse such trust, such offender and all persons knowingly and willfully aiding and abetting or otherwise assisting therein shall be guilty of a felony. If the value of the property is one hundred thousand dollars ($100,000) or more, a violation of this section is a Class C felony. If the value of the property is less than one hundred thousand dollars ($100,000), a violation of this section is a Class F felony. (1874-5, c. 52; Code, s. 1015; Rev., s. 3407; C.S., s. 4269; 1979, c. 716; c. 760, s. 5; 1979, 2nd Sess., c. 1316, s. 47; 1981, c. 63, s. 1; c. 179, s. 14; 1997-443, s. 19.25(e).)

§ 14-92. Embezzlement of funds by public officers and trustees.

If an officer, agent, or employee of an entity listed below, or a person having or holding money or property in trust for one of the listed entities, shall embezzle or otherwise willfully and corruptly use or misapply the same for any purpose other than that for which such moneys or property is held, such person shall be guilty of a felony. If the value of the money or property is one hundred thousand dollars ($100,000) or more, the person is guilty of a Class C felony. If the value of the money or property is less than one hundred thousand dollars ($100,000), the person is guilty of a Class F felony. If any clerk of the superior court or any sheriff, treasurer, register of deeds or other public officer of any county, unit or agency of local government, or local board of education shall embezzle or wrongfully convert to his own use, or corruptly use, or shall misapply for any purpose other than that for which the same are held, or shall fail to pay over and deliver to the proper persons entitled to receive the same when lawfully required so to do, any moneys, funds, securities or other property which such officer shall have received by virtue or color of his office in trust for any person or corporation, such officer shall be guilty of a felony. If the value of the money, funds, securities, or other property is one hundred thousand dollars ($100,000) or more, the person is guilty of a Class C felony. If the value of the money, funds, securities, or other property is less than one hundred thousand dollars ($100,000), the person is guilty of a Class F felony. The provisions of this section shall apply to all persons who shall go out of office and fail or neglect to account to or deliver over to their successors in office or other persons lawfully entitled to receive the same all such moneys, funds and securities or property aforesaid. The following entities are protected by this section: a county, a city or other unit or agency of local government, a local board of education, and a penal, charitable, religious, or educational institution. (1876-7, c. 47; Code, s. 1016; 1891, c. 241; Rev., s. 3408; C.S., s. 4270; 1979, c. 760, s. 5; 1979, 2nd Sess., c. 1316, s. 47; 1981, c. 63, s. 1; c. 179, s. 14; 1985, c. 509, s. 3; 1993, c. 539, s. 1177; 1994, Ex. Sess., c. 24, s. 14(c); 1997-443, s. 19.25(f).)

§ 14-93. Embezzlement by treasurers of charitable and religious organizations.

If any treasurer or other financial officer of any benevolent or religious institution, society or congregation shall lend any of the moneys coming into his hands to any other person or association without the consent of the institution, association or congregation to whom such moneys belong; or, if he shall fail to account for such moneys when called on, he shall be guilty of a felony. If the violation of this section involves money with a value of one hundred thousand dollars ($100,000) or more, the person is guilty of a Class C felony. If the violation of this section involves money with a value of less than one hundred thousand dollars ($100,000) or less, a violation of this section is a Class H felony. (1879, c. 105; Code, s. 1017; Rev., s. 3409; C.S., s. 4271; 1993, c. 539, s. 1178; 1994, Ex. Sess., c. 24, s. 14(c); 1997-443, s. 19.25(g).)

§ 14-94. Embezzlement by officers of railroad companies.

If any president, secretary, treasurer, director, engineer, agent or other officer of any railroad company shall embezzle any moneys, bonds or other valuable funds or securities, with which such president, secretary, treasurer, director, engineer, agent or other officer shall be charged by virtue of his office or agency, or shall in any way, directly or indirectly, apply or appropriate the same for the use or benefit of himself or any other person, state or corporation, other than the company of which he is president, secretary, treasurer, director, engineer, agent or other officer, for every such offense the person so offending shall be guilty of a felony, and on conviction in the superior or criminal court of any county through which the railroad of such company shall pass, shall be punished as a felon. If the value of the money, bonds, or other valuable funds or securities is one hundred thousand dollars ($100,000) or more, a violation of this section is a Class C felony. If the value of the money, bonds, or other valuable funds or securities is less than one hundred thousand dollars ($100,000), a violation of this section is a Class H felony. (1870-1, c. 103, s. 1; Code, s. 1018; Rev., s. 3403; C.S., s. 4272; 1979, c. 760, s. 5; 1979, 2nd Sess., c. 1316, s. 47; 1981, c. 63, s. 1; c. 179, s. 14; 1997-443, s. 19.25(h).)

§ 14-95: Repealed by Session Laws 1994, Ex. Sess., c. 14, s. 71(6).

§§ 14-96 through 14-96.1: Repealed by Session Laws 1989 (Reg. Sess., 1990), c. 1054, s. 6.

§ 14-97. Appropriation of partnership funds by partner to personal use.

Any person engaged in a partnership business in the State of North Carolina who shall, without the knowledge and consent of his copartner or copartners, take funds belonging to the partnership business and appropriate the same to his own personal use with the fraudulent intent of depriving his copartners of the use thereof, shall be guilty of a felony. Appropriation of partnership funds with a value of one hundred thousand dollars ($100,000) or more by a partner is a Class C felony. Appropriation of partnership funds with the value of less than one hundred thousand dollars ($100,000) by a partner is a Class H felony. (1921, c. 127; C.S., s. 4274(a); 1993, c. 539, s. 1179; 1994, Ex. Sess., c. 24, s. 14(c); 1997-443, s. 19.25(i).)

§ 14-98. Embezzlement by surviving partner.

If any surviving partner shall willfully and intentionally convert any of the property, money or effects belonging to the partnership to his own use, and refuse to account for the same on settlement, he shall be guilty of a felony. If the property, money, or effects has a value of one hundred thousand dollars ($100,000) or more, a violation of this section is a Class C felony. If the property, money, or effects has a value of less than one hundred thousand dollars ($100,000), a violation of this section is a Class H felony. (1901, c. 640, s. 9; Rev., s. 3405; C.S., s. 4275; 1979, c. 760, s. 5; 1979, 2nd Sess., c. 1316, s. 47; 1981, c. 63, s. 1; c. 179, s. 14; 1997-443, s. 19.25(j).)

§ 14-99. Embezzlement of taxes by officers.

If any officer appropriates to his own use the State, county, school, city or town taxes, he shall be guilty of embezzlement, and shall be punished as a felon. If the value of the taxes is one hundred thousand dollars ($100,000) or more, a violation of this section is a Class C felony. If the value of the taxes is less than one hundred thousand dollars ($100,000), a violation of this section is a Class F felony. (1883, c. 136, s. 49; Code, s. 3705; Rev., s. 3410; C.S., s. 4276; 1979, c.

760, s. 5; 1979, 2nd Sess., c. 1316, s. 47; 1981, c. 63, s. 1; c. 179, s. 14; 1993, c. 539, s. 1180; 1994, Ex. Sess., c. 24, s. 14(c); 1997-443, s. 19.25(k).)

Article 19.

False Pretenses and Cheats.

§ 14-100. Obtaining property by false pretenses.

(a)   If any person shall knowingly and designedly by means of any kind of false pretense whatsoever, whether the false pretense is of a past or subsisting fact or of a future fulfillment or event, obtain or attempt to obtain from any person within this State any money, goods, property, services, chose in action, or other thing of value with intent to cheat or defraud any person of such money, goods, property, services, chose in action or other thing of value, such person shall be guilty of a felony: Provided, that if, on the trial of anyone indicted for such crime, it shall be proved that he obtained the property in such manner as to amount to larceny or embezzlement, the jury shall have submitted to them such other felony proved; and no person tried for such felony shall be liable to be afterwards prosecuted for larceny or embezzlement upon the same facts: Provided, further, that it shall be sufficient in any indictment for obtaining or attempting to obtain any such money, goods, property, services, chose in action, or other thing of value by false pretenses to allege that the party accused did the act with intent to defraud, without alleging an intent to defraud any particular person, and without alleging any ownership of the money, goods, property, services, chose in action or other thing of value; and upon the trial of any such indictment, it shall not be necessary to prove either an intent to defraud any particular person or that the person to whom the false pretense was made was the person defrauded, but it shall be sufficient to allege and prove that the party accused made the false pretense charged with an intent to defraud. If the value of the money, goods, property, services, chose in action, or other thing of value is one hundred thousand dollars ($100,000) or more, a violation of this section is a Class C felony. If the value of the money, goods, property, services, chose in action, or other thing of value is less than one hundred thousand dollars ($100,000), a violation of this section is a Class H felony.

(b)   Evidence of nonfulfillment of a contract obligation standing alone shall not establish the essential element of intent to defraud.

(c) For purposes of this section, "person" means person, association, consortium, corporation, body politic, partnership, or other group, entity, or organization. (33 Hen. VIII, c. 1, ss. 1, 2; 30 Geo. II, c. 24, s. 1; 1811, c. 814, s. 2, P.R.; R.C., c. 34, s. 67; Code, s. 1025; Rev., s. 3432; C.S., s. 4277; 1975, c. 783; 1979, c. 760, s. 5; 1979, 2nd Sess., c. 1316, s. 47; 1981, c. 63, s. 1; c. 179, s. 14; 1997-443, s. 19.25(l).)

§ 14-100.1. Possession or manufacture of certain fraudulent forms of identification.

(a) Except as otherwise made unlawful by G.S. 20-30, it shall be unlawful for any person to knowingly possess or manufacture a false or fraudulent form of identification as defined in this section for the purpose of deception, fraud, or other criminal conduct.

(b) Except as otherwise made unlawful by G.S. 20-30, it shall be unlawful for any person to knowingly obtain a form of identification by the use of false, fictitious, or fraudulent information.

(c) Possession of a form of identification obtained in violation of subsection (b) of this section shall constitute a violation of subsection (a) of this section.

(d) For purposes of this section, a "form of identification" means any of the following or any replica thereof:

(1) An identification card containing a picture, issued by any department, agency, or subdivision of the State of North Carolina, the federal government, or any other state.

(2) A military identification card containing a picture.

(3) A passport.

(4) An alien registration card containing a picture.

(e) A violation of this section shall be punished as a Class 1 misdemeanor. (2001-461, s. 1; 2001-487, s. 42(a).)

§ 14-101. Obtaining signatures by false pretenses.

If any person, with intent to defraud or cheat another, shall designedly, by color of any false token or writing, or by any other false pretense, obtain the signature of any person to any written instrument, the false making of which would be punishable as forgery, he shall be punished as a Class H felon. (1871-2, c. 92; Code, s. 1026; Rev., s. 3433; C.S., s. 4278; 1945, c. 635; 1979, c. 760, s. 5; 1979 2nd Sess., c. 1316, s. 47; 1981, c. 63, s. 1, c. 179, s. 14; 1993, c. 539, s. 1181; 1994, Ex. Sess., c. 24, s. 14(c).)

§ 14-102. Obtaining property by false representation of pedigree of animals.

If any person shall, with intent to defraud or cheat, knowingly represent any animal for breeding purposes as being of greater degree of any particular strain of blood than such animal actually possesses, and by such representation obtain from any other person money or other thing of value, he shall be guilty of a Class 2 misdemeanor. (1891, c. 94, s. 2; Rev., s. 3307; C.S., s. 4279; 1993, c. 539, s. 40; 1994, Ex. Sess., c. 24, s. 14(c).)

§ 14-103. Obtaining certificate of registration of animals by false representation.

If any person shall, by any false representation or pretense, with intent to defraud or cheat, obtain from any club, association, society or company for the improvement of the breed of cattle, horses, sheep, swine, fowls or other domestic animals or birds, a certificate of registration of any animal in the herd register of any such association, society or company, or a transfer of any such registration, upon conviction thereof, the person is guilty of a Class 3 misdemeanor. (1891, c. 94, s. 1; Rev. s. 3308; C.S., s. 4280; 1993, c. 539, s. 41; 1994, Ex. Sess., c. 24, s. 14(c).)

§ 14-104. Obtaining advances under promise to work and pay for same.

If any person, with intent to cheat or defraud another, shall obtain any advances in money, provisions, goods, wares or merchandise of any description from any other person or corporation upon and by color of any promise or agreement that the person making the same will begin any work or labor of any description for such person or corporation from whom the advances are obtained, and the person making the promise or agreement shall willfully fail, without a lawful excuse, to commence or complete such work according to contract, he shall be guilty of a Class 2 misdemeanor. (1889, c. 444; 1891, c. 106; 1905, c. 411; Rev., s. 3431; C.S., s. 4281; 1993, c. 539, s. 42; 1994, Ex. Sess., c. 24, s. 14(c).)

§ 14-105. Obtaining advances under written promise to pay therefor out of designated property.

If any person shall obtain any advances in money, provisions, goods, wares or merchandise of any description from any other person or corporation, upon any written representation that the person making the same is the owner of any article of produce, or of any other specific chattel or personal property, which property, or the proceeds of which the owner in such representation thereby agrees to apply to the discharge of the debt so created, and the owner shall fail to apply such produce or other property, or the proceeds thereof, in accordance with such agreement, or shall dispose of the same in any other manner than is so agreed upon by the parties to the transaction, the person so offending shall be guilty of a misdemeanor, whether he shall or shall not have been the owner of any such property at the time such representation was made. Any person violating any provision of this section shall be guilty of a Class 2 misdemeanor. (1879, cc. 185, 186; Code, s. 1027; 1905, c. 104; Rev., s. 3434; C.S., s. 4282; 1969, c. 1224, s. 9; 1993, c. 539, s. 43; 1994, Ex. Sess., c. 24, s. 14(c).)

§ 14-106. Obtaining property in return for worthless check, draft or order.

Every person who, with intent to cheat and defraud another, shall obtain money, credit, goods, wares or any other thing of value by means of a check, draft or order of any kind upon any bank, person, firm or corporation, not indebted to the drawer, or where he has not provided for the payment or acceptance of the same, and the same be not paid upon presentation, shall be guilty of a Class 3 misdemeanor. The giving of the aforesaid worthless check, draft, or order shall be prima facie evidence of an intent to cheat and defraud. (1907, c. 975; 1909, c. 647; C.S., s. 4283; 1993, c. 539, s. 44; 1994, Ex. Sess., c. 24, s. 14(c); 2013-360, s. 18B.14(a).)

§ 14-107. Worthless checks; multiple presentment of checks.

(a) It is unlawful for any person, firm or corporation, to draw, make, utter or issue and deliver to another, any check or draft on any bank or depository, for the payment of money or its equivalent, knowing at the time of the making, drawing, uttering, issuing and delivering the check or draft, that the maker or drawer of it:

(1) Has not sufficient funds on deposit in or credit with the bank or depository with which to pay the check or draft upon presentation, or

(2) Has previously presented the check or draft for the payment of money or its equivalent.

(b) It is unlawful for any person, firm or corporation to solicit or to aid and abet any other person, firm or corporation to draw, make, utter or issue and deliver to any person, firm or corporation, any check or draft on any bank or depository for the payment of money or its equivalent, being informed, knowing or having reasonable grounds for believing at the time of the soliciting or the aiding and abetting that the maker or the drawer of the check or draft:

(1) Has not sufficient funds on deposit in, or credit with, the bank or depository with which to pay the check or draft upon presentation, or

(2) Has previously presented the check or draft for the payment of money or its equivalent.

(c) The word "credit" as used in this section means an arrangement or understanding with the bank or depository for the payment of a check or draft.

(d) A violation of this section is a Class I felony if the amount of the check or draft is more than two thousand dollars ($2,000). If the amount of the check or draft is two thousand dollars ($2,000) or less, a violation of this section is a misdemeanor punishable as follows:

(1) Except as provided in subdivision (3) or (4) of this subsection, the person is guilty of a Class 3 misdemeanor. Provided, however, if the person has been convicted three times of violating this section, the person shall on the fourth and all subsequent convictions (i) be punished as for a Class 1 misdemeanor and (ii) be ordered, as a condition of probation, to refrain from maintaining a checking account or making or uttering a check for three years.

(2) Repealed by Session Laws 1999-408, s. 1, effective December 1, 1999.

(3) If the check or draft is drawn upon a nonexistent account, the person is guilty of a Class 1 misdemeanor.

(4) If the check or draft is drawn upon an account that has been closed by the drawer, or that the drawer knows to have been closed by the bank or depository, prior to time the check is drawn, the person is guilty of a Class 1 misdemeanor.

(e) In deciding to impose any sentence other than an active prison sentence, the sentencing judge shall consider and may require, in accordance with the provisions of G.S. 15A-1343, restitution to the victim for (i) the amount of the check or draft, (ii) any service charges imposed on the payee by a bank or depository for processing the dishonored check, and (iii) any processing fees imposed by the payee pursuant to G.S. 25-3-506, and each prosecuting witness (whether or not under subpoena) shall be entitled to a witness fee as provided by G.S. 7A-314 which shall be taxed as part of the cost and assessed to the defendant. (1925, c. 14; 1927, c. 62; 1929, c. 273, ss. 1, 2; 1931, cc. 63, 138; 1933, cc. 43, 64, 93, 170, 265, 362, 458; 1939, c. 346; 1949, cc. 183, 332; 1951, c. 356; 1961, c. 89; 1963, cc. 73, 547, 870; 1967, c. 49, s. 1; c. 661, s. 1; 1969, c. 157; c. 876, s. 1; cc. 909, 1014; c. 1224, s. 10; 1971, c. 243, s. 1; 1977, c. 885; 1979, c. 837; 1983, c. 741; 1991, c. 523, s. 1; 1993, c. 374, s. 2; c. 539, ss. 45, 1182; 1994, Ex. Sess., c. 24, s. 14(c); 1995 (Reg. Sess., 1996), c. 742, s. 11; 1999-408, s. 1; 2013-244, s. 4; 2013-360, s. 18B.14(b).)

§ 14-107.1. Prima facie evidence in worthless check cases.

(a) Unless the context otherwise requires, the following definitions apply in this section:

(1) Check Passer. - A natural person who draws, makes, utters, or issues and delivers, or causes to be delivered to another any check or draft on any bank or depository for the payment of money or its equivalent.

(2) Acceptor. - A person, firm, corporation or any authorized employee thereof accepting a check or draft from a check passer.

(3) Check Taker. - A natural person who is an acceptor, or an employee or agent of an acceptor, of a check or draft in a face-to-face transaction.

(b) In prosecutions under G.S. 14-107 the prima facie evidence provisions of subsections (d) and (e) apply if all the conditions of subdivisions (1) through (7) below are met. The prima facie evidence provisions of subsection (e) apply if only conditions (5) through (7) are met. The conditions are:

(1) The check or draft is delivered to a check taker.

(2) The name and mailing address of the check passer are written or printed on the check or draft, and the check taker or acceptor shall not be required to write or print the race or gender of the check passer on the check or draft.

(3) The check taker identifies the check passer at the time of accepting the check by means of a North Carolina driver's license, a special identification card issued pursuant to G.S. 20-37.7, or other reliable serially numbered identification card containing a photograph and mailing address of the person in question.

(4) The license or identification card number of the check passer appears on the check or draft.

(5) After dishonor of the check or draft by the bank or depository, the acceptor sends the check passer a letter by certified mail, to the address recorded on the check, identifying the check or draft, setting forth the circumstances of dishonor, and requesting rectification of any bank error or other error in connection with the transaction within 10 days.

An acceptor may advise the check passer in a letter that legal action may be taken against him if payment is not made within the prescribed time period. Such letter, however, shall be in a form which does not violate applicable provisions of Article 2 of Chapter 75.

(6) The acceptor files the affidavit described in subdivision (7) with a judicial official, as defined in G.S. 15A-101(5), before issuance of the first process or pleading in the prosecution under G.S. 14-107. The affidavit must be kept in the case file (attached to the criminal pleading in the case).

(7) The affidavit of the acceptor, sworn to before a person authorized to administer oaths, must:

a. State the facts surrounding acceptance of the check or draft. If the conditions set forth in subdivisions (1) through (5) have been met, the specific facts demonstrating observance of those conditions must be stated.

b. Indicate that at least 15 days have elapsed since the mailing of the letter required under subdivision (5) and that the check passer has failed to rectify any error that may have occurred with respect to the dishonored check or draft.

c. Have attached a copy of the letter sent to the check passer pursuant to subdivision (5).

d. Have attached the receipt, or a copy of it, from the United States Postal Service certifying the mailing of the letter described in subdivision (5).

e. Have attached the check or draft or a copy thereof, including any stamp, marking or attachment indicating the reason for dishonor.

(c) In prosecutions under G.S. 14-107, where the check or draft is delivered to the acceptor by mail, or delivered other than in person, the prima facie evidence rule in subsections (d) and (e) shall apply if all the conditions below are met. The prima facie evidence rule in subsection (e) shall apply if conditions (5) through (7) below are met. The conditions are:

(1) The check or draft is delivered to the acceptor by United States mail, or by some person or instrumentality other than a check passer.

(2) The name and mailing address of the check passer are recorded on the check or draft.

(3) The acceptor has previously identified the check passer, at the time of opening the account, establishing the course of dealing, or initiating the lease or contract, by means of a North Carolina driver's license, a special identification card issued pursuant to G.S. 20-37.7, or other reliable serially numbered identification card containing a photograph and mailing address of the person in question, and obtained the signature of the person or persons who will be making payments on the account, course of dealing, lease or contract, and such signature is retained in the account file.

(4) The acceptor compares the name, address, and signature on the check with the name, address, and signature on file in the account, course of dealing, lease, or contract, and notes that the information contained on the check corresponds with the information contained in the file, and the signature on the check appears genuine when compared to the signature in the file.

(5) After dishonor of the check or draft by the bank or depository, the acceptor sends the check passer a letter by certified mail to the address recorded on the check or draft identifying the check or draft, setting forth the circumstances of dishonor and requesting rectification of any bank error or other error in connection with the transaction within 10 days.

An acceptor may advise the check passer in a letter that legal action may be taken against him if payment is not made within the prescribed time period. Such letter, however, shall be in a form which does not violate applicable provisions of Article 2 of Chapter 75.

(6) The acceptor files the affidavits described in subdivision (7) of this subsection with a judicial official, as defined in G.S. 15A-101(5), before issuance of the first process or pleading in the prosecution under G.S. 14-107. The affidavit must be kept in the case file (attached to the criminal pleading in the case).

(7) The affidavit of the acceptor, sworn to before a person authorized to administer oaths, must:

a. State the facts surrounding acceptance of the check or draft. If the conditions set forth in subdivisions (1) through (5) have been met, the specific facts demonstrating observance of those conditions must be stated.

b. Indicate that at least 15 days have elapsed since the mailing of the letter required under subdivision (5) and that the check passer has failed to rectify any error that may have occurred with respect to the dishonored check or draft.

c. Have attached a copy of the letter sent to the check passer pursuant to subdivision (5).

d. Have attached the receipt, or a copy of it, from the United States Postal Service certifying the mailing of the letter described in subdivision (5).

e. Have attached the check or draft or a copy thereof, including any stamp, marking or attachment indicating the reason for dishonor.

(d) If the conditions of subsection (b) or (c) have been met, proof of meeting them is prima facie evidence that the person charged was in fact the identified check passer.

(e) If the bank or depository dishonoring a check or draft has returned it in the regular course of business stamped or marked or with an attachment indicating the reason for dishonor, the check or draft and any attachment may be introduced in evidence and constitute prima facie evidence of the facts of dishonor if the conditions of subdivisions (5) through (7) of subsection (b) or subdivisions (5) through (7) of subsection (c) have been met. The reason for dishonor may be indicated with terms that include, but are not limited to, the following: "insufficient funds," "no account," "account closed," "NSF," "uncollected," "unable to locate," "stale dated," "postdated," "endorsement irregular," "signature irregular," "nonnegotiable," "altered," "unable to process," "refer to maker," "duplicate presentment," "forgery," "noncompliant," or "UCD noncompliant." The fact that the check or draft was returned dishonored may be received as evidence that the check passer had no credit with the bank or depository for payment of the check or draft.

(f) An affidavit by an employee of a bank or depository who has personal knowledge of the facts stated in the affidavit sworn to and properly executed before an official authorized to administer oaths is admissible in evidence without further authentication in a hearing or trial pursuant to a prosecution under G.S. 14-107 in the District Court Division of the General Court of Justice with respect to the facts of dishonor of the check or draft, including the existence of an account, the date the check or draft was processed, whether there were sufficient funds in an account to pay the check or draft, and other related matters. If the defendant requests that the bank or depository employee personally testify in the hearing or trial, the defendant may subpoena the employee. The defendant shall be provided a copy of the affidavit prior to trial and shall have the opportunity to subpoena the affiant for trial. (1979, c. 615, s. 1; 1985, c. 650, s. 1; 1989, c. 421; 1997-149, s. 1; 2013-244, s. 5.)

§ 14-107.2. Program for collection in worthless check cases.

(a) As used in this section, the terms "check passer" and "check taker" have the same meaning as defined in G.S. 14-107.1.

(a1) The Administrative Office of the Courts may authorize the establishment of a program for the collection of worthless checks in any prosecutorial district where economically feasible. The Administrative Office of the Courts may consider the following factors when making a feasibility determination:

(1) The population of the district.

(2) The number of worthless check prosecutions in the district.

(3) The availability of personnel and equipment in the district.

(b) Upon authorization by the Administrative Office of the Courts, a district attorney may establish a program for the collection of worthless checks in cases that may be prosecuted under G.S. 14-107. The district attorney may establish a program for the collection of worthless checks in cases that would be punishable as misdemeanors, in cases that would be punishable as felonies, or both. The district attorney shall establish criteria for the types of worthless check cases that will be eligible under the program.

(b1) A community mediation center may establish and charge fees for its services in the collection of worthless checks as part of a program established under this section and may assist the Administrative Office of the Courts and district attorneys in the establishment of worthless check programs in any districts in which worthless check programs have not been established.

(c) If a check passer participates in the program by paying the fee under G.S. 7A-308(c) and providing restitution to the check taker for (i) the amount of the check or draft, (ii) any service charges imposed on the check taker by a bank or depository for processing the dishonored check, and (iii) any processing fees imposed by the check taker pursuant to G.S. 25-3-506, then the district attorney shall not prosecute the worthless check case under G.S. 14-107.

(d) The Administrative Office of the Courts shall establish procedures for remitting the fee and providing restitution to the check taker.

(e) Repealed by Session Laws 2003-377, s. 3, effective August 1, 2003. (1997-443, s. 18.22(b); 1998-23, s. 11(a); 1998-212, s. 16.3(a); 1999-237, s.

17.7; 2000-67, s. 15.3A(a); 2001-61, s. 1; 2003-377, ss. 1, 2, 3; 2011-145, s. 31.24(a).)

§ 14-108. Obtaining property or services from slot machines, etc., by false coins or tokens.

Any person who shall operate, or cause to be operated, or who shall attempt to operate, or attempt to cause to be operated any automatic vending machine, slot machine, coin-box telephone or other receptacle designed to receive lawful coin of the United States of America in connection with the sale, use or enjoyment of property or service, by means of a slug or any false, counterfeited, mutilated, sweated or foreign coin, or by any means, method, trick or device whatsoever not lawfully authorized by the owner, lessee or licensee, of such machine, coin-box telephone or receptacle, or who shall take, obtain or receive from or in connection with any automatic vending machine, slot machine, coin-box telephone or other receptacle designed to receive lawful coin of the United States of America in connection with the sale, use or enjoyment of property or service, any goods, wares, merchandise, gas, electric current, article of value, or the use or enjoyment of any telephone or telegraph facilities or service, or of any musical instrument, phonograph or other property, without depositing in and surrendering to such machine, coin-box telephone or receptacle lawful coin of the United States of America to the amount required therefor by the owner, lessee or licensee of such machine, coin-box telephone or receptacle, shall be guilty of a Class 2 misdemeanor. (1927, c. 68, s. 1; 1969, c. 1224, s. 3; 1993, c. 539, s. 46, c. 553, s. 8; 1994, Ex. Sess., c. 24, s. 14(c).)

§ 14-109. Manufacture, sale, or gift of devices for cheating slot machines, etc.

Any person who, with intent to cheat or defraud the owner, lessee, licensee or other person entitled to the contents of any automatic vending machine, slot machine, coin-box telephone or other receptacle, depository or contrivance designed to receive lawful coin of the United States of America in connection with the sale, use or enjoyment of property or service, or who, knowing that the same is intended for unlawful use, shall manufacture for sale, or sell or give away any slug, device or substance whatsoever intended or calculated to be placed or deposited in any such automatic vending machine, slot machine, coin-box telephone or other such receptacle, depository or contrivance, shall be guilty of a Class 2 misdemeanor. (1927, c. 68, s. 2; 1969, c. 1224, s. 3; 1993, c. 539, s. 47; 1994, Ex. Sess., c. 24, s. 14(c).)

§ 14-110. Defrauding innkeeper or campground owner.

No person shall, with intent to defraud, obtain food, lodging, or other accommodations at a hotel, inn, boardinghouse, eating house, or campground. Whoever violates this section shall be guilty of a Class 2 misdemeanor. Obtaining such lodging, food, or other accommodation by false pretense, or by false or fictitious show of pretense of baggage or other property, or absconding without paying or offering to pay therefor, or surreptitiously removing or attempting to remove such baggage, shall be prima facie evidence of such fraudulent intent, but this section shall not apply where there has been an agreement in writing for delay in such payment. (1907, c. 816; C.S., s. 4284; 1969, c. 947; c. 1224, s. 3; 1985, c. 391; 1993, c. 539, s. 48; 1994, Ex. Sess., c. 24, s. 14(c).)

§ 14-111: Repealed by Session Laws 1994, Ex. Sess., c. 14, s. 72(4).

§ 14-111.1. Obtaining ambulance services without intending to pay therefor - Buncombe, Haywood and Madison Counties.

Any person who with the intent to defraud shall obtain ambulance services for himself or other persons without intending at the time of obtaining such services to pay a reasonable charge therefor, shall be guilty of a Class 2 misdemeanor. If a person or persons obtaining such services willfully fails to pay for the services within a period of 90 days after request for payment, such failure shall raise a presumption that the services were obtained with the intention to defraud, and with the intention not to pay therefor.

This section shall apply only to the Counties of Buncombe, Haywood and Madison. (1965, c. 976, s. 1; 1969, c. 1224, s. 4; 1993, c. 539, s. 49; 1994, Ex. Sess., c. 24, s. 14(c).)

§ 14-111.2. Obtaining ambulance services without intending to pay therefor - certain named counties.

Any person who with intent to defraud shall obtain ambulance services without intending at the time of obtaining such services to pay, if financially able, any reasonable charges therefor shall be guilty of a Class 2 misdemeanor. A determination by the court that the recipient of such services has willfully failed to pay for the services rendered for a period of 90 days after request for payment, and that the recipient is financially able to do so, shall raise a presumption that the recipient at the time of obtaining the services intended to defraud the provider of the services and did not intend to pay for the services.

The section shall apply to Alamance, Anson, Ashe, Beaufort, Cabarrus, Caldwell, Camden, Carteret, Caswell, Catawba, Chatham, Cherokee, Clay, Cleveland, Cumberland, Davie, Duplin, Durham, Forsyth, Gaston, Graham, Guilford, Halifax, Haywood, Henderson, Hoke, Hyde, Iredell, Macon, Mecklenburg, Montgomery, New Hanover, Onslow, Orange, Pasquotank, Pender, Person, Polk, Randolph, Robeson, Rockingham, Scotland, Stanly, Surry, Transylvania, Union, Vance, Washington, Wilkes and Yadkin Counties only. (1967, c. 964; 1969, cc. 292, 753; c. 1224, s. 4; 1971, cc. 125, 203, 300, 496; 1973, c. 880, s. 2; 1977, cc. 63, 144; 1983, c. 42, s. 1; 1985, c. 335, s. 1; 1987 (Reg. Sess., 1988), c. 910, s. 1; 1993, c. 539, s. 50; 1994, Ex. Sess., c. 24, s. 14(c); 1995, c. 9, s. 2; 1999-64, s. 1; 2000-15, s. 1; 2001-106, s. 1.)

§ 14-111.3. Making unneeded ambulance request in certain counties.

It shall be unlawful for any person or persons to willfully obtain or attempt to obtain ambulance service that is not needed, or to make a false request or report that an ambulance is needed. Every person convicted of violating this section shall be guilty of a Class 3 misdemeanor.

This section shall apply only to the Counties of Alamance, Ashe, Buncombe, Cabarrus, Camden, Carteret, Cherokee, Clay, Cleveland, Davie, Duplin, Durham, Graham, Greene, Halifax, Haywood, Hoke, Macon, Madison, New Hanover, Onslow, Pender, Polk, Robeson, Rockingham, Washington, Wilkes and Yadkin. (1965, c. 976, s. 2; 1971, c. 496; 1977, c. 96; 1983, c. 42, s. 2; 1985, c. 335, s. 2; 1987 (Reg. Sess., 1988), c. 910, s. 2; 1989, c. 514; 1989 (Reg. Sess., 1990), c. 834; 1993, c. 539, s. 51; 1994, Ex. Sess., c. 24, s. 14(c); 1995, c. 9, s. 3; 1999-64, s. 2; 2000-15, s. 2; 2001-106, s. 2.)

§ 14-111.4. Misuse of 911 system.

It is unlawful for an individual who is not seeking public safety assistance, is not providing 911 service, or is not responding to a 911 call to access or attempt to access the 911 system for a purpose other than an emergency communication. A person who knowingly violates this section commits a Class 1 misdemeanor. (2007-383, s. 1(b); 2013-286, s. 1.)

§ 14-112. Obtaining merchandise on approval.

If any person, with intent to cheat and defraud, shall solicit and obtain from any merchant any article of merchandise on approval, and shall thereafter, upon demand, refuse or fail to return the same to such merchant in an unused and undamaged condition, or to pay for the same, such person so offending shall be guilty of a Class 2 misdemeanor. Evidence that a person has solicited a merchant to deliver to him any article of merchandise for examination or approval and has obtained the same upon such solicitation, and thereafter, upon demand, has refused or failed to return the same to such merchant in an unused and undamaged condition, or to pay for the same, shall constitute prima facie evidence of the intent of such person to cheat and defraud, within the meaning of this section: Provided, this section shall not apply to merchandise sold upon a written contract which is signed by the purchaser. (1911, c. 185; C.S., s. 4285; 1941, c. 242; 1969, c. 1224, s. 2; 1993, c. 539, s. 52; 1994, Ex. Sess., c. 24, s. 14(c).)

§ 14-112.1. Repealed by Session Laws 1967, c. 1088, s. 2.

§ 14-112.2. Exploitation of an older adult or disabled adult.

(a) The following definitions apply in this section:

(1) Disabled adult. - A person 18 years of age or older or a lawfully emancipated minor who is present in the State of North Carolina and who is physically or mentally incapacitated as defined in G.S. 108A-101(d).

(2) Older adult. - A person 65 years of age or older.

(b) It is unlawful for a person: (i) who stands in a position of trust and confidence with an older adult or disabled adult, or (ii) who has a business relationship with an older adult or disabled adult to knowingly, by deception or intimidation, obtain or use, or endeavor to obtain or use, an older adult's or disabled adult's funds, assets, or property with the intent to temporarily or permanently deprive the older adult or disabled adult of the use, benefit, or possession of the funds, assets, or property, or to benefit someone other than the older adult or disabled adult.

(c) It is unlawful for a person to knowingly, by deception or intimidation, obtain or use, endeavor to obtain or use, or conspire with another to obtain or use an older adult's or disabled adult's funds, assets, or property with the intent to temporarily or permanently deprive the older adult or disabled adult of the use, benefit, or possession of the funds, assets, or property, or benefit someone other than the older adult or disabled adult. This subsection shall not apply to a person acting within the scope of that person's lawful authority as the agent for the older adult or disabled adult.

(d) A violation of subsection (b) of this section is punishable as follows:

(1) If the funds, assets, or property involved in the exploitation of the older adult or disabled adult is valued at one hundred thousand dollars ($100,000) or more, then the offense is a Class F felony.

(2) If the funds, assets, or property involved in the exploitation of the older adult or disabled adult is valued at twenty thousand dollars ($20,000) or more but less than one hundred thousand dollars ($100,000), then the offense is a Class G felony.

(3) If the funds, assets, or property involved in the exploitation of the older adult or disabled adult is valued at less than twenty thousand dollars ($20,000), then the offense is a Class H felony.

(e) A violation of subsection (c) of this section is punishable as follows:

(1) If the funds, assets, or property involved in the exploitation of the older adult or disabled adult is valued at one hundred thousand dollars ($100,000) or more, then the offense is a Class G felony.

(2) If the funds, assets, or property involved in the exploitation of the older adult or disabled adult is valued at twenty thousand dollars ($20,000) or more but less than one hundred thousand dollars ($100,000), then the offense is a Class H felony.

(3) If the funds, assets, or property involved in the exploitation of the older adult or disabled adult is valued at less than twenty thousand dollars ($20,000), then the offense is a Class I felony.

(f) If a person is charged with a violation of this section that involves funds, assets, or property valued at more than five thousand dollars ($5,000), the district attorney may file a petition in the pending criminal proceeding before the court with jurisdiction over the pending charges to freeze the funds, assets, or property of the defendant in an amount up to one hundred fifty percent (150%) of the alleged value of funds, assets, or property in the defendant's pending criminal proceeding for purposes of restitution to the victim. The standard of proof required to freeze the defendant's funds, assets, or property shall be by clear and convincing evidence. The procedure for petitioning the court under this subsection shall be governed by G.S. 14-112.3. (2005-272, s. 2; 2006-264, s. 99; 2013-203, s. 1; 2013-337, s. 1.)

§ 14-112.3. Asset freeze or seizure; proceeding.

(a) For purposes of this section, the term "assets" includes funds and property as well as other assets that may be involved in a violation of G.S. 14-112.2.

(b) Whenever it appears by clear and convincing evidence that any defendant is about to or intends to divest himself or herself of assets in a manner that would render the defendant insolvent for purposes of restitution, the district attorney may make an application to the court with jurisdiction over the pending charges to freeze or seize the assets of the defendant. Upon a showing by clear and convincing evidence in the hearing, the court shall issue an order to freeze or seize the assets of the defendant in the amount calculated pursuant to G.S. 14-112.2(f). The procedure for petitioning the court under this section shall be governed by G.S. 1A-1, Rule 65, except as otherwise provided in this section.

(c) At any time after service of the order to freeze or seize assets, the defendant or any person claiming an interest in the assets may file a motion to release the assets.

(d) In any proceeding to release assets, the burden of proof shall be by clear and convincing evidence and shall be on the State to show that the defendant is about to, intends to, or did divest himself or herself of assets in a manner that would render the defendant insolvent for purposes of restitution. If the court finds that the defendant is about to, intends to, or did divest himself or herself of assets in a manner that would render the defendant insolvent for purposes of restitution, the court shall order the assets frozen or held until further order of the court. The rules of evidence that apply to this proceeding are the rules that would apply in a proceeding pursuant to G.S. 1A-1, Rule 65.

(e) If the prosecution of the charge under G.S. 14-112.2 is terminated by voluntary dismissal by the State or if a judgment of acquittal is entered, the court shall vacate the order to freeze or seize the assets.

(f) Any person holding any interest in the frozen or seized assets may commence a separate civil proceeding in the manner provided by law. (2013-203, s. 2.)

§ 14-113. Obtaining money by false representation of physical disability.

It shall be unlawful for any person to falsely represent himself or herself in any manner whatsoever as blind, deaf, unable to speak, or otherwise physically disabled for the purpose of obtaining money or other thing of value or of making sales of any character of personal property. Any person so falsely representing himself or herself and securing aid or assistance on account of such representation, shall be deemed guilty of a Class 2 misdemeanor. (1919, c. 104; C.S., s. 4286; 1969, c. 1224, s. 1; 1993, c. 539, s. 53; 1994, Ex. Sess., c. 24, s. 14(c); 2011-29, s. 3.)

Article 19A.

Obtaining Property or Services by False or Fraudulent Use of Credit Device or Other Means.

§ 14-113.1. Use of false or counterfeit credit device; unauthorized use of another's credit device; use after notice of revocation.

It shall be unlawful for any person knowingly to obtain or attempt to obtain credit, or to purchase or attempt to purchase any goods, property or service, by the use of any false, fictitious, or counterfeit telephone number, credit number or other credit device, or by the use of any telephone number, credit number or other credit device of another without the authority of the person to whom such number or device was issued, or by the use of any telephone number, credit number or other credit device in any case where such number or device has been revoked and notice of revocation has been given to the person to whom issued or he has knowledge or reason to believe that such revocation has occurred. (1961, c. 223, s. 1; 1965, c. 1147; 1967, c. 1244, s. 1; 1971, c. 1213, s. 1.)

§ 14-113.2. Notice defined; prima facie evidence of receipt of notice.

The word "notice" as used in G.S. 14-113.1 shall be construed to include either notice given in person or notice given in writing to the person to whom the number or device was issued. The sending of a notice in writing by registered or certified mail in the United States mail, duly stamped and addressed to such person at his last address known to the issuer, shall be prima facie evidence that such notice was duly received after five days from the date of the deposit in the mail. (1961, c. 223, s. 3; 1965, c. 1147; 1967, c. 1244, s. 1.)

§ 14-113.3. Use of credit device as prima facie evidence of knowledge.

The presentation or use of a revoked, false, fictitious or counterfeit telephone number, credit number, or other credit device for the purpose of obtaining credit or the privilege of making a deferred payment for the article or service purchased shall be prima facie evidence of knowledge that the said credit device is revoked, false, fictitious or counterfeit; and the unauthorized use of any telephone number, credit number or other credit device of another shall be prima facie evidence of knowledge that such use was without the authority of the person to whom such number or device was issued. (1961, c. 223, s. 4; 1965, c. 1147; 1967, c. 1244, s. 1.)

§ 14-113.4. Avoiding or attempting to avoid payment for telecommunication services.

It shall be unlawful for any person to avoid or attempt to avoid, or to cause another to avoid, the lawful charges, in whole or in part, for any telephone or telegraph service or for the transmission of a message, signal or other communication by telephone or telegraph, or over telephone or telegraph facilities by the use of any fraudulent scheme, device, means or method. (1961, c. 223, s. 2; 1965, c. 1147.)

§ 14-113.5. Making, distributing, possessing, transferring, or programming device for theft of telecommunication service; publication of information regarding schemes, devices, means, or methods for such theft; concealment of existence, origin or destination of any telecommunication.

(a) It shall be unlawful for any person knowingly to:

(1) Make, distribute, possess, use, or assemble an unlawful telecommunications device or modify, alter, program, or reprogram a telecommunication device designed, adapted, or which is used:

a. For commission of a theft of telecommunication service or to acquire or facilitate the acquisition of telecommunications service without the consent of the telecommunication service provider in violation of this Article, or

b. To conceal, or assist another to conceal, from any supplier of a telecommunication service provider or from any lawful authority the existence or place of origin or of destination of any telecommunication, or

(2) Sell, possess, distribute, give, transport, or otherwise transfer to another or offer or advertise for sale any:

a. Unlawful telecommunication device, or plans or instructions for making or assembling the same under circumstances evincing an intent to use or employ the unlawful telecommunication device, or to allow the same to be used or employed, for a purpose described in (1)a or (1)b above, or knowing or having reason to believe that the same is intended to be so used, or that the aforesaid plans or instructions are intended to be used for making or assembling the unlawful telecommunication device; or

b. Material, including hardware, cables, tools, data, computer software or other information or equipment, knowing that the purchaser or a third person intends to use the material in the manufacture of an unlawful telecommunication device; or

(3) Publish plans or instructions for making or assembling or using any unlawful telecommunication device, or

(4) Publish the number or code of an existing, cancelled, revoked or nonexistent telephone number, credit number or other credit device, or method of numbering or coding which is employed in the issuance of telephone numbers, credit numbers or other credit devices with knowledge or reason to believe that it may be used to avoid the payment of any lawful telephone or telegraph toll charge under circumstances evincing an intent to have the telephone number, credit number, credit device or method of numbering or coding so used.

(5) Repealed by Session Laws 1995, c. 425, s. 1.

(b) Any unlawful telecommunication device, plans, instructions, or publications described in this section may be seized under warrant or incident to a lawful arrest for a violation of this section. Upon the conviction of a person for a violation of this section, the court may order the sheriff of the county in which the person was convicted to destroy as contraband or to otherwise lawfully dispose of the unlawful telecommunication device, plans, instructions, or publication.

(c) The following definitions apply in this section and in G.S. 14-113.6:

(1) Manufacture of an unlawful telecommunication device. - The production or assembly of an unlawful telecommunication device or the modification, alteration, programming or reprogramming of a telecommunication device to be capable of acquiring or facilitating the acquisition of telecommunication service without the consent of the telecommunication service provider.

(2) Publish. - The communication or dissemination of information to any one or more persons, either orally, in person or by telephone, radio or television, or in a writing of any kind, including without limitation a letter or memorandum, circular or handbill, newspaper or magazine article, or book.

(3) Telecommunication device. - Any type of instrument, device, machine or equipment that is capable of transmitting or receiving telephonic, electronic or radio communications, or any part of such instrument, device, machine or equipment, or any computer circuit, computer chip, electronic mechanism or other component that is capable of facilitating the transmission or reception of telephonic, electronic or radio communications.

(4) Telecommunication service. - Any service provided for a charge or compensation to facilitate the origination, transmission, emission or reception of signs, signals, data, writings, images, sounds or intelligence of any nature of telephone, including cellular or other wireless telephones, wire, radio, electromagnetic, photoelectronic or photo-optical system.

(5) Telecommunication service provider. - A person or entity providing telecommunication service, including, a cellular, paging or other wireless communications company or other person or entity which, for a fee, supplies the facility, cell site, mobile telephone switching office or other equipment or telecommunication service.

(6) Unlawful telecommunication device. - Any telecommunication device that is capable, or has been altered, modified, programmed or reprogrammed alone or in conjunction with another access device or other equipment so as to be capable, of acquiring or facilitating the acquisition of any electronic serial number, mobile identification number, personal identification number or any telecommunication service without the consent of the telecommunication service provider. The term includes, telecommunications devices altered to obtain service without the consent of the telecommunication service provider, tumbler phones, counterfeit or clone microchips, scanning receivers of wireless telecommunication service of a telecommunication service provider and other instruments capable of disguising their identity or location or of gaining access to a communications system operated by a telecommunication service provider. This section shall not apply to any device operated by a law enforcement agency in the normal course of its activities. (1965, c. 1147; 1971, c. 1213, s. 2; 1995, c. 425, s. 1.)

§ 14-113.6. Penalties for violation; civil action.

(a) Any person violating any of the provisions of this Article shall be guilty of a Class 2 misdemeanor. However, if the offense is a violation of G.S. 14-113.5 and involves five or more unlawful telecommunication devices the person shall be guilty of a Class G felony.

(b) The court may, in addition to any other sentence authorized by law, order a person convicted of violating G.S. 14-113.5 to make restitution for the offense.

(c) Any person or entity aggrieved by a violation of G.S. 14-113.5 may, in a civil action in any court of competent jurisdiction, obtain appropriate relief, including preliminary and other equitable or declaratory relief, compensatory and punitive damages, reasonable investigation expenses, costs of suit and any attorney fees as may be provided by law. (1961, c. 223, s. 5; 1965, c. 1147; 1969, c. 1224, s. 6; 1993, c. 539, s. 54; 1994, Ex. Sess., c. 24, s. 14(c); 1995, c. 425, s. 2.)

§ 14-113.6A. Venue of offenses.

(a) Any of the offenses described in Article 19A which involve the placement of telephone calls may be deemed to have been committed at either the place at which the telephone call or calls were made or at the place where the telephone call or calls were received.

(b) An offense under former G.S. 14-113.5(3) or 14-113.5(4) (see now G.S. 14-113.5(a)(3) or 14-113.5(a)(4)) may be deemed to have been committed at either the place at which the publication was initiated or at which the publication was received or at which the information so published was utilized to avoid or attempt to avoid the payment of any lawful telephone or telegraph toll charge. (1971, c. 1213, s. 3.)

§ 14-113.7. Article not construed as repealing § 14-100.

This Article shall not be construed as repealing G.S. 14-100. (1961, c. 223, s. 6; 1065, c. 1147.)

§ 14-113.7A. Application of Article to credit cards.

This Article shall not be construed as being applicable to any credit card as the term is defined in G.S. 14-113.8. (1967, c. 1244, s. 1.)

Article 19B.

Financial Transaction Card Crime Act.

§ 14-113.8. Definitions.

The following words and phrases as used in this Chapter, unless a different meaning is plainly required by the context, shall have the following meanings:

(1)   Acquirer. - "Acquirer" means a business organization, financial institution, or an agent of a business organization or financial institution that authorizes a merchant to accept payment by financial transaction card for money, goods, services or anything else of value.

(1a)   Automated Banking Device. - "Automated banking device" means any machine which when properly activated by a financial transaction card and/or personal identification code may be used for any of the purposes for which a financial transaction card may be used.

(2)   Cardholder. - "Cardholder" means the person or organization named on the face of a financial transaction card to whom or for whose benefit the financial transaction card is issued by an issuer.

(3)   Expired Financial Transaction Card. - "Expired financial transaction card" means a financial transaction card which is no longer valid because the term shown on it has elapsed.

(4)   Financial Transaction Card. - "Financial transaction card" or "FTC" means any instrument or device whether known as a credit card, credit plate, bank services card, banking card, check guarantee card, debit card, or by any other name, issued with or without fee by an issuer for the use of the cardholder:

a.   In obtaining money, goods, services, or anything else of value on credit; or

b.   In certifying or guaranteeing to a person or business the availability to the cardholder of funds on deposit that are equal to or greater than the amount necessary to honor a draft or check payable to the order of such person or business; or

c.   In providing the cardholder access to a demand deposit account or time deposit account for the purpose of:

1. Making deposits of money or checks therein; or

2. Withdrawing funds in the form of money, money orders, or traveler's checks therefrom; or

3. Transferring funds from any demand deposit account or time deposit account to any other demand deposit account or time deposit account; or

4. Transferring funds from any demand deposit account or time deposit account to any credit card accounts, overdraft privilege accounts, loan accounts, or any other credit accounts in full or partial satisfaction of any outstanding balance owed existing therein; or

5. For the purchase of goods, services or anything else of value; or

6. Obtaining information pertaining to any demand deposit account or time deposit account;

d. But shall not include a telephone number, credit number, or other credit device which is covered by the provisions of Article 19A of this Chapter.

(5) Issuer. - "Issuer" means the business organization or financial institution or its duly authorized agent which issues a financial transaction card.

(6) Personal Identification Code. - "Personal identification code" means a numeric and/or alphabetical code assigned to the cardholder of a financial transaction card by the issuer to permit authorized electronic use of that FTC.

(7) Presenting. - "Presenting" means, as used herein, those actions taken by a cardholder or any person to introduce a financial transaction card into an automated banking device, including utilization of a personal identification code, or merely displaying or showing a financial transaction card to the issuer, or to any person or organization providing money, goods, services, or anything else of value, or any other entity with intent to defraud.

(8) Receives. - "Receives" or "receiving" means acquiring possession or control or accepting a financial transaction card as security for a loan.

(9) Revoked Financial Transaction Card. - "Revoked financial transaction card" means a financial transaction card which is no longer valid because permission to use it has been suspended or terminated by the issuer.

(10) Scanning Device. - "Scanning device" means a scanner, reader, or any other device that is used to access, read, scan, obtain, memorize, or store, temporarily or permanently, information encoded on a financial transaction card. (1967, c. 1244, s. 2; 1971, c. 1213, s. 4; 1979, c. 741, s. 1; 1989, c. 161, s. 1; 2002-175, s. 2.)

§ 14-113.9. Financial transaction card theft.

(a) A person is guilty of financial transaction card theft when the person does any of the following:

(1) Takes, obtains or withholds a financial transaction card from the person, possession, custody or control of another without the cardholder's consent and with the intent to use it; or who, with knowledge that it has been so taken, obtained or withheld, receives the financial transaction card with intent to use it or to sell it, or to transfer it to a person other than the issuer or the cardholder.

(2) Receives a financial transaction card that he knows to have been lost, mislaid, or delivered under a mistake as to the identity or address of the cardholder, and who retains possession with intent to use it or to sell it or to transfer it to a person other than the issuer or the cardholder.

(3) Not being the issuer, sells a financial transaction card or buys a financial transaction card from a person other than the issuer.

(4) Not being the issuer, during any 12-month period, receives financial transaction cards issued in the names of two or more persons which he has reason to know were taken or retained under circumstances which constitute a violation of G.S. 14-113.13(a)(3) and subdivision (3) of subsection (a) of this section.

(5) With the intent to defraud any person, either (i) uses a scanning device to access, read, obtain, memorize, or store, temporarily or permanently, information encoded on another person's financial transaction card, or (ii) receives the encoded information from another person's financial transaction card.

(b) Credit card theft is punishable as provided by G.S. 14-113.17(b). (1967, c. 1244, s. 2; 1979, c. 741, s. 1; c. 760, s. 5; 1979, 2nd Sess., c. 1316, s. 47; 1981, c. 63, s. 1; c. 179, s. 14; 2002-175, s. 3.)

§ 14-113.10. Prima facie evidence of theft.

When a person has in his possession or under his control financial transaction cards issued in the names of two or more other persons other than members of his immediate family, such possession shall be prima facie evidence that such financial transaction cards have been obtained in violation of G.S. 14-113.9(a). (1967, c. 1244, s. 2; 1979, c. 741, s. 1.)

§ 14-113.11. Forgery of financial transaction card.

(a) A person is guilty of financial transaction card forgery when:

(1) With intent to defraud a purported issuer, a person or organization providing money, goods, services or anything else of value, or any other person, he falsely makes or falsely embosses a purported financial transaction card or utters such a financial transaction card; or

(2) With intent to defraud a purported issuer, a person or organization providing money, goods, services or anything else of value, or any other person, he falsely encodes, duplicates or alters existing encoded information on a financial transaction card or utters such a financial transaction card; or

(3) He, not being the cardholder or a person authorized by him, with intent to defraud the issuer, or a person or organization providing money, goods, services or anything else of value, or any other person, signs a financial transaction card.

(b) A person falsely makes a financial transaction card when he makes or draws, in whole or in part, a device or instrument which purports to be the financial transaction card of a named issuer but which is not such a financial transaction card because the issuer did not authorize the making or drawing, or alters a financial transaction card which was validly issued.

(c) A person falsely embosses a financial transaction card when, without authorization of the named issuer, he completes a financial transaction card by adding any of the matter, other than the signature of the cardholder, which an issuer requires to appear on the financial transaction card before it can be used by a cardholder.

(d) A person falsely encodes a financial transaction card when, without authorization of the purported issuer, he records magnetically, electronically, electro-magnetically or by any other means whatsoever, information on a financial transaction card which will permit acceptance of that card by any automated banking device. Conviction of financial transaction card forgery shall be punishable as provided in G.S. 14-113.17(b). (1967, c. 1244, s. 2; 1979, c. 741, s. 1.)

§ 14-113.12. Prima facie evidence of forgery.

(a) When a person, other than the purported issuer, possesses two or more financial transaction cards which are falsely made or falsely embossed, such possession shall be prima facie evidence that said cards were obtained in violation of G.S. 14-113.11(a)(1) or 14-113.11(a)(2).

(b) When a person, other than the cardholder or a person authorized by him possesses two or more financial transaction cards which are signed, such possession shall be prima facie evidence that said cards were obtained in violation of G.S. 14-113.11(a)(3). (1967, c. 1244, s. 2; 1979, c. 741, s. 1.)

§ 14-113.13. Financial transaction card fraud.

(a) A person is guilty of financial transaction card fraud when, with intent to defraud the issuer, a person or organization providing money, goods, services or anything else of value, or any other person, he

(1) Uses for the purpose of obtaining money, goods, services or anything else of value a financial transaction card obtained or retained, or which was received with knowledge that it was obtained or retained, in violation of G.S. 14-113.9 or 14-113.11 or a financial transaction card which he knows is forged,

altered, expired, revoked or was obtained as a result of a fraudulent application in violation of G.S. 14-113.13(c); or

(2) Obtains money, goods, services, or anything else of value by:

a. Representing without the consent of the cardholder that he is the holder of a specified card; or

b. Presenting the financial transaction card without the authorization or permission of the cardholder; or

c. Representing that he is the holder of a card and such card has not in fact been issued; or

d. Using a financial transaction card to knowingly and willfully exceed:

1. The actual balance of a demand deposit account or time deposit account; or

2. An authorized credit line in an amount which exceeds such authorized credit line in the amount of five hundred dollars ($500.00), or fifty percent (50%) of such authorized credit line, whichever is greater; or

(3) Obtains control over a financial transaction card as security for debt; or

(4) Deposits into his account or any account, by means of an automated banking device, a false, fictitious, forged, altered or counterfeit check, draft, money order, or any other such document not his lawful or legal property; or

(5) Receives money, goods, services or anything else of value as a result of a false, fictitious, forged, altered, or counterfeit check, draft, money order or any other such document having been deposited into an account via an automated banking device, knowing at the time of receipt of the money, goods, services, or item of value that the document so deposited was false, fictitious, forged, altered or counterfeit or that the above deposited item was not his lawful or legal property.

(b) A person who is authorized by an issuer to furnish money, goods, services or anything else of value upon presentation of a financial transaction card by the cardholder, or any agent or employee of such person is guilty of a financial transaction card fraud when, with intent to defraud the issuer or the cardholder, he

(1)   Furnishes money, goods, services or anything else of value upon presentation of a financial transaction card obtained or retained in violation of G.S. 14-113.9, or a financial transaction card which he knows is forged, expired or revoked; or

(2)   Fails to furnish money, goods, services or anything else of value which he represents in writing to the issuer that he has furnished.

Conviction of financial transaction card fraud as provided in subsection (a) or (b) of this section is punishable as provided in G.S. 14-113.17(a) if the value of all money, goods, services and other things of value furnished in violation of this section, or if the difference between the value actually furnished and the value represented to the issuer to have been furnished in violation of this section, does not exceed five hundred dollars ($500.00) in any six-month period. Conviction of financial transaction card fraud as provided in subsection (a) or (b) of this section is punishable as provided in G.S. 14-113.17(b) if such value exceeds five hundred dollars ($500.00) in any six-month period.

(c)   A person is guilty of financial transaction card fraud when, upon application for a financial transaction card to an issuer, he knowingly makes or causes to be made a false statement or report relative to his name, occupation, financial condition, assets, or liabilities; or willfully and substantially overvalues any assets, or willfully omits or substantially undervalues any indebtedness for the purpose of influencing the issuer to issue a financial transaction card.

Conviction of financial transaction card fraud as provided in this subsection is punishable as provided in G.S. 14-113.17(a).

(c1)   A person authorized by an acquirer to furnish money, goods, services or anything else of value upon presentation of a financial transaction card or a financial transaction card account number by a cardholder, or any agent or employee of such person, who, with intent to defraud the issuer, acquirer, or cardholder, remits to an issuer or acquirer, for payment, a financial transaction card record of a sale, which sale was not made by such person, his agent or employee, is guilty of financial transaction card fraud.

Conviction of financial transaction card fraud as provided in this subsection is punishable as provided in G.S. 14-113.17(a).

(d) A cardholder is guilty of financial transaction card fraud when he willfully, knowingly, and with an intent to defraud the issuer, a person or organization providing money, goods, services, or anything else of value, or any other person, submits, verbally or in writing, to the issuer or any other person, any false notice or report of the theft, loss, disappearance, or nonreceipt of his financial transaction card.

Conviction of financial transaction card fraud as provided in this subsection is punishable as provided in G.S. 14-113.17(a).

(e) In any prosecution for violation of G.S. 14-113.13, the State is not required to establish and it is no defense that some of the acts constituting the crime did not occur in this State or within one city, county, or local jurisdiction.

(f) For purposes of this section, revocation shall be construed to include either notice given in person or notice given in writing to the person to whom the financial transaction card and/or personal identification code was issued. Notice of revocation shall be immediate when notice is given in person. The sending of a notice in writing by registered or certified mail in the United States mail, duly stamped and addressed to such person at his last address known to the issuer, shall be prima facie evidence that such notice was duly received after seven days from the date of the deposit in the mail. If the address is located outside the United States, Puerto Rico, the Virgin Islands, the Canal Zone and Canada, notice shall be presumed to have been received 10 days after mailing by registered or certified mail. (1967, c. 1244, s. 2; 1979, c. 741, s. 1; 1989, c. 161, s. 2.)

§ 14-113.14. Criminal possession of financial transaction card forgery devices.

(a) A person is guilty of criminal possession of financial transaction card forgery devices when:

(1) He is a person other than the cardholder and possesses two or more incomplete financial transaction cards, with intent to complete them without the consent of the issuer; or

(2) He possesses, with knowledge of its character, machinery, plates, or any other contrivance designed to reproduce instruments purporting to be

financial transaction cards of an issuer who has not consented to the preparation of such financial transaction cards.

(b)   A financial transaction card is incomplete if part of the matter other than the signature of the cardholder, which an issuer requires to appear on the financial transaction card before it can be used by a cardholder, has not yet been stamped, embossed, imprinted, encoded or written upon it.

Conviction of criminal possession of financial transaction card forgery devices is punishable as provided in G.S. 14-113.17(b). (1967, c. 1244, s. 2; 1979, c. 741, s. 1.)

§ 14-113.15. Criminal receipt of goods and services fraudulently obtained.

A person is guilty of criminally receiving goods and services fraudulently obtained when he receives money, goods, services or anything else of value obtained in violation of G.S. 14-113.13(a) with the knowledge or belief that the same were obtained in violation of G.S. 14-113.13(a). Conviction of criminal receipt of goods and services fraudulently obtained is punishable as provided in G.S. 14-113.17(a) if the value of all the money, goods, services and anything else of value, obtained in violation of this section, does not exceed five hundred dollars ($500.00) in any six-month period; conviction of criminal receipt of goods and services fraudulently obtained is punishable as provided in G.S. 14-113.17(b) if such value exceeds five hundred dollars ($500.00) in any six-month period. (1967, c. 1244, s. 2; 1979, c. 741, s. 1.)

§ 14-113.15A. Criminal factoring of financial transaction card records.

Any person who, without the acquirer's express authorization, employs or solicits an authorized merchant, or any agent or employee of such merchant, to remit to an issuer or acquirer, for payment, a financial transaction card record of a sale, which sale was not made by such merchant, his agent or employee, is guilty of a felony punishable as provided in G.S. 14-113.17(b). (1989, c. 161, s. 3.)

§ 14-113.16. Presumption of criminal receipt of goods and services fraudulently obtained.

A person who obtains at a discount price a ticket issued by an airline, railroad, steamship or other transportation company from other than an authorized agent of such company which was acquired in violation of G.S. 14-113.13(a) without reasonable inquiry to ascertain that the person from whom it was obtained had a legal right to possess it shall be presumed to know that such ticket was acquired under circumstances constituting a violation of G.S. 14-113.13(a). (1967, c. 1244, s. 2; 1979, c. 741, s. 1.)

§ 14-113.17. Punishment and penalties.

(a) A person who is subject to the punishment and penalties of this Article shall be guilty of a Class 2 misdemeanor.

(b) A crime punishable under this Article is punishable as a Class I felony. (1967, c. 1244, s. 2; 1979, c. 741, s. 1; c. 760, s. 5; 1993, c. 539, ss. 55, 1183; 1994, Ex. Sess., c. 24, s. 14(c).)

§ 14-113.18. Reserved for future codification purposes.

§ 14-113.19. Reserved for future codification purposes.

Article 19C.

Identity Theft.

§ 14-113.20. Identity theft.

(a) A person who knowingly obtains, possesses, or uses identifying information of another person, living or dead, with the intent to fraudulently represent that the person is the other person for the purposes of making financial or credit transactions in the other person's name, to obtain anything of value, benefit, or advantage, or for the purpose of avoiding legal consequences is guilty of a felony punishable as provided in G.S. 14-113.22(a).

(b) The term "identifying information" as used in this Article includes the following:

(1) Social security or employer taxpayer identification numbers.

(2) Drivers license, State identification card, or passport numbers.

(3) Checking account numbers.

(4) Savings account numbers.

(5) Credit card numbers.

(6) Debit card numbers.

(7) Personal Identification (PIN) Code as defined in G.S. 14-113.8(6).

(8) Electronic identification numbers, electronic mail names or addresses, Internet account numbers, or Internet identification names.

(9) Digital signatures.

(10) Any other numbers or information that can be used to access a person's financial resources.

(11) Biometric data.

(12) Fingerprints.

(13) Passwords.

(14) Parent's legal surname prior to marriage.

(c) It shall not be a violation under this Article for a person to do any of the following:

(1) Lawfully obtain credit information in the course of a bona fide consumer or commercial transaction.

(2) Lawfully exercise, in good faith, a security interest or a right of offset by a creditor or financial institution.

(3) Lawfully comply, in good faith, with any warrant, court order, levy, garnishment, attachment, or other judicial or administrative order, decree, or directive, when any party is required to do so. (1999-449, s. 1; 2000-140, s. 37; 2002-175, s. 4; 2005-414, s. 6.)

§ 14-113.20A. Trafficking in stolen identities.

(a) It is unlawful for a person to sell, transfer, or purchase the identifying information of another person with the intent to commit identity theft, or to assist another person in committing identity theft, as set forth in G.S. 14-113.20.

(b) A violation of this section is a felony punishable as provided in G.S. 14-113.22(a1). (2002-175, s. 5; 2005-414, s. 7(2).)

§ 14-113.21. Venue of offenses.

In any criminal proceeding brought under G.S. 14-113.20, the crime is considered to be committed in the county where the victim resides, where the perpetrator resides, where any part of the identity theft took place, or in any other county instrumental to the completion of the offense, regardless of whether the defendant was ever actually present in that county. (1999-449, s. 1; 2005-414, ss. 2, 7.)

§ 14-113.21A. Investigation of offenses.

(a) A person who has learned or reasonably suspects that the person has been the victim of identity theft may contact the local law enforcement agency that has jurisdiction over the person's actual residence. Notwithstanding the fact that jurisdiction may lie elsewhere for investigation and prosecution of a crime of identity theft, the local law enforcement agency may take the complaint, issue an incident report, and provide the complainant with a copy of the report and may refer the report to a law enforcement agency in that different jurisdiction.

(b) Nothing in this section interferes with the discretion of a local law enforcement agency to allocate resources for investigations of crimes. A complaint filed or report issued under this section is not required to be counted as an open case for purposes of compiling open case statistics. (2005-414, s. 3.)

§ 14-113.22. Punishment and liability.

(a) A violation of G.S.14-113.20(a) is punishable as a Class G felony, except it is punishable as a Class F felony if: (i) the victim suffers arrest, detention, or conviction as a proximate result of the offense, or (ii) the person is in possession of the identifying information pertaining to three or more separate persons.

(a1) A violation of G.S. 14-113.20A is punishable as a Class E felony.

(a2) The court may order a person convicted under G.S. 14-113.20 or G.S. 14-113.20A to pay restitution pursuant to Article 81C of Chapter 15A of the General Statutes for financial loss caused by the violation to any person. Financial loss included under this subsection may include, in addition to actual losses, lost wages, attorneys' fees, and other costs incurred by the victim in correcting his or her credit history or credit rating, or in connection with any criminal, civil, or administrative proceeding brought against the victim resulting from the misappropriation of the victim's identifying information.

(b) Notwithstanding subsection (a), (a1), or (a2) of this section, any person who commits an act made unlawful by G.S. 14-113.20 or G.S. 14-113.20A may also be liable for damages under G.S. 1-539.2C.

(c) In any case in which a person obtains identifying information of another person in violation of this Article, uses that information to commit a crime in addition to a violation of this Article, and is convicted of that additional crime, the court records shall reflect that the person whose identity was falsely used to commit the crime did not commit the crime. (1999-449, s. 1; 2002-175, ss. 6, 7; 2003-206, s. 3.)

§ 14-113.23. Authority of the Attorney General.

The Attorney General may investigate any complaint regarding identity theft under this Article. In conducting these investigations, the Attorney General has all the investigative powers available to the Attorney General under Article 1 of Chapter 75 of the General Statutes. The Attorney General shall refer all cases of identity theft under G.S. 14-113.20 to the district attorney in the county where the crime was deemed committed in accordance with G.S. 14-113.21. (1999-449, s. 1; 2005-414, s. 7(2).)

§ 14-113.24. Credit, charge, or debit card numbers on receipts.

(a)   For purposes of this section, the word "person" means the person that owns or leases the cash register or other machine or device that electronically prints receipts of credit, charge, or debit card transactions.

(b)   Except as provided in this section, no person that accepts credit, charge, or debit cards for the transaction of business shall print more than five digits of the credit, charge, or debit card account number or the expiration date upon any receipt with the intent to provide the receipt to the cardholder at the point of sale. This section applies to a person who employs a cash register or other machine or device that electronically prints receipts for credit, charge, or debit card transactions. This section does not apply to a person whose sole means of recording a credit, charge, or debit card number for the transaction of business is by handwriting or by an imprint or copy of the credit, charge, or debit card.

(c)   A person who violates this section commits an infraction as defined in G.S. 14-3.1 and is subject to a penalty of up to five hundred dollars ($500.00) per violation, not to exceed five hundred dollars ($500.00) in any calendar month or two thousand dollars ($2,000) in any calendar year. A person who receives a citation for violation of this section is not subject to the penalty provided in this subsection if the person establishes in court that the person came into compliance with this section within 30 days of the issuance of the citation and the person has remained in compliance with this section. (2003-206, s. 1; 2003-206, s. 2.)

§ 14-113.25. Sale of certain cash registers and other receipt printing machines.

(a) No person shall sell or offer to sell a cash register or other machine or device that electronically prints receipts of credit, charge, or debit card transactions that cannot be programmed or operated to produce a receipt with five or fewer digits of the credit, charge, or debit card account number and no expiration date printed on the receipt. This subsection applies to cash registers or other machines or devices sold or offered for sale for use in the ordinary course of business in this State.

(b) A person who violates this section commits an infraction as defined in G.S. 14-3.1 and is subject to a penalty of up to five hundred dollars ($500.00) per violation. For purposes of assessing penalties pursuant to this subsection, the sale or offer for sale of each individual cash register or other machine or device that electronically prints receipts of credit, charge, or debit card transactions in violation of this section is treated as a separate violation. (2003-206, s. 1.)

§ 14-113.26. Reserved for future codification purposes.

§ 14-113.27. Reserved for future codification purposes.

§ 14-113.28. Reserved for future codification purposes.

§ 14-113.29. Reserved for future codification purposes.

Article 19D.

Telephone Records Privacy Protection Act.

§ 14-113.30. Definitions.

The following definitions apply in this Article:

(1) Caller identification record. - A record collected and retained by or on behalf of a customer utilizing caller identification or similar technology that is delivered electronically to the recipient of a telephone call simultaneously with the reception of the telephone call and that indicates the telephone number from which the telephone call was initiated or similar information regarding the telephone call.

(2) Customer. - A person or the legal guardian of a person or a representative of a business to whom a telephone service provider provides telephone service to a number subscribed or listed in the name of the person or business.

(3) Person. - An individual, business association, partnership, limited partnership, corporation, limited liability company, or other legal entity.

(4) Telephone record. - A record in written, electronic, or oral form, except a caller identification record, Directory Assistance information, and subscriber list information, that is created by a telephone service provider and that contains any of the following information with respect to a customer:

a. Telephone numbers that have been dialed by the customer.

b. Telephone numbers that pertain to calls made to the customer.

c. The time when calls were made by the customer or to the customer.

d. The duration of calls made by the customer or to the customer.

e. The charges applied to calls, if any.

(5) Telephone service. - The conveyance of two-way communication in analog, digital, or other form by any medium, including wire, cable, fiber optics, cellular, broadband personal communications services, or other wireless technologies, satellite, microwave, or at any frequency over any part of the electromagnetic spectrum. The term also includes the conveyance of voice communication over the Internet and telephone relay service.

(6) Telephone service provider. - A person who provides telephone service to a customer without regard to the form of technology used, including traditional wire-line or cable communications service; cellular, broadband PCS, or other wireless communications service; microwave, satellite, or other terrestrial communications service; or voice over Internet communications service. (2007-374, s. 1.)

§ 14-113.31. Prohibition of falsely obtaining, selling, or soliciting telephone records.

(a) No person shall obtain, or attempt to obtain, by any means, whether electronically, in writing, or in oral form, with or without consideration, a telephone record that pertains to a customer who is a resident of this State without the customer's consent by doing any of the following:

(1) Making a false statement or representation to an agent, representative, or employee of a telephone service provider.

(2) Making a false statement or representation to a customer of a telephone service provider.

(3) Knowingly providing to a telephone service provider a document that is fraudulent, that has been lost or stolen, or that has been obtained by fraud, or that contains a false, fictitious, or fraudulent statement or representation.

(4) Accessing customer accounts of a telephone service provider via the Internet without prior authorization from the customer to whom the telephone records relate.

(b) No person shall knowingly purchase, receive, or solicit another to purchase or receive a telephone record that pertains to a customer without the prior authorization of that customer, or if the purchaser or receiver knows or has reason to know that the record has been obtained fraudulently.

(c) No person shall sell or offer to sell a telephone record that was obtained without the customer's prior consent, or if the person knows or has reason to know that the telephone record was obtained fraudulently. (2007-374, s. 1.)

§ 14-113.32. Exceptions.

(a) The provisions of G.S. 14-113.31 shall not apply to any of the following:

(1) Any lawfully authorized investigative, protective, or intelligence activity of a law enforcement agency in connection with the official duties of the law enforcement agency.

(2) A disclosure by a telephone service provider if the telephone service provider reasonably believes the disclosure is necessary to: (i) provide telephone service to a customer, including sharing telephone records with one

of the provider's affiliates or (ii) protect an individual or service provider from fraudulent, abusive, or unlawful use of telephone service or a telephone record.

(3) A disclosure by a telephone service provider to the National Center for Missing and Exploited Children.

(4) A disclosure by a telephone service provider that is authorized by State or federal law or regulation.

(5) A disclosure by a telephone service provider to a governmental entity if the provider reasonably believes there is an emergency involving immediate danger of death or serious physical injury.

(6) Testing of a telephone service provider's security procedures or systems for maintaining the confidentiality of customers' telephone records.

(b) Nothing in this Article shall be construed to expand the obligation or duty of a telephone service provider to maintain the confidentiality of telephone records beyond the requirements of this Article or federal law or regulation. Any telephone service provider or agent, employee, or representative of a telephone service provider who reasonably and in good faith discloses telephone records shall not be criminally or civilly liable if the disclosure is later determined to be in violation of this Article. (2007-374, s. 1.)

§ 14-113.33. Punishment; liability.

(a) Unless the conduct is covered under some other provision of law providing greater punishment, any person who violates this Article is guilty of a Class H felony. In any criminal proceeding brought under this Article, the crime is considered to be committed in the county where the customer resides, where the defendant resides, where any part of the offense took place, or in any other county instrumental to the completion of the offense, regardless of whether the defendant was ever actually present in that county.

(b) A violation of G.S. 14-331.31 is a violation of G.S. 75-1.1, except that a customer whose telephone records were obtained, sold, or solicited in violation of this Article shall be entitled to damages pursuant to G.S. 75-16, or one thousand dollars ($1,000), whichever is greater. (2007-374, s. 1.)

Article 20.

Frauds.

§ 14-114. Fraudulent disposal of personal property on which there is a security interest.

(a)   If any person, after executing a security agreement on personal property for a lawful purpose, shall make any disposition of any property embraced in such security agreement, with intent to defeat the rights of the secured party, every person so offending and every person with a knowledge of the security interest buying any property embraced in which security agreement, and every person assisting, aiding or abetting the unlawful disposition of such property, with intent to defeat the rights of any secured party in such security agreement, shall be guilty of a Class 2 misdemeanor.

A person's refusal to turn over secured property to a secured party who is attempting to repossess the property without a judgment or order for possession shall not, by itself, be a violation of this section.

(b)   Intent to commit the crime as set forth in subsection (a) may be presumed from proof of possession of the property embraced in such security agreement by the grantor thereof after execution of the security agreement, and while it is in force, the further proof of the fact that the sheriff or other officer charged with the execution of process cannot after due diligence find such property under process directed to him for its seizure, for the satisfaction of such security agreement. However, this presumption may be rebutted by evidence that the property has, through no fault of the defendant, been stolen, lost, damaged beyond repair, or otherwise disposed of by the defendant without intent to defeat the rights of the secured party. (1873-4, c. 31; 1874-5, c. 215; 1883, c. 61; Code, s. 1089; 1887, c. 14; Rev., s. 3435; C.S., s. 4287; 1969, c. 984, s. 2; c. 1224, s. 4; 1987 (Reg. Sess., 1988), c. 1065, s. 1; 1993, c. 539, s. 56; 1994, Ex. Sess., c. 24, s. 14(c).)

§ 14-115. Secreting property to hinder enforcement of lien or security interest.

Any person who, with intent to prevent or hinder the enforcement of a lien or security interest after a judgment or order has been issued for possession for that personal property subject to said lien or security interest, either refuses to surrender such personal property in his possession to a law enforcement officer, or removes, or exchanges, or secretes such personal property, shall be guilty of a Class 2 misdemeanor. (1887, c. 14; Rev., s. 3436; C.S., s. 4288; 1969, c. 984, s. 3; c. 1224, s. 1; 1987 (Reg. Sess., 1988), c. 1065, s. 2; 1989, c. 401; 1993, c. 539, s. 57; 1994, Ex. Sess., c. 24, s. 14(c).)

§ 14-116: Repealed by Session Laws 1993 (Reg. Sess., 1994), c. 767, s. 30(1).

§ 14-117. Fraudulent and deceptive advertising.

It shall be unlawful for any person, firm, corporation or association, with intent to sell or in anywise to dispose of merchandise, securities, service or any other thing offered by such person, firm, corporation or association, directly or indirectly, to the public for sale or distribution, or with intent to increase the consumption thereof, or to induce the public in any manner to enter into any obligation relating thereto, or to acquire title thereto, or an interest therein, to make public, disseminate, circulate or place before the public or cause directly or indirectly to be made, published, disseminated, circulated or placed before the public in this State, in a newspaper or other publication, or in the form of a book, notice, handbill, poster, bill, circular, pamphlet or letter, or in any other way, an advertisement of any sort regarding merchandise, securities, service or any other thing so offered to the public, which advertisement contains any assertion, representation or statement of fact which is untrue, deceptive or misleading: Provided, that such advertising shall be done willfully and with intent to mislead. Any person who shall violate the provisions of this section shall be guilty of a Class 2 misdemeanor. (1915, c. 218; C.S., s. 4290; 1993, c. 539, s. 59; 1994, Ex. Sess., c. 24, s. 14(c).)

§ 14-117.1: Repealed by Session Laws 1994, Ex. Sess., c. 14, s. 72(5).

§ 14-117.2. Gasoline price advertisements.

(a) Advertisements by any person or firm of the price of any grade of motor fuel must clearly so indicate if such price is dependent upon purchaser himself drawing or pumping the fuel.

(b) Any person or firm violating the provisions of this section shall be guilty of a Class 3 misdemeanor. (1971, c. 324, ss. 1, 2; 1993, c. 539, s. 60; 1994, Ex. Sess., c. 24, s. 14(c).)

§ 14-118. Blackmailing.

If any person shall knowingly send or deliver any letter or writing demanding of any other person, with menaces and without any reasonable or probable cause, any chattel, money or valuable security; or if any person shall accuse, or threaten to accuse, or shall knowingly send or deliver any letter or writing accusing or threatening to accuse any other person of any crime punishable by law with death or by imprisonment in the State's prison, with the intent to extort or gain from such person any chattel, money or valuable security, every such offender shall be guilty of a Class 1 misdemeanor. (R.C., c. 34, s. 110; Code, s. 989; Rev., s. 3428; C.S., s. 4291; 1993, c. 539, s. 61; 1994, Ex. Sess., c. 24, s. 14(c).)

§ 14-118.1. Simulation of court process in connection with collection of claim, demand or account.

It shall be unlawful for any person, firm, corporation, association, agent or employee in any manner to coerce, intimidate, or attempt to coerce or intimidate any person in connection with any claim, demand or account, by the issuance, utterance or delivery of any matter, printed, typed or written, which (i) simulates or resembles a summons, warrant, writ or other court process or pleading; or (ii) by its form, wording, use of the name of North Carolina or any officer, agency or subdivision thereof, use of seals or insignia, or general appearance has a tendency to create in the mind of the ordinary person the false impression that it has judicial or other official authorization, sanction or approval. Any violation of the provisions of this section shall be a Class I felony. (1961, c. 1188; 1979, c. 263; 1993, c. 539, s. 62; 1994, Ex. Sess., c. 24, s. 14(c); 2012-150, s. 3.)

§ 14-118.2. Assisting, etc., in obtaining academic credit by fraudulent means.

(a) It shall be unlawful for any person, firm, corporation or association to assist any student, or advertise, offer or attempt to assist any student, in obtaining or in attempting to obtain, by fraudulent means, any academic credit, grade or test score, or any diploma, certificate or other instrument purporting to confer any literary, scientific, professional, technical or other degree in any course of study in any university, college, academy or other educational institution. The activity prohibited by this subsection includes, but is not limited to, preparing or advertising, offering, or attempting to prepare a term paper, thesis, or dissertation for another; impersonating or advertising, offering or attempting to impersonate another in taking or attempting to take an examination; and the giving or changing of a grade or test score or offering to give or change a grade or test score in exchange for an article of value or money.

(b) Any person, firm, corporation or association violating any of the provisions of this section shall be guilty of a Class 2 misdemeanor. This section includes the acts of a teacher or other school official; however, the provisions of this section shall not apply to the acts of one student in assisting another student as herein defined if the former is duly registered in an educational institution in North Carolina and is subject to the disciplinary authority thereof. (1963, c. 781; 1969, c. 1224, s. 7; 1989, c. 144; 1993, c. 539, s. 63; 1994, Ex. Sess., c. 24, s. 14(c).)

§ 14-118.3. Acquisition and use of information obtained from patients in hospitals for fraudulent purposes.

It shall be unlawful for any person, firm or corporation, or any officer, agent or other representative of any person, firm or corporation to obtain or seek to obtain from any person while a patient in any hospital information concerning any illness, injury or disease of such patient, other than information concerning the illness, injury or disease for which such patient is then hospitalized and being treated, for a fraudulent purpose, or to use any information so obtained in regard to such other illness, injury or disease for a fraudulent purpose.

Any person, firm or corporation violating the provisions of this section shall be guilty of a Class 2 misdemeanor. (1967, c. 974; 1969, c. 1224, s. 5; 1993, c. 539, s. 64; 1994, Ex. Sess., c. 24, s. 14(c).)

§ 14-118.4. Extortion.

Any person who threatens or communicates a threat or threats to another with the intention thereby wrongfully to obtain anything of value or any acquittance, advantage, or immunity is guilty of extortion and such person shall be punished as a Class F felon. (1973, c. 1032; 1979, c. 760, s. 5; 1979, 2nd Sess., c. 1316, s. 47; 1981, c. 63, s. 1, c. 179, s. 14; 1993, c. 539, s. 1184; 1994, Ex. Sess., c. 24, s. 14(c).)

§ 14-118.5. Theft of cable television service.

(a) Any person, firm or corporation who, after October 1, 1984, knowingly and willfully attaches or maintains an electronic, mechanical or other connection to any cable, wire, decoder, converter, device or equipment of a cable television system or removes, tampers with, modifies or alters any cable, wire, decoder, converter, device or equipment of a cable television system for the purpose of intercepting or receiving any programming or service transmitted by such cable television system which person, firm or corporation is not authorized by the cable television system to receive, is guilty of a Class 3 misdemeanor which may include a fine not exceeding five hundred dollars ($500.00). Each unauthorized connection, attachment, removal, modification or alteration shall constitute a separate violation.

(b) Any person, firm or corporation who knowingly and willfully, without the authorization of a cable television system, distributes, sells, attempts to sell or possesses for sale in North Carolina any converter, decoder, device, or kit, that is designed to decode or descramble any encoded or scrambled signal transmitted by such cable television system, is guilty of a Class 3 misdemeanor which may include a fine not exceeding five hundred dollars ($500.00). The term "encoded or scrambled signal" shall include any signal or transmission that is not intended to produce an intelligible program or service without the aid of a decoder, descrambler, filter, trap or other electronic or mechanical device.

(c) Any cable television system may institute a civil action to enjoin and restrain any violation of this section, and in addition, such cable television system shall be entitled to civil damages in the following amounts:

(1) For each violation of subsection (a), three hundred dollars ($300.00) or three times the amount of actual damages, if any, sustained by the plaintiff, whichever amount is greater.

(2) For each violation of subsection (b), one thousand dollars ($1,000) or three times the amount of actual damages, if any, sustained by the plaintiff, whichever amount is greater.

(d) It is not a necessary prerequisite to a civil action instituted pursuant to this section that the plaintiff has suffered or will suffer actual damages.

(e) Proof that any equipment, cable, wire, decoder, converter or device of a cable television system was modified, removed, altered, tampered with or connected without the consent of such cable system in violation of this section shall be prima facie evidence that such action was taken knowingly and willfully by the person or persons in whose name the cable system's equipment, cable, wire, decoder, converter or device is installed or the person or persons regularly receiving the benefits of cable services resulting from such unauthorized modification, removal, alteration, tampering or connection.

(f) The receipt, decoding or converting of a signal from the air by the use of a satellite dish or antenna shall not constitute a violation of this section.

(g) Cable television systems may refuse to provide service to anyone who violates subsection (a) of this section whether or not the alleged violator has been prosecuted thereunder. (1977, 2nd Sess., c. 1185, s. 1; 1983 (Reg. Sess., 1984), c. 1088, s. 1; 1993, c. 539, s. 65; 1994, Ex. Sess., c. 24, s. 14(c).)

§ 14-118.6. Filing false lien or encumbrance.

(a) It shall be unlawful for any person to present for filing in a public record or a private record generally available to the public a false lien or encumbrance against the real or personal property of a public officer, a public employee, or an immediate family member of the public officer or public employee on account of the performance of the public officer or public employee's official duties, knowing or having reason to know that the lien or encumbrance is false or contains a materially false, fictitious, or fraudulent statement or representation. For purposes of this subsection, the term "immediate family member" means a spouse or a child. Any person who violates this subsection shall be guilty of a Class I felony.

(b) In the case of a lien or encumbrance presented to the register of deeds for filing, if the register of deeds has a reasonable suspicion that the lien or encumbrance is false, the register of deeds may refuse to file the lien or encumbrance. Neither the register of deeds nor any other entity shall be liable for filing or refusing to file a lien or encumbrance under this section. If the filing of the lien or encumbrance is denied, the register of deeds shall allow the filing of a Notice of Denied Lien or Encumbrance Filing on a form adopted by the Secretary of State, for which no filing fee shall be collected. The Notice of Denied Lien or Encumbrance Filing shall not itself constitute a lien or encumbrance. If the filing of the lien or encumbrance is denied, any interested person may file a special proceeding in the county where the filing was denied within ten (10) business days of the filing of the Notice of Denied Lien or Encumbrance Filing asking the court to find that the proposed filing has a statutory or contractual basis and to order that the document be filed. If, after hearing, upon a minimum of five (5) days' notice and opportunity to be heard to all interested persons and all persons claiming an ownership interest in the property, the court finds that there is a statutory or contractual basis for the proposed filing, the court shall order the document filed. A lien or encumbrance filed upon order of the court under this subsection shall have a priority interest as of the time of the filing of the Notice of Denied Lien or Encumbrance Filing. If the court finds that there is no statutory or contractual basis for the proposed filing, the court shall order that the proposed filing is null and void and that it shall not be filed, indexed, or recorded and a copy of that order shall be filed by the register of deeds that originally denied the filing. The review by the judge under this subsection shall not be deemed a finding as to any underlying claim of the parties involved. If a special proceeding is not filed under this subsection within ten (10) business days of the filing of the Notice of Denied Lien or Encumbrance Filing, the lien or encumbrance is deemed null and void.

(c) Upon being presented with an order duly issued by a court of this State declaring that a filed lien or encumbrance is false, and therefore null and void, the register of deeds that received the filing, in addition to filing the order, shall conspicuously mark on the first page of the original record previously filed the following statement: "THE CLAIM ASSERTED IN THIS DOCUMENT IS FALSE AND IS NOT PROVIDED FOR BY THE GENERAL LAWS OF THIS STATE."

(d) In addition to any criminal penalties provided for in this section, a violation of this section shall constitute a violation of G.S. 75-1.1.

(e)   Subsections (b) and (c) of this section shall not apply to filings under Article 9 of Chapter 25 of the General Statutes or under Chapter 44A of the General Statutes. (2012-150, s. 4; 2013-170, s. 1; 2013-410, s. 27.8.)

§ 14-118.7. Possession, transfer, or use of automated sales suppression device.

(a)   Definitions. - The following definitions apply in this section:

(1)   Automated sales suppression device or zapper. - A software program that falsifies the electronic records of electronic cash registers and other point-of-sale systems, including transaction data and transaction reports. The term includes the software program, any device that carries the software program, or an Internet link to the software program.

(2)   Electronic cash register. - A device that keeps a register or supporting documents through the use of an electronic device or computer system designed to record transaction data for the purpose of computing, compiling, or processing retail sales transaction data in whatever manner.

(3)   Phantom-ware. - A hidden programming option embedded in the operating system of an electronic cash register or hardwired into the electronic cash register that can be used to create a second set of records or may eliminate or manipulate transaction records, which may or may not be preserved in digital formats, to represent the true or manipulated record of transactions in the electronic cash register.

(4)   Transaction data. - The term includes items purchased by a customer, the price for each item, a taxability determination for each item, a segregated tax amount for each of the taxed items, the amount of cash or credit tendered, the net amount returned to the customer in change, the date and time of the purchase, the name, address, and identification number of the vendor, and the receipt or invoice number of the transaction.

(5)   Transaction report. - A report that documents, but is not limited to documenting, the sales, taxes, or fees collected, media totals, and discount voids at an electronic cash register and that is printed on cash register tape at the end of a day or shift, or a report that documents every action at an electronic cash register and that is stored electronically.

(b) Offense. - No person shall knowingly sell, purchase, install, transfer, possess, use, or access any automated sales suppression device, zapper, or phantom-ware.

(c) Penalty. - Any person convicted of a violation of this section is guilty of a Class H felony with a fine of up to ten thousand dollars ($10,000).

(d) Liability. - Any person who violates this section is liable for all taxes, fees, penalties, and interest due the State as the result of the use of an automated sales suppression device, zapper, or phantom-ware and shall forfeit to the State as an additional penalty all profits associated with the sale or use of an automated sales suppression device, zapper, or phantom-ware.

(e) Contraband. - An automated sales suppression device, zapper, or phantom-ware, or any device containing such device or software, is contraband. (2013-301, s. 1.)

§ 14-118.8. Reserved for future codification purposes.

§ 14-118.9. Reserved for future codification purposes.

Article 20A.

Residential Mortgage Fraud Act.

§ 14-118.10. Title.

This Article shall be known and cited as the "Residential Mortgage Fraud Act." (2007-163, s. 1.)

§ 14-118.11. Definitions.

Unless otherwise provided in this Article, the following definitions apply in this Article:

(1) Mortgage lending process. - The process through which a person seeks or obtains a mortgage loan including solicitation, application, origination,

negotiation of terms, underwriting, signing, closing, and funding of a mortgage loan and services provided incident to a mortgage loan, including the appraisal of the residential real property. Documents involved in the mortgage lending process include (i) uniform residential loan applications or other loan applications, (ii) appraisal reports, (iii) settlement statements, (iv) supporting personal documentation for loan applications, including W-2 or other earnings or income statements, verifications of rent, income, and employment, bank statements, tax returns, and payroll stubs, and (v) any required mortgage-related disclosures.

(2) Mortgage loan. - A loan primarily secured by either (i) a mortgage or a deed of trust on residential real property or (ii) a security interest in a manufactured home (as defined by G.S. 143-145(7)) located or to be located on residential real property.

(3) Pattern of residential mortgage fraud. - Residential mortgage fraud that involves five or more mortgage loans, which have the same or similar intents, results, accomplices, victims, or methods of commission or otherwise are interrelated by distinguishing characteristics.

(4) Person. - An individual, partnership, limited liability company, limited partnership, corporation, association, or other entity, however organized.

(5) Residential real property. - Real property located in the State of North Carolina upon which there is located or is to be located a structure or structures designed principally for residential purposes, including, but not limited to, individual units of townhouses, condominiums, and cooperatives. (2007-163, s. 1.)

§ 14-118.12. Residential mortgage fraud.

(a) A person is guilty of residential mortgage fraud when, for financial gain and with the intent to defraud, that person does any of the following:

(1) Knowingly makes or attempts to make any material misstatement, misrepresentation, or omission within the mortgage lending process with the intention that a mortgage lender, mortgage broker, borrower, or any other person or entity that is involved in the mortgage lending process relies on it.

(2) Knowingly uses or facilitates or attempts to use or facilitate the use of any misstatement, misrepresentation, or omission within the mortgage lending process with the intention that a mortgage lender, borrower, or any other person or entity that is involved in the mortgage lending process relies on it.

(3) Receives or attempts to receive proceeds or any other funds in connection with a residential mortgage closing that the person knew, or should have known, resulted from a violation of subdivision (1) or (2) of this subsection.

(4) Conspires or solicits another to violate any of the provisions of subdivision (1), (2), or (3) of this subsection.

(5) Knowingly files in a public record or a private record generally available to the public a document falsely claiming that a mortgage loan has been satisfied, discharged, released, revoked, or terminated or is invalid.

(b) It shall be sufficient in any prosecution under this Article for residential mortgage fraud to show that the party accused did the act with the intent to deceive or defraud. It shall be unnecessary to show that any particular person or entity was harmed financially in the transaction or that the person or entity to whom the deliberate misstatement, misrepresentation, or omission was made relied upon the misstatement, misrepresentation, or omission. (2007-163, s. 1; 2012-150, s. 5.)

§ 14-118.13. Venue.

In any criminal proceeding brought under this Article, the crime shall be construed to have been committed:

(1) In the county in which the residential real property for which a mortgage loan is being sought is located;

(2) In any county in which any act was performed in furtherance of the violation;

(3) In any county in which any person alleged to have violated this Article had control or possession of any proceeds of the violation;

(4) If a closing occurred, in any county in which the closing occurred; or

(5)   In any county in which a document containing a deliberate misstatement, misrepresentation, or omission is filed with the official registrar of deeds or with the Division of Motor Vehicles. (2007-163, s. 1.)

§ 14-118.14. Authority to investigate and prosecute.

Upon its own investigation or upon referral by the Office of the Commissioner of Banks, the North Carolina Real Estate Commission, the Attorney General, the North Carolina Appraisal Board, or other parties, of available evidence concerning violations of this Article, the proper district attorney may institute the appropriate criminal proceedings under this Article. (2007-163, s. 1.)

§ 14-118.15. Penalty for violation of Article.

(a)   Unless the conduct is prohibited by some other provision of law providing for greater punishment, a violation of this Article involving a single mortgage loan is a Class H felony.

(b)   Unless the conduct is prohibited by some other provision of law providing for greater punishment, a violation of this Article involving a pattern of residential mortgage fraud is a Class E felony. (2007-163, s. 1.)

§ 14-118.16. Forfeiture.

(a)   All real and personal property of every kind used or intended for use in the course of, derived from, or realized through a violation of this Article shall be subject to forfeiture to the State as set forth in G.S. 14-2.3 and G.S. 14-7.20. However, the forfeiture of any real or personal property shall be subordinate to any security interest in the property taken by a lender in good faith as collateral for the extension of credit and recorded as provided by law, and no real or personal property shall be forfeited under this section against an owner who made a bona fide purchase of the property without knowledge of a violation of this Article.

(b) In addition to the provisions of subsection (a) of this section, courts may order restitution to any person that has suffered a financial loss due to violation of this Article. (2007-163, s. 1.)

§ 14-118.17. Liability for reporting suspected mortgage fraud.

In the absence of fraud, bad faith, or malice, a person shall not be subject to an action for civil liability for filing reports or furnishing other information regarding suspected residential mortgage fraud to a regulatory or law enforcement agency. (2007-163, s. 1.)

Article 21.

Forgery.

§ 14-119. Forgery of notes, checks, and other securities; counterfeiting of instruments.

(a) It is unlawful for any person to forge or counterfeit any instrument, or possess any counterfeit instrument, with the intent to injure or defraud any person, financial institution, or governmental unit. Any person in violation of this subsection is guilty of a Class I felony.

(b) Any person who transports or possesses five or more counterfeit instruments with the intent to injure or defraud any person, financial institution, or governmental unit is guilty of a Class G felony.

(c) As used in this Article, the term:

(1) "Counterfeit" means to manufacture, copy, reproduce, or forge an instrument that purports to be genuine, but is not, because it has been falsely copied, reproduced, forged, manufactured, embossed, encoded, duplicated, or altered.

(2) "Financial institution" means any mutual fund, money market fund, credit union, savings and loan association, bank, or similar institution, either foreign or domestic.

(3) "Governmental unit" means the United States, any United States territory, any state of the United States, any political subdivision, agency, or instrumentality of any state, or any foreign jurisdiction.

(4) "Instrument" means (i) any currency, bill, note, warrant, check, order, or similar instrument of or on any financial institution or governmental unit, or any cashier or officer of the institution or unit; or (ii) any security issued by, or on behalf of, any corporation, financial institution, or governmental unit. (1819, c. 994, s. 1, P.R.; R.C., c. 34, s. 60; Code, s. 1030; Rev., s. 3419; C.S., s. 4293; 1979, c. 760, s. 5; 1979, 2nd Sess., c. 1316, s. 47; 1981, c. 63, s. 1; c. 179, s. 14; 1983, c. 397, s. 1; 2002-175, s. 1.)

§ 14-120. Uttering forged paper or instrument containing a forged endorsement.

If any person, directly or indirectly, whether for the sake of gain or with intent to defraud or injure any other person, shall utter or publish any such false, forged or counterfeited instrument as is mentioned in G.S. 14-119, or shall pass or deliver, or attempt to pass or deliver, any of them to another person (knowing the same to be falsely forged or counterfeited) the person so offending shall be punished as a Class I felon. If any person, directly or indirectly, whether for the sake of gain or with intent to defraud or injure any other person, shall falsely make, forge or counterfeit any endorsement on any instrument described in the preceding section, whether such instrument be genuine or false, or shall knowingly utter or publish any such instrument containing a false, forged or counterfeited endorsement or, knowing the same to be falsely endorsed, shall pass or deliver or attempt to pass or deliver any such instrument containing a forged endorsement to another person, the person so offending shall be guilty of a Class I felony. (1819, c. 994, s. 2, P.R.; R.C., c. 34, s. 61; Code, s. 1031; Rev., s. 3427; 1909, c. 666; C.S., s. 4294; 1961, c. 94; 1979, c. 760, s. 5; 1979, 2nd Sess., c. 1316, s. 47; 1981, c. 63, s. 1, c. 179, s. 14; 1983, c. 397, s. 2; 1993, c. 539, s. 1185; 1994, Ex. Sess., c. 24, s. 14(c).)

§ 14-121. Selling of certain forged securities.

If any person shall sell, by delivery, endorsement or otherwise, to any other person, any judgment for the recovery of money purporting to have been rendered by a magistrate, or any bond, promissory note, bill of exchange, order, draft or liquidated account purporting to be signed by the debtor (knowing the same to be forged), the person so offending shall be punished as a Class H felon. (R.C., c. 34, s. 63; Code, s. 1033; Rev., s. 3425; C.S., s. 4295; 1973, c. 108, s. 2; 1979, c. 760, s. 5; 1979, 2nd Sess., c. 1316, s. 47; 1981, c. 63, s. 1, c. 179, s. 14; 1993, c. 539, s. 1186; 1994, Ex. Sess., c. 24, s. 14(c).)

§ 14-122. Forgery of deeds, wills and certain other instruments.

If any person, of his own head and imagination, or by false conspiracy or fraud with others, shall wittingly and falsely forge and make, or shall cause or wittingly assent to the forging or making of, or shall show forth in evidence, knowing the same to be forged, any deed, lease or will, or any bond, writing obligatory, bill of exchange, promissory note, endorsement or assignment thereof; or any acquittance or receipt for money or goods; or any receipt or release for any bond, note, bill or any other security for the payment of money; or any order for the payment of money or delivery of goods, with intent, in any of said instances, to defraud any person or corporation, and thereof shall be duly convicted, the person so offending shall be punished as a Class H felon. (5 Eliz., c. 14, ss. 2, 3; 21 James I, c. 26; 1801, c. 572, P.R.; R.C., c. 34, s. 59; Code, s. 1029; Rev., s. 3424; C.S., s. 4296; 1979, c. 760, s. 5; 1979, 2nd Sess., c. 1316, s. 47; 1981, c. 63, s. 1, c. 179, s. 14; 1993, c. 539, s. 1187; 1994, Ex. Sess., c. 24, s. 14(c).)

§ 14-122.1. Falsifying documents issued by a secondary school, postsecondary educational institution, or governmental agency.

(a)   It shall be unlawful for any person knowingly and willfully:

(1)   To make falsely or alter falsely, or to procure to be made falsely or altered falsely, or to aid or assist in making falsely or altering falsely, a diploma, certificate, license, or transcript signifying merit or achievement in an educational program issued by a secondary school, a postsecondary educational institution, or a governmental agency;

(2)   To sell, give, buy, or obtain, or to procure to be sold, given, bought, or obtained, or to aid or assist in selling, giving, buying, or obtaining, a diploma, certificate, license, or transcript, which he knows is false, signifying merit or achievement in an educational program issued by a secondary school, a postsecondary educational institution, or a governmental agency;

(3) To use, offer, or present as genuine a falsely made or falsely altered diploma, certificate, license, or transcript signifying merit or achievement in an educational program issued by a secondary school, a postsecondary educational institution, or a governmental agency, which he knows is false; or

(4) To make a false written representation of fact that he has received a degree or other certification signifying merit, achievement, or completion of an educational program involving study, experience, or testing from a secondary school, a postsecondary educational institution or governmental agency in an application for:

(a) Employment;

(b) Admission to an educational program;

(c) Award; or

(d) For the purpose of inducing another to issue a diploma, certificate, license, or transcript signifying merit or achievement in an educational program of a secondary school, postsecondary educational institution, or a governmental agency.

(b) As used in this section, "postsecondary educational institution" means a technical college, community college, junior college, college, or university. As used in this section, "governmental agency" means any agency of a State or local government or of the federal government. As used in this section, "secondary school" means grades 9 through 12.

(c) Any person who violates a provision of this section shall be guilty of a Class 1 misdemeanor. (1981, c. 146, s. 1; 1987, c. 388; 1993, c. 539, s. 66; 1994, Ex. Sess., c. 24, s. 14(c).)

§ 14-123. Forging names to petitions and uttering forged petitions.

If any person shall willfully sign, or cause to be signed, or willfully assent to the signing of the name of any person without his consent, or of any deceased or fictitious person, to any petition or recommendation with the intent of procuring any commutation of sentence, pardon or reprieve of any person convicted of any crime or offense, or for the purpose of procuring such pardon, reprieve or commutation to be refused or delayed by any public officer, or with the intent of procuring from any person whatsoever, either for himself or another, any appointment to office, or to any position of honor or trust, or with the intent to influence the official action of any public officer in the management, conduct or decision of any matter affecting the public, he shall be punished as a Class I felon; and if any person shall willfully use any such paper for any of the purposes or intents above recited, knowing that any part of the signatures to such petition or recommendation has been signed thereto without the consent of the alleged signers, or that names of any dead or fictitious persons are signed thereto, he shall be guilty of a felony, and shall be punished in like manner. (1883, c. 275; Code, s. 1034; Rev., s. 3426; C.S., s. 4297; 1979, c. 760, s. 5; 1979, 2nd Sess., c. 1316, s. 47; 1981, c. 63, s. 1; c. 179, s. 14.)

§ 14-124. Forging certificate of corporate stock and uttering forged certificates.

If any officer or agent of a corporation shall, falsely and with a fraudulent purpose, make, with the intent that the same shall be issued and delivered to any other person by name or as holder or bearer thereof, any certificate or other writing, whereby it is certified or declared that such person, holder or bearer is entitled to or has an interest in the stock of such corporation, when in fact such person, holder or bearer is not so entitled, or is not entitled to the amount of stock in such certificate or writing specified; or if any officer or agent of such corporation, or other person, knowing such certificate or other writing to be false or untrue, shall transfer, assign or deliver the same to another person, for the sake of gain, or with the intent to defraud the corporation, or any member thereof, or such person to whom the same shall be transferred, assigned or delivered, the person so offending shall be punished as a Class I felon. (R.C., c. 34, s. 62; Code, s. 1032; Rev., s. 3421; C.S., s. 4298; 1979, c. 760, s. 5; 1979, 2nd Sess., c. 1316, s. 47; 1981, c. 63, s. 1; c. 179, s. 14.)

§ 14-125. Forgery of bank notes and other instruments by connecting genuine parts.

If any person shall fraudulently connect together different parts of two or more bank notes, or other genuine instruments, in such a manner as to produce another note or instrument, with intent to pass all of them as genuine, the same shall be deemed a forgery, and the instrument so produced a forged note, or forged instrument, in like manner as if each of them had been falsely made or forged. (R.C., c. 34, s. 66; Code, s. 1037; Rev., s. 3420; C.S., s. 4299.)

SUBCHAPTER VI. CRIMINAL TRESPASS.

Article 22.

Damages and Other Offenses to Land and Fixtures.

§ 14-126: Repealed by Session Laws 1987, c. 700, s. 2.

§ 14-127. Willful and wanton injury to real property.

If any person shall willfully and wantonly damage, injure or destroy any real property whatsoever, either of a public or private nature, he shall be guilty of a Class 1 misdemeanor. (R.C., c. 34, s. 111; 1873-4, c. 176, s. 5; Code, s. 1081; Rev., s. 3677; C.S., s. 4301; 1967, c. 1083; 1993, c. 539, s. 67; 1994, Ex. Sess., c. 24, s. 14(c).)

§ 14-128. Injury to trees, crops, lands, etc., of another.

Any person, not being on his own lands, who shall without the consent of the owner thereof, willfully commit any damage, injury, or spoliation to or upon any tree, wood, underwood, timber, garden, crops, vegetables, plants, lands, springs, or any other matter or thing growing or being thereon, or who cuts, breaks, injures, or removes any tree, plant, or flower, shall be guilty of a Class 1 misdemeanor: Provided, however, that this section shall not apply to the officers, agents, and employees of the Department of Transportation while in the discharge of their duties within the right-of-way or easement of the Department of Transportation. (Ex. Sess. 1924, c. 54; 1957, c. 65, s. 11, c. 754; 1965, c. 300, s. 1; 1969, c. 22, s. 1; 1973, c. 507, s. 5; 1977, c. 464, s. 34; 1993, c. 539, s. 68; 1994, Ex. Sess., c. 24, s. 14(c).)

§ 14-128.1. Repealed by Session Laws 1979, c. 964, s. 2.

§ 14-129. Taking, etc., of certain wild plants from land of another.

No person, firm or corporation shall dig up, pull up or take from the land of another or from any public domain, the whole or any part of any Venus flytrap (Dionaea muscipula), trailing arbutus, Aaron's Rod (Thermopsis caroliniana), Bird-foot Violet (Viola pedata), Bloodroot (Sanguinaria canadensis), Blue Dogbane (Amsonia tabernaemontana), Cardinal-flower (Lobelia cardinalis), Columbine (Aquilegia canadensis), Dutchman's Breeches (Dicentra cucullaria), Maidenhair Fern (Adiantum pedatum), Walking Fern (Camptosorus rhizophyllus), Gentians (Gentiana), Ground Cedar, Running Cedar, Hepatica (Hepatica americana and acutiloba), Jack-in-the-Pulpit (Arisaema triphyllum), Lily (Lilium), Lupine (Lupinus), Monkshood (Aconitum uncinatum and reclinatum), May Apple (Podophyllum peltatum), Orchids (all species), Pitcher Plant (Sarracenia), Shooting Star (Dodecatheon meadia), Oconee Bells (Shortia galacifolia), Solomon's Seal (Polygonatum), Trailing Christmas (Greens-Lycopodium), Trillium (Trillium), Virginia Bluebells (Mertensia virginica), and Fringe Tree (Chionanthus virginicus), American holly, white pine, red cedar, hemlock or other coniferous trees, or any flowering dogwood, any mountain laurel, any rhododendron, or any ground pine, or any Christmas greens, or any Judas tree, or any leucothea, or any azalea, without having in his possession a permit to dig up, pull up or take such plants, signed by the owner of such land, or by his duly authorized agent. Any person convicted of violating the provisions of this section shall be guilty of a Class 3 misdemeanor only punished by a fine of not less than ten dollars ($10.00) nor more than fifty dollars ($50.00) for each offense. The provisions of this section shall not apply to the Counties of Cabarrus, Carteret, Catawba, Cherokee, Chowan, Cumberland, Currituck, Dare, Duplin, Edgecombe, Franklin, Gaston, Granville, Hertford, McDowell, Pamlico, Pender, Person, Richmond, Rockingham, Rowan and Swain. (1941, c. 253; 1951, c. 367, s. 1; 1955, cc. 251, 962; 1961, c. 1021; 1967, c. 355; 1971, c. 951; 1993, c. 539, s. 69; c. 553, s. 9; 1994, Ex. Sess., c. 24, s. 14(c); 2001-93, s. 1; 2001-487, s. 43(a).)

§ 14-129.1. Repealed by Session Laws 1979, c. 964, s. 2.

§ 14-129.2. Unlawful to take sea oats.

(a) It is unlawful to dig up, pull up, or take from the land of another or from any public domain the whole or any part of any Sea Oats (Uniola paniculata) without the consent of the owner of that land.

(b) Any person convicted of violating the provisions of this section shall be guilty of a Class 3 misdemeanor and shall be punished by a fine of not less than twenty-five dollars ($25.00) nor more than two hundred dollars ($200.00) for each offense. (2001-93, s. 2.)

§ 14-130. Trespass on public lands.

If any person shall erect a building on any state-owned lands, or cultivate or remove timber from any such lands, without the permission of the State, he shall be guilty of a Class 1 misdemeanor. Moreover, the State can recover from any person cutting timber on its land three times the value of the timber which is cut. (1823, c. 1190, P.R.; 1842, c. 36, s. 4; R.C., c. 34, s. 42; Code, s. 1121; Rev., s. 3746; 1909, c. 891; C.S., s. 4302; 1979, c. 15; 1993, c. 539, s. 70; 1994, Ex. Sess., c. 24, s. 14(c).)

§ 14-131. Trespass on land under option by the federal government.

On lands under option which have formally or informally been offered to and accepted by the North Carolina Department of Environment and Natural Resources by the acquiring federal agency and tentatively accepted by said Department for administration as State forests, State parks, State game refuges or for other public purposes, it shall be unlawful to cut, dig, break, injure or remove any timber, lumber, firewood, trees, shrubs or other plants; or any fence, house, barn or other structure; or to pursue, trap, hunt or kill any bird or other wild animals or take fish from streams or lakes within the boundaries of such areas without the written consent of the local official of the United States having charge of the acquisition of such lands.

Any person, firm or corporation convicted of the violation of this section shall be guilty of a Class 3 misdemeanor.

The Department of Environment and Natural Resources through its legally appointed forestry, fish and game wardens is hereby authorized and empowered to assist the county law-enforcement officers in the enforcement of this section. (1935, c. 317; 1973, c. 1262, s. 86; 1977, c. 771, s. 4; 1989, c. 727, s. 218(2); 1993, c. 539, s. 71; 1994, Ex. Sess., c. 24, s. 14(c); 1997-443, s. 11A.119(a).)

§ 14-132. Disorderly conduct in and injuries to public buildings and facilities.

(a) It is a misdemeanor if any person shall:

(1) Make any rude or riotous noise, or be guilty of any disorderly conduct, in or near any public building or facility; or

(2) Unlawfully write or scribble on, mark, deface, besmear, or injure the walls of any public building or facility, or any statue or monument situated in any public place; or

(3) Commit any nuisance in or near any public building or facility.

(b) Any person in charge of any public building or facility owned or controlled by the State, any subdivision of the State, or any other public agency shall have authority to arrest summarily and without warrant for a violation of this section.

(c) The term "public building or facility" as used in this section includes any building or facility which is:

(1) One to which the public or a portion of the public has access and is owned or controlled by the State, any subdivision of the State, any other public agency, or any private institution or agency of a charitable, educational, or eleemosynary nature; or

(2) Dedicated to the use of the general public for a purpose which is primarily concerned with public recreation, cultural activities, and other events of a public nature or character.

(3) Designated by the Attorney General in accordance with G.S. 114-20.1.

The term "building or facility" as used in this section also includes the surrounding grounds and premises of any building or facility used in connection with the operation or functioning of such building or facility.

(d)   Any person who violates any provision of this section is guilty of a Class 2 misdemeanor. (1829, c. 29, ss. 1, 2; 1842, c. 47; R.C., c. 103, ss. 7, 8; Code, s. 2308; Rev., s. 3742; 1915, c. 269; C.S., s. 4303; 1969, c. 869, s. 7 1/2, c. 1224, s. 2; 1981, c. 499, s. 2; 1993, c. 539, s. 72; 1994, Ex. Sess., c. 24, s. 14(c).)

§ 14-132.1. Repealed by Session Laws 1987, c. 700, s. 2.

§ 14-132.2. Willfully trespassing upon, damaging, or impeding the progress of a public school bus.

(a)   Any person who shall unlawfully and willfully demolish, destroy, deface, injure, burn or damage any public school bus or public school activity bus shall be guilty of a Class 1 misdemeanor.

(b)   Any person who shall enter a public school bus or public school activity bus after being forbidden to do so by the authorized school bus driver in charge thereof, or the school principal to whom the public school bus or public school activity bus is assigned, shall be guilty of a Class 1 misdemeanor.

(c)   Any occupant of a public school bus or public school activity bus who shall refuse to leave said bus upon demand of the authorized driver in charge thereof, or upon demand of the principal of the school to which said bus is assigned, shall be guilty of a Class 1 misdemeanor.

(c1)   Any person who shall unlawfully and willfully stop, impede, delay, or detain any public school bus or public school activity bus being operated for public school purposes shall be guilty of a Class 1 misdemeanor.

(d)   Subsections (b) and (c) of this section shall not apply to a child less than 12 years of age, or authorized professional school personnel. (1975, c. 191, s. 1; 1993, c. 539, s. 73; 1994, Ex. Sess., c. 24, s. 14(c); 2001-26, s. 1.)

§ 14-133: Repealed by Session Laws 1993 (Reg. Sess., 1994), c. 767, s. 30(2).

§ 14-134. Repealed by Session Laws 1987, c. 700, s. 2.

§ 14-134.1. Repealed by Session Laws 1977, c. 887, s. 2.

§ 14-134.2. Operating motor vehicle upon utility easements after being forbidden to do so.

If any person, without permission, shall ride, drive or operate a minibike, motorbike, motorcycle, jeep, dune buggy, automobile, truck or any other motor vehicle, other than a motorized all terrain vehicle as defined in G.S. 14-159.3, upon a utility easement upon which the owner or holder of the easement or agent of the owner or holder of the easement has posted on the easement a "no trespassing" sign or has otherwise given oral or written notice to the person not to so ride, drive or operate such a vehicle upon the said easement, he shall be guilty of a Class 3 misdemeanor, provided, however, neither the owner of the property nor the holder of the easement or their agents, employees, guests, invitees or permittees shall be guilty of a violation under this section. (1975, c. 636, s. 1; 1993, c. 539, s. 75; 1994, Ex. Sess., c. 24, s. 14(c); 1997-487, s. 2.)

§ 14-134.3. Domestic criminal trespass.

(a) Any person who enters after being forbidden to do so or remains after being ordered to leave by the lawful occupant, upon the premises occupied by a present or former spouse or by a person with whom the person charged has lived as if married, shall be guilty of a misdemeanor if the complainant and the person charged are living apart; provided, however, that no person shall be guilty if said person enters upon the premises pursuant to a judicial order or written separation agreement which gives the person the right to enter upon said premises for the purpose of visiting with minor children. Evidence that the parties are living apart shall include but is not necessarily limited to:

(1) A judicial order of separation;

(2) A court order directing the person charged to stay away from the premises occupied by the complainant;

(3) An agreement, whether verbal or written, between the complainant and the person charged that they shall live separate and apart, and such parties are in fact living separate and apart; or

(4) Separate places of residence for the complainant and the person charged.

Except as provided in subsection (b) of this section, upon conviction, said person is guilty of a Class 1 misdemeanor.

(b) A person convicted of a violation of this section is guilty of a Class G felony if the person is trespassing upon property operated as a safe house or haven for victims of domestic violence and the person is armed with a deadly weapon at the time of the offense. (1979, c. 561, s. 2; 1993, c. 539, s. 76; 1994, Ex. Sess., c. 24, s. 14(c); 1998-212, s. 17.19(a).)

§ 14-135. Cutting, injuring, or removing another's timber.

If any person not being the bona fide owner thereof, shall knowingly and willfully cut down, injure or remove any standing, growing or fallen tree or log off the property of another, the person shall be punished the same as in G.S. 14-72. (1889, c. 168; Rev., s. 3687; C.S., s. 4306; 1957, c. 1437, s. 1; 1993, c. 539, s. 77; 1994, Ex. Sess., c. 24, s. 14(c); 2009-508, s. 1.)

§ 14-136. Setting fire to grass and brushlands and woodlands.

If any person shall intentionally set fire to any grassland, brushland or woodland, except it be his own property, or in that case without first giving notice to all persons owning or in charge of lands adjoining the land intended to be fired, and without also taking care to watch such fire while burning and to extinguish it before it shall reach any lands near to or adjoining the lands so fired, he shall for every such offense be guilty of a Class 2 misdemeanor for the first offense, and for a second or any subsequent similar offense shall be guilty of a Class 1 misdemeanor. If intent to damage the property of another shall be shown, said person shall be punished as a Class I felon. This section shall not prevent an action for the damages sustained by the owner of any property from such fires. For the purposes of this section, the term "woodland" is to be taken to include all forest areas, both timber and cutover land, and all second-growth stands on areas that have at one time been cultivated. Any person who shall furnish to the State, evidence sufficient for the conviction of a violation of this section shall receive the sum of five hundred dollars ($500.00) to be paid from the State Fire Suppression Fund. (1777, c. 123, ss. 1, 2, P.R.; R.C., c. 16, ss. 1, 2; Code, ss. 52, 53; Rev., s. 3346; 1915, c. 243, ss. 8, 11; 1919, c. 318; C.S., s. 4309; 1925, c. 61, s. 1; 1943, c. 661; 1979, c. 760, s. 5; 1979, 2nd Sess., c. 1316, s. 47; 1981, c. 63, s. 1, c. 179, s. 14, c. 892; 1993, c. 539, ss. 78, 1188; 1994, Ex. Sess., c. 24, s. 14(c).)

§ 14-137. Willfully or negligently setting fire to woods and fields.

If any person, firm or corporation shall willfully or negligently set on fire, or cause to be set on fire, any woods, lands or fields, whatsoever, every such offender shall be guilty of a Class 2 misdemeanor. This section shall apply only in those counties under the protection of the Department of Environment and Natural Resources in its work of forest fire control. It shall not apply in the case of a landowner firing, or causing to be fired, his own open, nonwooded lands, or fields in connection with farming or building operations at the time and in the manner now provided by law: Provided, he shall have confined the fire at his own expense to said open lands or fields. (1907, c. 320, ss. 4, 5; C.S., s. 4310; 1925, c. 61, s. 2; 1941, c. 258; 1973, c. 1262, s. 86; 1977, c. 771, s. 4; 1989, c. 727, s. 218(3); 1993, c. 539, s. 79; 1994, Ex. Sess., c. 24, s. 14(c); 1997-443, s. 11A.119(a).)

§ 14-138: Repealed by Session Laws 1994, Ex. Sess., c. 14, s. 72(6).

§ 14-138.1. Setting fire to grassland, brushland, or woodland.

Any person, firm, corporation, or other legal entity who shall in any manner whatsoever start any fire upon any grassland, brushland, or woodland without fully extinguishing the same, shall be guilty of a Class 3 misdemeanor which may include a fine of not less than ten dollars ($10.00) or more than fifty dollars ($50.00). For the purpose of this section, the term "woodland" includes timber and cutover land and all second growth stands on areas that were once cultivated. (1995, c. 210, s. 1.)

§ 14-139. Repealed by Session Laws 1981, c. 1100, s. 1.

§ 14-140: Repealed by Session Laws 1993 (Reg. Sess., 1994), c. 767, s. 30(3).

§ 14-140.1. Certain fire to be guarded by watchman.

Any person, firm, corporation, or other legal entity who shall burn any brush, grass, or other material whereby any property may be endangered or destroyed, without keeping and maintaining a careful watchman in charge of the burning, shall be guilty of a Class 3 misdemeanor which may include a fine of not less than ten dollars ($10.00) or more than fifty dollars ($50.00). Fire escaping from the brush, grass, or other material while burning shall be prima facie evidence of violation of this provision. (1995, c. 210, s. 2.)

§ 14-141. Burning or otherwise destroying crops in the field.

Any person who shall willfully burn or destroy any other person's lawfully grown crop, pasture, or provender shall be punished as follows:

(1)   If the damage is two thousand dollars ($2,000) or less, the person is guilty of a Class 1 misdemeanor.

(2)   If the damage is more than two thousand dollars ($2,000), the person is guilty of a Class I felony. (1874-5, c. 133; Code, s. 985, subsec. 2; 1885, c. 42; Rev., s. 3339; C.S., s. 4313; 1979, c. 760, s. 5; 1979, 2nd Sess., c. 1316, s. 47; 1981, c. 63, s. 1, c. 179, s. 14; 1991, c. 534; 1993, c. 539, s. 81; 1994, Ex. Sess., c. 24, s. 14(c).)

§ 14-142. Injuries to dams and water channels of mills and factories.

If any person shall cut away, destroy or otherwise injure any dam, or part thereof, or shall obstruct or damage any race, canal or other water channel erected, opened, used or constructed for the purpose of furnishing water for the operation of any mill, factory or machine works, or for the escape of water therefrom, he shall be guilty of a Class 2 misdemeanor. (1866, c. 48; Code, s.

1087; Rev., s. 3678; C.S., s. 4315; 1969, c. 1224, s. 13; 1993, c. 539, s. 82; 1994, Ex. Sess., c. 24, s. 14(c).)

§ 14-143. Repealed by Session Laws 1987, c. 700, s. 2.

§ 14-144. Injuring houses, churches, fences and walls.

If any person shall, by any other means than burning or attempting to burn, unlawfully and willfully demolish, destroy, deface, injure or damage any of the houses or other buildings mentioned in Article 15 (Arson and Other Burnings) of this Chapter; or shall by any other means than burning or attempting to burn unlawfully and willfully demolish, pull down, destroy, deface, damage or injure any church, uninhabited house, outhouse or other house or building not mentioned in such article; or shall unlawfully and willfully burn, destroy, pull down, injure or remove any fence, wall or other enclosure, or any part thereof, surrounding or about any yard, garden, cultivated field or pasture, or about any church or graveyard, or about any factory or other house in which machinery is used, every person so offending shall be punished as follows:

(1)   If the damage is five thousand dollars ($5,000) or less, the person is guilty of a Class 2 misdemeanor.

(2)   If the damage is more than five thousand dollars ($5,000), the person is guilty of a Class I felony. (R.C., c. 34, s. 103; Code, s. 1062; Rev., s. 3673; C.S., s. 4317; 1957, c. 250, s. 2; 1969, c. 1224, s. 1; 1993, c. 539, s. 83; 1994, Ex. Sess., c. 24, s. 14(c); 2008-15, s. 1; 2009-570, s. 3.)

§ 14-145. Unlawful posting of advertisements.

Any person who in any manner paints, prints, places, or affixes, or causes to be painted, printed, placed, or affixed, any business or commercial advertisement on or to any stone, tree, fence, stump, pole, automobile, building, or other object, which is the property of another without first obtaining the written consent of such owner thereof, or who in any manner paints, prints, places, puts, or affixes, or causes to be painted, printed, placed, or affixed, such an advertisement on or to any stone, tree, fence, stump, pole, mile-board, milestone, danger-sign, danger-signal, guide-sign, guide-post, automobile, building or other object within the limits of a public highway, shall be guilty of a Class 3 misdemeanor. (Ex. Sess. 1924, c. 109; 1993, c. 539, s. 84; 1994, Ex. Sess., c. 24, s. 14(c).)

§ 14-146. Injuring bridges.

If any person shall unlawfully and willfully demolish, destroy, break, tear down, injure or damage any bridge across any of the creeks or rivers or other streams in the State, he shall be guilty of a Class 1 misdemeanor. (1883, c. 271; Code, s. 993; Rev., s. 3771; C.S., s. 4318; 1993, c. 539, s. 85; 1994, Ex. Sess., c. 24, s. 14(c).)

§ 14-147. Removing, altering or defacing landmarks.

If any person, firm or corporation shall knowingly remove, alter or deface any landmark in anywise whatsoever, or shall knowingly cause such removal, alteration or defacement to be done, such person, firm or corporation shall be guilty of a Class 2 misdemeanor. This section shall not apply to landmarks, such as creeks and other small streams, which the interest of agriculture may require to be altered or turned from their channels, nor to such persons, firms or corporations as own the fee simple in the lands on both sides of the lines designated by the landmarks removed, altered or defaced. Nor shall this section apply to those adjoining landowners who may by agreement remove, alter or deface landmarks in which they alone are interested. (1858-9, c. 17; Code, s. 1063; Rev., s. 3674; 1915, c. 248; C.S., s. 4319; 1993, c. 539, s. 86; 1994, Ex. Sess., c. 24, s. 14(c).)

§ 14-148. Defacing or desecrating grave sites.

(a)   It is unlawful to willfully:

(1)   Throw, place or put any refuse, garbage or trash in or on any cemetery.

(2)   Take away, disturb, vandalize, destroy or change the location of any stone, brick, iron or other material or fence enclosing a cemetery without

authorization of law or consent of the surviving spouse or next of kin of the deceased.

(3) Take away, disturb, vandalize, destroy, or tamper with any shrubbery, flowers, plants or other articles planted or placed within any cemetery to designate where human remains are interred or to preserve and perpetuate the memory and name of any person, without authorization of law or the consent of the surviving spouse or next of kin.

(b) The provisions of this section shall not apply to:

(1) Ordinary maintenance and care of a cemetery by the owner, caretaker, or other person acting to facilitate cemetery operations by keeping the cemetery free from accumulated debris or other signs of neglect.

(2) Conduct that is punishable under G.S. 14-149.

(3) A professional archaeologist as defined in G.S. 70-28(4) acting pursuant to the provisions of Article 3 of Chapter 70 of the General Statutes.

(c) Violation of this section is a Class I felony if the damage caused by the violation is one thousand dollars ($1,000) or more. Any other violation of this section is a Class 1 misdemeanor. In passing sentence, the court shall consider the appropriateness of restitution or reparation as a condition of probation under G.S. 15A-1343(b)(9) as an alternative to actual imposition of a fine, jail term, or both. (1840, c. 6; R.C., c. 34, s. 102; Code, s. 1088; Rev., s. 3680; C.S., s. 4320; 1969, c. 987; 1981, c. 752, s. 1; c. 853, s. 4; 1993, c. 539, s. 87; 1994, Ex. Sess., c. 24, s. 14(c); 2007-122, s. 1.)

§ 14-149. Desecrating, plowing over or covering up graves; desecrating human remains.

(a) It is a Class I felony, without authorization of law or the consent of the surviving spouse or next of kin of the deceased, to knowingly and willfully:

(1) Open, disturb, destroy, remove, vandalize or desecrate any casket or other repository of any human remains, by any means including plowing under, tearing up, covering over or otherwise obliterating or removing any grave or any portion thereof.

(2) Take away, disturb, vandalize, destroy, tamper with, or deface any tombstone, headstone, monument, grave marker, grave ornamentation, or grave artifacts erected or placed within any cemetery to designate the place where human remains are interred or to preserve and perpetuate the memory and the name of any person. This subdivision shall not apply to the ordinary maintenance and care of a cemetery.

(3) Repealed by Session Laws 2007-122, s. 2, effective December 1, 2007, and applicable to offenses committed on or after that date.

(a1) It is a Class H felony, without authorization of law or the consent of the surviving spouse or next of kin of the deceased, to knowingly and willfully disturb, destroy, remove, vandalize, or desecrate any human remains that have been interred in a cemetery.

(b) The provisions of this section shall not apply to a professional archaeologist as defined in G.S. 70-28(4) acting pursuant to the provisions of Article 3 of Chapter 70 of the General Statutes. (1889, c. 130; Rev., s. 3681; 1919, c. 218; C.S., s. 4321; 1981, c. 752, s. 2; c. 853, s. 5; 2007-122, s. 2.)

§§ 14-150 through 14-150.1. Repealed by Session Laws 1981, c. 752, s. 3, effective October 1, 1981.

§ 14-151. Interfering with gas, electric and steam appliances or meters; penalties.

(a) It shall be unlawful for any person to willfully, with intent to injure or defraud, commit any of the following acts:

(1) Connect a tube, pipe, wire or other instrument or contrivance with a pipe or wire used for conducting or supplying illuminating gas, fuel, natural gas or electricity in such a manner as to supply such gas or electricity to any burner, orifice, lamp or motor where the same is or can be burned or used without passing through the meter or other instrument provided for registering the quantity consumed.

(2) Obstruct, alter, bypass, tamper with, injure or prevent the action of a meter or other instrument used to measure or register the quantity of illuminating fuel, natural gas, water, or electricity passing through such meter by a person other than an employee of the company owning or supplying any gas, water, or electric meter, who willfully shall detach or disconnect such meter, or

make or report any test of, or examine for the purpose of testing any meter so detached or disconnected.

(3)   In any manner whatever change, extend or alter any service or other pipe, wire or attachment of any kind, connecting with or through which natural or artificial gas or electricity is furnished from the gas mains or pipes of any person, without first procuring from said person written permission to make such change, extension or alterations.

(4)   Make any connection or reconnection with the gas mains, water pipes, service pipes or wires of any person, furnishing to consumers natural or artificial gas, water, or electricity, or turn on or off or in any manner interfere with any valve or stopcock or other appliance belonging to such person, and connected with his service or other pipes or wires, or enlarge the orifices of mixers, or use natural gas for heating purposes except through mixers, or electricity for any purpose without first procuring from such person a written permit to turn on or off such stopcock or valve, or to make such connection or reconnections, or to enlarge the orifice of mixers, or to use for heating purposes without mixers, or to interfere with the valves, stopcocks, wires or other appliances of such, as the case may be.

(5)   Retain possession of or refuse to deliver any mixer, meter, lamp or other appliance which may be leased or rented by any person, for the purpose of furnishing gas, water, electricity or power through the same, or sell, lend or in any other manner dispose of the same to any person other than such person entitled to the possession of the same.

(6)   Set on fire any gas escaping from wells, broken or leaking mains, pipes, valves or other appliances used by any person in conveying gas to consumers, or interfere in any manner with the wells, pipes, mains, gateboxes, valves, stopcocks, wires, cables, conduits or any other appliances, machinery or property of any person engaged in furnishing gas to consumers unless employed by or acting under the authority and direction of such person.

(7)   Open or cause to be opened, or reconnect or cause to be reconnected any valve lawfully closed or disconnected by a district steam corporation.

(8)   Turn on steam or cause it to be turned on or to reenter any premises when the same has been lawfully stopped from entering such premises.

(9) Reconnect electricity, gas, or water connections or otherwise turn back on one or more of those utilities when they have been lawfully disconnected or turned off by the provider of the utility.

(10) Alter, bypass, interfere with, or cut off any load management device, equipment, or system which has been installed by the electricity supplier for the purpose of limiting the use of electricity at peak-load periods, provided, however, if there has been a written request to remove the load management device, equipment, or system to the electric supplier and the electric supplier has not removed the device within two working days, there shall be no violation of this section.

(b) Any meter or service entrance facility found to have been altered, tampered with, or bypassed in a manner that would cause such meter to inaccurately measure and register the electricity, gas, or water consumed or which would cause the electricity, gas, or water to be diverted from the recording apparatus of the meter shall be prima facie evidence of intent to violate and of the violation of this section by the person in whose name such meter is installed or the person or persons so using or receiving the benefits of such unmetered, unregistered, or diverted electricity, gas, or water.

(c) For the purposes of this section, the term "gas" shall mean all types and forms of gas, including, but not limited to, natural gas.

(d) Criminal violations of this section shall be punishable as follows:

(1) A violation of this section is a Class 1 misdemeanor.

(2) A second or subsequent violation of this section is a Class H felony.

(3) A violation of this section that results in significant property damage or public endangerment is a Class F felony.

(4) Unless the conduct is covered under some other provision of law providing greater punishment, a violation that results in the death of another is a Class D felony.

(e) [Whoever is found in a civil action to have violated any provision] of this section [shall be liable to the electric, gas or water supplier in triple the amount of losses and damages sustained or five] thousand [dollars] ($5,000), [whichever is greater].

(f) Nothing in this section shall be construed to apply to licensed contractors while performing usual and ordinary services in accordance with recognized customs and standards. (1901, c. 735; Rev., s. 3666; C.S., s. 4323; 1993, c. 539, s. 88; 1994, Ex. Sess., c. 24, s. 14(c); 2013-88, s. 1.)

§ 14-151.1: Repealed by Session Laws 2013-88, s. 2, effective December 1, 2013, and applicable to offenses committed on or after that date.

§ 14-152. Injuring fixtures and other property of gas companies; civil liability.

If any person shall willfully, wantonly or maliciously remove, obstruct, injure or destroy any part of the plant, machinery, fixtures, structures or buildings, or anything appertaining to the works of any gas company, or shall use, tamper or interfere with the same, he shall be deemed guilty of a Class 3 misdemeanor. Such person shall also forfeit and pay to the company so injured, to be sued for and recovered in a civil action, double the amount of the damages sustained by any such injury. (1889 (Pr.), c. 35, s. 3; Rev., s. 3671; C.S., s. 4324; 1993, c. 539, s. 90; 1994, Ex. Sess., c. 24, s. 14(c).)

§ 14-153. Tampering with engines and boilers.

If any person shall willfully turn out water from any boiler or turn the bolts of any engine or boiler, or meddle or tamper with such boiler or engine, or any other machinery in connection with any boiler or engine, causing loss, damage, danger or delay to the owner in the prosecution of his work, he shall be guilty of a Class 2 misdemeanor. (1901, c. 733; Rev., s. 3667; C.S., s. 4325; 1993, c. 539, s. 91; 1994, Ex. Sess., c. 24, s. 14(c).)

§ 14-154. Injuring wires and other fixtures of telephone, telegraph, and electric-power companies.

If any person shall willfully injure, destroy or pull down any telegraph, telephone, cable telecommunications, or electric-power-transmission pedestal or pole, or any telegraph, telephone, cable telecommunications, or electric power line, wire or fiber insulator, power supply, transformer, transmission or other apparatus, equipment or fixture used in the transmission of telegraph, telephone, cable telecommunications, or electrical power service or any equipment related to wireless communications regulated by the Federal Communications Commission, that person shall be guilty of a Class I Felony. (1881, c. 4; 1883, c. 103; Code, s. 1118; Rev., s. 3847; 1907, c. 827, s. 1; C.S., s. 4326; 1993, c. 539, s. 92; 1994, Ex. Sess., c. 24, s. 14(c); 2007-301, s. 2.)

§ 14-155. Unauthorized connections with telephone or telegraph.

It shall be unlawful for any person to tap or make any connection with any wire or apparatus of any telephone or telegraph company operating in this State, except such connection as may be authorized by the person or corporation operating such wire or apparatus. Any person violating this section shall be guilty of a Class 3 misdemeanor. Each day's continuance of such unlawful connection shall be a separate offense. No connection approved by the Federal Communications Commission or the North Carolina Utilities Commission shall be a violation of this section. (1911, c. 113; C.S., s. 4327; 1973, c. 648; 1977, 2nd Sess., c. 1185, s. 2; 1993, c. 539, s. 93; 1994, Ex. Sess., c. 24, s. 14(c).)

§ 14-156. Injuring fixtures and other property of electric-power companies.

It shall be unlawful for any person willfully and wantonly, and without the consent of the owner, to take down, remove, injure, obstruct, displace or destroy any line erected or constructed for the transmission of electrical current, or any poles, towers, wires, conduits, cables, insulators or any support upon which wires or cables may be suspended, or any part of any such line or appurtenances or apparatus connected therewith, or to sever any wire or cable thereof, or in any manner to interrupt the transmission of electrical current over and along any such line, or to take down, remove, injure or destroy any house, shop, building or other structure or machinery connected with or necessary to the use of any line erected or constructed for the transmission of electrical current, or to wantonly or willfully cause injury to any of the property mentioned in this section by means of fire. Any person violating any of the provisions of this section shall be guilty of a Class 2 misdemeanor. (1907, c. 919; C.S., s. 4328; 1993, c. 539, s. 94; 1994, Ex. Sess., c. 24, s. 14(c).)

§ 14-157. Felling trees on telephone and electric-power wires.

If any person shall negligently and carelessly cut or fell any tree, or any limb or branch therefrom, in such a manner as to cause the same to fall upon and across any telephone, electric light or electric-power-transmission wire, from which any injury to such wire shall be occasioned, he shall be guilty of a Class 3 misdemeanor, and shall also be liable to penalty of fifty dollars ($50.00) for each and every offense. (1903, c. 616; Rev., s. 3849; 1907, c. 827, s. 2; C.S., s. 4329; 1969, c. 1224, s. 9; 1993, c. 539, s. 95; 1994, Ex. Sess., c. 24, s. 14(c).)

§ 14-158. Interfering with telephone lines.

If any person shall unnecessarily disconnect the wire or in any other way render any telephone line, or any part of such line, unfit for use in transmitting messages, or shall unnecessarily cut, tear down, destroy or in any way render unfit for the transmission of messages any part of the wire of a telephone line, he shall be guilty of a Class 2 misdemeanor. (1901, c. 318; Rev., s. 3845; C.S., s. 4330; 1969, c. 1224, s. 3; 1993, c. 539, s. 96; 1994, Ex. Sess., c. 24, s. 14(c).)

§ 14-159. Injuring buildings or fences; taking possession of house without consent.

If any person shall deface, injure or damage any house, uninhabited house or other building belonging to another; or deface, damage, pull down, injure, remove or destroy any fence or wall enclosing, in whole or in part, the premises belonging to another; or shall move into, take possession of and/or occupy any house, uninhabited house or other building situated on the premises belonging to another, without having first obtained authority so to do and consent of the owner or agent thereof, he shall be guilty of a Class 3 misdemeanor. (1929, c. 192, s. 1; 1993, c. 539, s. 97; 1994, Ex. Sess., c. 24, s. 14(c).)

§ 14-159.1. Contaminating a public water system.

(a) A person commits the offense of contaminating a public water system, as defined in G.S. 130A-313(10), if he willfully or wantonly:

(1) Contaminates, adulterates or otherwise impurifies or attempts to contaminate, adulterate or otherwise impurify the water in a public water system, including the water source, with any toxic chemical, biological agent or radiological substance that is harmful to human health, except those added in approved concentrations for water treatment operations; or

(2) Damages or tampers with the property or equipment of a public water system with the intent to impair the services of the public water system.

(b) Any person who commits the offense defined in this section is guilty of a Class C felony. (1983, c. 507, s. 1; 1985, c. 509, s. 4, c. 689, s. 5; 1993, c. 539, s. 1189; 1994, Ex. Sess., c. 24, s. 14(c).)

§ 14-159.2. Interference with animal research.

(a) It is unlawful for a person willfully to commit any of the following acts:

(1) The unauthorized entry into any research facility where animals are kept within the facility for research in the advancement of medical, veterinary, dental, or biological sciences, with the intent to (i) disrupt the normal operation of the research facility, or (ii) damage the research facility or any personal property located thereon, or (iii) release from any enclosure or restraining device any animal kept within the research facility, or (iv) interfere with the care of any animal kept within the research facility;

(2) The damaging of any such research facility or any personal property located thereon;

(3) The unauthorized release from any enclosure or restraining device of any animal kept within any research facility; or

(4) The interference with the care of any animal kept within any research facility.

(b) Any person who commits an offense under subsection (a) of this section shall be guilty of a Class 1 misdemeanor.

(c) Any person who commits an offense under subsection (a) of this section that involves the release from any enclosure or restraining device of any animal having an infectious disease shall be guilty of a Class I felony.

(d) As a condition of probation, the court may order a person convicted under this section to make restitution to the owner of the animal for damages, including the cost of restoring the animal to confinement and of restoring the animal to its health condition prior to any release, and for damages to personal property, including materials, equipment, data, and records, and real property caused by the interference. If the interference causes the failure of an experiment, the restitution may include all costs of repeating the experiment, including replacement of the animals, labor, and materials.

(e) Nothing in this section shall be construed to affect any rights or causes of action of a person damaged through interference with animal research. (1991, c. 203; 1993, c. 539, ss. 98, 1190; 1994, Ex. Sess., c. 24, s. 14(c).)

§ 14-159.3. Trespass to land on motorized all terrain vehicle.

(a) No person shall operate any motorized all terrain vehicle:

(1) On any private property not owned by the operator, without the consent of the owner; or

(2) Within the banks of any stream or waterway, but excluding a sound or the Atlantic Ocean, the adjacent lands of which are not owned by the operator, without the consent of the owner or outside the restrictions imposed by the owner.

(b) A "motorized all terrain vehicle", as used in this section, is a two or more wheeled vehicle designed for recreational off-road use.

(c) A violation of this section shall be a Class 2 misdemeanor. (1997-456, s. 56.8; 1997-487, s. 1.)

§ 14-159.4. Cutting, mutilating, defacing, or otherwise injuring property to obtain nonferrous metals.

(a) Definition of Nonferrous Metals. - For purposes of this section, the term "nonferrous metals" means metals not containing significant quantities of iron or steel, including, but not limited to, copper wire, copper clad steel wire, copper pipe, copper bars, copper sheeting, aluminum other than aluminum cans, a product that is a mixture of aluminum and copper, catalytic converters, lead-acid batteries, and stainless steel beer kegs or containers.

(b) Prohibited Act. - It is unlawful for a person to willfully and wantonly cut, mutilate, deface, or otherwise injure any personal or real property of another, including any fixtures or improvements, for the purpose of obtaining nonferrous metals in any amount.

(c) Punishment. - Violations of this section are punishable as follows:

(1) Default. - If the direct injury is to property, and the amount of loss in value to the property, the amount of repairs necessary to return the property to its condition before the act, or the property loss (including fixtures or improvements) is less than one thousand dollars ($1,000), a violation shall be punishable as a Class 1 misdemeanor. If the applicable amount is one thousand dollars ($1,000) or more, but less than ten thousand dollars ($10,000), a violation shall be punishable as a Class H felony. If the applicable amount is ten thousand dollars ($10,000) or more, a violation shall be deemed an aggravated offense and shall be punishable as a Class F felony.

(2) When person suffers serious injury. - Unless the conduct is covered under some other provision of law providing greater punishment, a violation of this section that results in a serious injury to another person is punishable as a Class A1 misdemeanor.

(3) When person suffers a serious bodily injury. - Unless the conduct is covered under some other provision of law providing greater punishment, a violation of this section that results in serious bodily injury to another person is punishable as a Class F felony. For purposes of this subdivision, "serious bodily injury" is as defined in G.S. 14-32.4.

(4) When person is killed. - Unless the conduct is covered under some other provision of law providing greater punishment, a violation of this section that results in the death of another person is punishable as a Class D felony.

(5) When critical infrastructure affected. - Unless the conduct is covered under some other provision of law providing greater punishment, a violation of

this section that results in the disruption of communication or electrical service to critical infrastructure or to more than 10 customers of the communication or electrical service is guilty of a Class 1 misdemeanor.

(d) Liability. - This section does not create or impose a duty of care upon the owner of personal or real property that would not otherwise exist under common law. A public or private owner of personal or real property shall not be civilly liable:

(1) To a person who is injured while committing or attempting to commit a violation of this section.

(2) To a person who is injured while a third party is committing or attempting to commit a violation of this section.

(3) For a person's injuries caused by a dangerous condition created as a result of a violation of this section, when the owner does not know and could not have reasonably known of the dangerous condition. (2012-46, s. 31.)

§ 14-159.5: Reserved for future codification purposes.

Article 22A.

Trespassing upon "Posted" Property to Hunt, Fish, Trap, or Remove Pine Needles/Straw.

§ 14-159.6. Trespass for purposes of hunting, etc., without written consent a misdemeanor; defense.

(a) Any person who willfully goes on the land, waters, ponds, or a legally established waterfowl blind of another that has been posted in accordance with the provisions of G.S. 14-159.7, to hunt, fish or trap without written permission of the landowner, lessee, or his agent shall be guilty of a Class 2 misdemeanor. Written permission shall be carried on one's person, signed by the landowner, lessee, or agent, and dated within the last 12 months. The written permission shall be displayed upon request of any law enforcement officer of the Wildlife Resources Commission, sheriff or deputy sheriff, or other law enforcement officer with general subject matter jurisdiction. A person shall have written permission for purposes of this section if a landowner, lessee, or agent has granted permission to a club to hunt, fish, or trap on the land and the person is carrying both a current membership card demonstrating the person's membership in the club and a copy of written permission granted to the club that complies with the requirements of this section.

(b)   Any person who willfully goes on the land of another that has been posted in accordance with the provisions of G.S. 14-159.7(1), to rake or remove pine needles or pine straw without the written consent of the owner or his agent shall be guilty of a Class 1 misdemeanor.

(c)   It is an affirmative defense to a prosecution under subsection (a) or (b) of this section that the person had in fact obtained prior permission of the owner, lessee, or agent as required by those subsections but did not have on his or her person valid written permission at the time of citation or arrest. (1949, c. 887, s. 1; 1953, c. 1226; 1965, c. 1134; 1975, c. 280, s. 1; 1979, c. 830, s. 11; 1991, c. 435, s. 4; 1993, c. 539, s. 99; 1994, Ex. Sess., c. 24, s. 14(c); 1997-443, s. 19.25(z); 2011-231, s. 1.)

§ 14-159.7. Regulations as to posting of property.

For purposes of posting property under G.S. 14-159.7, the owner or lessee of the property may use either of the following methods:

(1)   The owner or lessee of the property may place notices, signs, or posters on the property. The notices, signs or posters shall measure not less than 120 square inches and shall be conspicuously posted on private lands not more than 200 yards apart close to and along the boundaries. At least one such notice, sign, or poster shall be posted on each side of such land, and one at each corner thereof, provided that said corner can be reasonably ascertained. For the purpose of prohibiting fishing, or the taking of fish by any means, in any stream, lake, or pond, it shall only be necessary that the signs, notices, or posters be posted along the stream or shoreline of a pond or lake at intervals of not more than 200 yards apart.

(2)   The owner or lessee of the property may place identifying purple paint marks on trees or posts around the area to be posted. Each paint mark shall be a vertical line of at least eight inches in length, and the bottom of the mark shall be no less than three feet nor more than five feet from the base of the tree or

post. The paint marks shall be placed no more than 100 yards apart and shall be readily visible to any person approaching the property. For the purpose of prohibiting fishing, or the taking of fish by any means, in any stream, lake, or pond, it shall only be necessary that the paint marks be placed along the stream or shoreline of a pond or lake at intervals of not more than 100 yards apart. (1949, c. 887, s. 2; 1953, c. 1226; 1965, c. 923; 1975, c. 280, ss. 2, 3; 1979, c. 830, s. 11; 2011-231, s. 2.)

§ 14-159.8. Mutilation, etc., of "posted" signs; posting signs without consent of owner or agent.

Any person who shall mutilate, destroy or take down any "posted," "no hunting" or similar notice, sign or poster on the lands, waters, or legally established waterfowl blind of another, or who shall post such sign or poster on the lands, waters or legally established waterfowl blind of another, without the consent of the owner or his agent, shall be deemed guilty of a Class 3 misdemeanor and only punished by a fine of not more than one hundred dollars ($100.00). (1949, c. 887, s. 3; 1953, c. 1226; 1969, c. 51; 1979, c. 830, s. 11; 1993, c. 539, s. 100; 1994, Ex. Sess., c. 24, s. 14(c).)

§ 14-159.9. Entrance on navigable waters, etc., for purpose of fishing, hunting or trapping not prohibited.

Nothing in this Article shall be construed to prohibit the entrance of any person upon navigable waters and the bays and sounds adjoining such waters for the purpose of fishing, hunting or trapping. (1949, c. 887, s. 4; 1953, c. 1226; 1979, c. 830, s. 11.)

§ 14-159.10. Enforcement of Article.

This Article may be enforced by sheriffs or deputy sheriffs, law enforcement officers of the Wildlife Resources Commission, and other peace officers with general subject matter jurisdiction. (1979, c. 830, s. 11; 2011-231, s. 3.)

Article 22B.

First and Second Degree Trespass.

§ 14-159.11. Definition.

As used in this Article, "building" means any structure or part of a structure, other than a conveyance, enclosed so as to permit reasonable entry only through a door and roofed to protect it from the elements. (1987, c. 700, s. 1.)

§ 14-159.12. First degree trespass.

(a) Offense. - A person commits the offense of first degree trespass if, without authorization, he enters or remains:

(1) On premises of another so enclosed or secured as to demonstrate clearly an intent to keep out intruders; or

(2) In a building of another.

(b) Except as otherwise provided in subsection (c) or (d) of this section, first degree trespass is a Class 2 misdemeanor.

(c) Except as otherwise provided in subsection (d) of this section, a violation of subsection (a) of this section is a Class A1 misdemeanor if all of the following circumstances exist:

(1) The offense is committed on the premises of any of the following:

a. A facility that is owned or operated by an electric power supplier as defined in G.S. 62-133.8(a)(3) and that is either an electric generation facility, a transmission substation, a transmission switching station, a transmission switching structure, or a control center used to manage transmission operations or electrical power generating at multiple plant locations.

b. Any facility used or available for use in the collection, treatment, testing, storing, pumping, or distribution of water for a public water system.

c. Any facility, including any liquefied natural gas storage facility or propane air facility, that is owned or operated by a natural gas local distribution company, natural gas pipeline carrier operating under a certificate of public convenience and necessity from the Utilities Commission, municipal corporation operating a municipally owned gas distribution system, or regional natural gas district organized and operated pursuant to Article 28 of Chapter 160A of the General Statutes used for transmission, distribution, measurement, testing, regulating, compression, control, or storage of natural gas.

(2) The person actually entered a building, or it was necessary for the person to climb over, go under, or otherwise surmount a fence or other barrier to reach the facility.

(d) If, in addition to the circumstances set out in subsection (c) of this section, the violation also includes any of the following elements, then the offense is a Class H felony:

(1) The offense is committed with the intent to disrupt the normal operation of any of the facilities described in subdivision (1) of subsection (c) of this section.

(2) The offense involves an act that places either the offender or others on the premises at risk of serious bodily injury.

(e) As used in subsections (c) and (d) of this section, the term "facility" shall mean a building or other infrastructure. (1987, c. 700, s. 1; 1993, c. 539, s. 101; 1994, Ex. Sess., c. 24, s. 14(c); 2012-168, s. 1.)

§ 14-159.13. Second degree trespass.

(a) Offense. - A person commits the offense of second degree trespass if, without authorization, he enters or remains on premises of another:

(1) After he has been notified not to enter or remain there by the owner, by a person in charge of the premises, by a lawful occupant, or by another authorized person; or

(2) That are posted, in a manner reasonably likely to come to the attention of intruders, with notice not to enter the premises.

(b)   Classification. - Second degree trespass is a Class 3 misdemeanor. (1987, c. 700, s. 1; 1993, c. 539, s. 102; 1994, Ex. Sess., c. 24, s. 14(c).)

§ 14-159.14. Lesser included offenses.

The offenses created by this act shall constitute lesser included offenses of breaking or entering as provided in G.S. 14-54 and G.S. 14-56. (1987, c. 700, s. 1.)

§§ 14-159.15 through 14-159.19. Reserved for future codification purposes.

Article 22C.

Cave Protection Act.

§ 14-159.20. Definitions.

The terms listed below have the following definitions as used in this Article, unless the context clearly requires a different meaning:

(1)   "Cave" means any naturally occurring subterranean cavity. The word "cave" includes or is synonymous with cavern, pit, well, sinkhole, and grotto;

(2)   "Commercial cave" means any cave with improved trails and lighting utilized by the owner for the purpose of exhibition to the general public as a profit or nonprofit enterprise, wherein a fee is collected for entry;

(3)   "Gate" means any structure or device located to limit or prohibit access or entry to any cave;

(4) "Person" means any individual, partnership, firm, association, trust or corporation;

(5) "Speleothem" means a natural mineral formation or deposit occurring in a cave. This includes or is synonymous with stalagmites, stalactites, helectites, anthodites, gypsum flowers, needles, angel's hair, soda straws, draperies, bacon, cave pearls, popcorn (coral), rimstone dams, columns, palettes, and flowstone. Speleothems are commonly composed of calcite, epsomite, gypsum, aragonite, celestite and other similar minerals; and

(6) "Owner" means a person who has title to land where a cave is located, including a person who owns title to a leasehold estate in such land. (1987, c. 449.)

§ 14-159.21. Vandalism; penalties.

It is unlawful for any person, without express, prior, written permission of the owner, to willfully or knowingly:

(1) Break, break off, crack, carve upon, write, burn or otherwise mark upon, remove, or in any manner destroy, disturb, deface, mar or harm the surfaces of any cave or any natural material therein, including speleothems;

(2) Disturb or alter in any manner the natural condition of any cave;

(3) Break, force, tamper with or otherwise disturb a lock, gate, door or other obstruction designed to control or prevent access to any cave, even though entrance thereto may not be gained.

Any person violating a provision of this section shall be guilty of a Class 3 misdemeanor. (1987, c. 449; 1993, c. 539, s. 103; 1994, Ex. Sess., c. 24, s. 14(c).)

§ 14-159.22. Sale of speleothems unlawful; penalties.

It is unlawful to sell or offer for sale any speleothems in this State, or to export them for sale outside the State. A person who violates any of the provisions of this section shall be guilty of a Class 3 misdemeanor. (1987, c. 449; 1993, c. 539, s. 104; 1994, Ex. Sess., c. 24, s. 14(c).)

§ 14-159.23. Limitation of liability of owners and agents.

The owner of a cave, and his agents and employees, shall not be liable for any injury to, or for the death of any person, or for any loss or damage to property, by reason of any act or omission unless it is established that the injury, death, loss, or damage occurred as a result of gross negligence, wanton conduct, or intentional wrongdoing. The limitation of liability provided by this section applies only with respect to injury, death, loss, or damage occurring within a cave, or in connection with entry into or exit from a cave, and applies only with respect to persons to whom no charge has been made for admission to the cave. (1987, c. 449.)

Article 23.

Trespasses to Personal Property.

§ 14-160. Willful and wanton injury to personal property; punishments.

(a) If any person shall wantonly and willfully injure the personal property of another he shall be guilty of a Class 2 misdemeanor.

(b) Notwithstanding the provisions of subsection (a), if any person shall wantonly and willfully injure the personal property of another, causing damage in an amount in excess of two hundred dollars ($200.00), he shall be guilty of a Class 1 misdemeanor.

(c) This section applies to injuries to personal property without regard to whether the property is destroyed or not. (1876-7, c. 18; Code, s. 1082; 1885, c. 53; Rev., s. 3676; C.S., s. 4331; 1969, c. 1224, s. 14; 1993, c. 539, s. 105; 1994, Ex. Sess., c. 24, s. 14(c).)

§ 14-160.1. Alteration, destruction or removal of permanent identification marks from personal property.

(a)   It shall be unlawful for any person to alter, deface, destroy or remove the permanent serial number, manufacturer's identification plate or other permanent, distinguishing number or identification mark from any item of personal property with the intent thereby to conceal or misrepresent the identity of said item.

(b)   It shall be unlawful for any person knowingly to sell, buy or be in possession of any item of personal property, not his own, on which the permanent serial number, manufacturer's identification plate or other permanent, distinguishing number or identification mark has been altered, defaced, destroyed or removed for the purpose of concealing or misrepresenting the identity of said item.

(c)   Unless the conduct is covered under some other provision of law providing greater punishment, a violation of any of the provisions of this section shall be a Class 1 misdemeanor.

(d)   This section shall not in any way affect the provisions of G.S. 20-108, 20-109(a) or 20-109(b). (1977, c. 767, s. 1; 1993, c. 539, s. 106; 1994, Ex. Sess., c. 24, s. 14(c); 2009-204, s. 1.)

§ 14-160.2. Alteration, destruction, or removal of serial number from firearm; possession of firearm with serial number removed.

(a)   It shall be unlawful for any person to alter, deface, destroy, or remove the permanent serial number, manufacturer's identification plate, or other permanent distinguishing number or identification mark from any firearm with the intent thereby to conceal or misrepresent the identity of the firearm.

(b)   It shall be unlawful for any person knowingly to sell, buy, or be in possession of any firearm on which the permanent serial number, manufacturer's identification plate, or other permanent distinguishing number or identification mark has been altered, defaced, destroyed, or removed for the purpose of concealing or misrepresenting the identity of the firearm.

(c) A violation of any of the provisions of this section shall be a Class H felony. (2009-204, s. 2.)

§ 14-161: Repealed by Session Laws 1994, Ex. Sess., c. 14, s. 72(7).

§ 14-162. Removing boats.

If any person shall loose, unmoor, or turn adrift from any landing or other place wherever the same shall be, any boat, canoe, or other marine vessel, or if any person shall direct the same to be done without the consent of the owner, or the person having the lawful custody or possession of such vessel, he shall be guilty of a Class 2 misdemeanor. The owner may also have his action for such injury. The penalties aforesaid shall not extend to any person who shall press any such property by public authority. (R.C., c. 14, ss. 1, 3; Code, s. 2288; 1889, c. 378; Rev., s. 3544; C.S., s. 4333; 1977, c. 729; 1993, c. 539, s. 107; 1994, Ex. Sess., c. 24, s. 14(c).)

§ 14-163. Poisoning livestock.

If any person shall willfully and unlawfully poison any horse, mule, hog, sheep or other livestock, the property of another, such person shall be punished as a Class I felon. (1898-9, c. 253; Code, s. 1003; Rev., s. 3313; C.S., s. 4334; 1969, c. 1224, s. 3; 1973, c. 1388; 1979, c. 760, s. 5; 1979, 2nd Sess., c. 1316, s. 47; 1981, c. 63, s. 1, c. 179, s. 14.)

§ 14-163.1. Assaulting a law enforcement agency animal, an assistance animal, or a search and rescue animal.

(a) The following definitions apply in this section:

(1) Assistance animal. - An animal that is trained and may be used to assist a "person with a disability" as defined in G.S. 168A-3. The term "assistance animal" is not limited to a dog and includes any animal trained to assist a person with a disability as provided in Article 1 of Chapter 168 of the General Statutes.

(2) Law enforcement agency animal. - An animal that is trained and may be used to assist a law enforcement officer in the performance of the officer's official duties.

(3) Harm. - Any injury, illness, or other physiological impairment; or any behavioral impairment that impedes or interferes with duties performed by a law enforcement agency animal or an assistance animal.

(3a) Search and rescue animal. - An animal that is trained and may be used to assist in a search and rescue operation.

(4) Serious harm. - Harm that does any of the following:

a. Creates a substantial risk of death.

b. Causes maiming or causes substantial loss or impairment of bodily function.

c. Causes acute pain of a duration that results in substantial suffering.

d. Requires retraining of the law enforcement agency animal or assistance animal.

e. Requires retirement of the law enforcement agency animal or assistance animal from performing duties.

(a1) Any person who knows or has reason to know that an animal is a law enforcement agency animal, an assistance animal, or a search and rescue animal and who willfully kills the animal is guilty of a Class H felony.

(b) Any person who knows or has reason to know that an animal is a law enforcement agency animal, an assistance animal, or a search and rescue animal and who willfully causes or attempts to cause serious harm to the animal is guilty of a Class I felony.

(c) Unless the conduct is covered under some other provision of law providing greater punishment, any person who knows or has reason to know that an animal is a law enforcement agency animal, an assistance animal, or a search and rescue animal and who willfully causes or attempts to cause harm to the animal is guilty of a Class 1 misdemeanor.

(d) Unless the conduct is covered under some other provision of law providing greater punishment, any person who knows or has reason to know that an animal is a law enforcement agency animal, an assistance animal, or a search and rescue animal and who willfully taunts, teases, harasses, delays, obstructs, or attempts to delay or obstruct the animal in the performance of its duty as a law enforcement agency animal, an assistance animal, or a search and rescue animal is guilty of a Class 2 misdemeanor.

(d1) A defendant convicted of a violation of this section shall be ordered to make restitution to the person with a disability, or to a person, group, or law enforcement agency who owns or is responsible for the care of the law enforcement agency animal or search and rescue animal for any of the following as appropriate:

(1) Veterinary, medical care, and boarding expenses for the law enforcement agency animal, the assistance animal, or the search and rescue animal.

(2) Medical expenses for the person with the disability relating to the harm inflicted upon the assistance animal.

(3) Replacement and training or retraining expenses for the law enforcement agency animal, the assistance animal, or the search and rescue animal.

(4) Expenses incurred to provide temporary mobility services to the person with a disability.

(5) Wages or income lost while the person with a disability is with the assistance animal receiving training or retraining.

(6) The salary of the law enforcement agency animal handler as a result of the lost services to the agency during the time the handler is with the law enforcement agency animal receiving training or retraining.

(6a) The salary of the search and rescue animal handler as a result of the search and rescue services lost during the time the handler is with the search and rescue animal receiving training or retraining.

(7) Any other expense reasonably incurred as a result of the offense.

(e) This section shall not apply to a licensed veterinarian whose conduct is in accordance with Article 11 of Chapter 90 of the General Statutes.

(f) Self-defense is an affirmative defense to a violation of this section.

(g) Nothing in this section shall affect any civil remedies available for violation of this section. (1983, c. 646, s. 1; 1993, c. 539, s. 108; 1994, Ex. Sess., c. 24, s. 14(c); 1995, c. 258, s. 1; 2001-411, s. 1; 2005-184, s. 1; 2007-80, s. 1; 2009-460, s. 1.)

§ 14-164: Repealed by Session Laws 1994, Ex. Sess., c. 14, s. 72(8).

Article 24.

Vehicles and Draft Animals-Protection of Bailor against Acts of Bailee.

§ 14-165. Malicious or willful injury to hired personal property.

Any person who shall rent or hire from any person, firm or corporation, any horse, mule or like animal, or any buggy, wagon, truck, automobile, or other like vehicle, aircraft, motor, trailer, appliance, equipment, tool, or other thing of value, who shall maliciously or willfully injure or damage the same by in any way using or driving the same in violation of any statute of the State of North Carolina, or who shall permit any other person so to do, shall be guilty of a Class 2 misdemeanor. (1927, c. 61, s. 1; 1965, c. 1073, s. 1; 1993, c. 539, s. 109; 1994, Ex. Sess., c. 24, s. 14(c).)

§ 14-166. Subletting of hired property.

Any person who shall rent or hire, any horse, mule, or other like animal, or any buggy, wagon, truck, automobile, or other like vehicle, aircraft, motor, trailer, appliance, equipment, tool, or other thing of value, who shall, without the permission of the person, firm or corporation from whom such property is rented or hired, sublet or rent the same to any other person, firm or corporation, shall be guilty of a Class 2 misdemeanor. (1927, c. 61, s. 2; 1965, c. 1073, s. 2; 1969, c. 1224, s. 15; 1993, c. 539, s. 110; 1994, Ex. Sess., c. 24, s. 14(c).)

§ 14-167. Failure to return hired property.

Any person who shall rent or hire, any horse, mule or other like animal, or any buggy, wagon, truck, automobile, or other vehicle, aircraft, motor, trailer, appliance, equipment, tool, or other thing of value, and who shall willfully fail to return the same to the possession of the person, firm or corporation from whom such property has been rented or hired at the expiration of the time for which such property has been rented or hired, shall be guilty of a Class 3 misdemeanor.

If the value at the time of the rental or hiring of the truck, automobile, or other motor vehicle that is not returned is in excess of four thousand dollars ($4,000), the person who rented or hired it and failed to return it shall be guilty of a Class H felony. (1927, c. 61, s. 3; 1965, c. 1073, s. 3; 1969, c. 1224, s. 15; 1993, c. 539, s. 111; 1994, Ex. Sess., c. 24, s. 14(c); 2005-182, s. 1; 2013-360, s. 18B.14(c).)

§ 14-168. Hiring with intent to defraud.

Any person who shall, with intent to cheat and defraud the owner thereof of the rental price therefor, hire or rent any horse or mule or any other like animal, or any buggy, wagon, truck, automobile or other like vehicle, aircraft, motor, trailer, appliance, equipment, tool, or other thing of value, or who shall obtain the possession of the same by false and fraudulent statements made with intent to deceive, which are calculated to deceive, and which do deceive, shall be guilty of a Class 2 misdemeanor. (1927, c. 61, s. 4; 1965, c. 1073, s. 4; 1969, c. 1224, s. 15; 1993, c. 539, s. 112; 1994, Ex. Sess., c. 24, s. 14(c).)

§ 14-168.1. Conversion by bailee, lessee, tenant or attorney-in-fact.

Every person entrusted with any property as bailee, lessee, tenant or lodger, or with any power of attorney for the sale or transfer thereof, who fraudulently converts the same, or the proceeds thereof, to his own use, or secretes it with a fraudulent intent to convert it to his own use, shall be guilty of a Class 3 misdemeanor.

If, however, the value of the property converted or secreted, or the proceeds thereof, is in excess of four hundred dollars ($400.00), every person so converting or secreting it is guilty of a Class H felony. In all cases of doubt the jury shall, in the verdict, fix the value of the property converted or secreted. (1965, c. 1073, s. 5; 1979, c. 468; 1979, 2nd Sess., c. 1316, s. 13; 1981, c. 63, s. 1; c. 179, s. 14; 1993, c. 539, s. 113; 1994, Ex. Sess., c. 24, s. 14(c); 2013-360, s. 18B.14(d).)

§ 14-168.2. Definitions.

For the purposes of this Article, the terms "rent," "hire" and "lease" are used to designate the letting for hire of any horse, mule or other like animal, or any buggy, wagon, truck, automobile, aircraft, motor, trailer, appliance, equipment, tool, or other thing of value by lease, bailment, or rental agreement. (1965, c. 1073, s. 5.)

§ 14-168.3. Prima facie evidence of intent to convert property.

It shall be prima facie evidence of intent to commit a crime as set forth in G.S. 14-167, 14-168, and 14-168.1 with respect to any property other than a truck, automobile, or other motor vehicle when one who has, by written instrument, leased or rented the personal property of another:

(1)   Failed or refused to return such property to its owner after the lease, bailment, or rental agreement has expired,

a.   Within 10 days, and

b.   Within 48 hours after written demand for return thereof is personally served or given by registered mail delivered to the last known address provided in such lease or rental agreement, or

(2)   When the leasing or rental of such personal property is obtained by presentation of identification to the lessor or rentor thereof which is false, fictitious, or knowingly not current as to name, address, place of employment, or other identification. (1965, c. 1118; 2005-182, s. 2.)

§ 14-168.4. Failing to return rented property on which there is purchase option.

(a) It shall be a Class 3 misdemeanor for any person to fail to return rented property with intent to defeat the rights of the owner, which is rented pursuant to a written rental agreement in which there is an option to purchase the property, after the date of termination provided in the agreement has occurred or, if the termination date is the occurrence of a specified event, then that such event has in fact occurred.

(b) Intent to commit the crime set forth in subsection (a) may be presumed from the following evidence:

(1) Evidence that the defendant has disposed of the property, or has encumbered the property by allowing a security interest to be placed on the property or by delivering the property to a pawnbroker; or

(2) Evidence that the defendant has refused to deliver the property to the sheriff or other officer charged with the execution of process directed to him for its seizure, after a judgment for possession of the property or a claim and delivery order for the property has been issued; or

(3) Evidence that the defendant has moved the rented property out of state and has failed to notify the owner of the new location of the property.

However, this presumption may be rebutted by evidence from the defendant that he has no intent to defeat the rights of the owner of the property.

(c) Violations of this Article for failure to return rented property which is rented pursuant to a written rental agreement in which there is an option to purchase shall be prosecuted only under this section. (1987 (Reg. Sess., 1988), c. 1065, s. 3; 1993, c. 539, s. 114; 1994, Ex. Sess., c. 24, s. 14(c); 2013-360, s. 18B.14(e).)

§ 14-168.5. Prima facie evidence of intent to convert a truck, automobile, or other motor vehicle; demand for return or payment.

(a) Prima Facie Evidence. - It shall be prima facie evidence of intent to commit a crime as set forth in G.S. 14-167, 14-168, and 14-168.1 when one who has, by written instrument, leased or rented a truck, automobile, or other motor vehicle owned by another:

(1) Failed or refused to return the vehicle to the lessor or rentor at the place specified after the lease, bailment, or rental agreement has expired, within 72 hours after written demand for the vehicle is made in accordance with subsection (b) of this section; or

(2) When the leasing or rental of the vehicle is obtained by presentation of identification to the lessor or rentor of the vehicle which is false, fictitious, or knowingly not current as to name, address, place of employment, or other identification.

(b) Method of Demand; When Effective. -

(1) Demand for return of a leased or rented truck, automobile, or other motor vehicle may be made in one of three ways:

a. By personal service in accordance with Rule 4(j) of the North Carolina Rules of Civil Procedure.

b. By certified mail, return receipt requested, addressed to the last known address provided in the lease, bailment, or rental agreement.

c. By depositing the demand with a designated delivery service authorized pursuant to 26 U.S.C. § 7502(f)(2) addressed to the last known address provided in the lease, bailment, or rental agreement.

(2) Demand is effective upon hand delivery to the last known address, three days after deposit by mail (even if the demand is returned as undeliverable), or upon delivery by a designated delivery service to the last known address. (2005-182, s. 3.)

§ 14-169. Violation made misdemeanor.

Except as otherwise provided, any person violating the provisions of this Article shall be guilty of a Class 1 misdemeanor. (1927, c. 61, s. 5; 1929, c. 38, s. 1; 1969, c. 1224, s. 15; 1993, c. 539, s. 115; 1994, Ex. Sess., c. 24, s. 14(c).)

Article 25.

Regulating the Leasing of Storage Batteries.

§§ 14-170 through 14-176: Repealed by Session Laws 1993 (Reg. Sess., 1994), c. 767, s. 30(4)-(10).

SUBCHAPTER VII. OFFENSES AGAINST PUBLIC MORALITY AND DECENCY.

Article 26.

Offenses against Public Morality and Decency.

§ 14-177. Crime against nature.

If any person shall commit the crime against nature, with mankind or beast, he shall be punished as a Class I felon. (5 Eliz., c. 17; 25 Hen. VIII, c. 6; R.C., c. 34, s. 6; 1868-9, c. 167, s. 6; Code, s. 1010; Rev., s. 3349; C.S., s. 4336; 1965, c. 621, s. 4; 1979, c. 760, s. 5; 1979, 2nd Sess., c. 1316, s. 47; 1981, c. 63, s. 1, c. 179, s. 14; 1993, c. 539, s. 1191; 1994, Ex. Sess., c. 24, s. 14(c).)

§ 14-178. Incest.

(a) Offense. - A person commits the offense of incest if the person engages in carnal intercourse with the person's (i) grandparent or grandchild, (ii) parent or child or stepchild or legally adopted child, (iii) brother or sister of the half or whole blood, or (iv) uncle, aunt, nephew, or niece.

(b) Punishment and Sentencing. -

(1) A person is guilty of a Class B1 felony if either of the following occurs:

a. The person commits incest against a child under the age of 13 and the person is at least 12 years old and is at least four years older than the child when the incest occurred.

b. The person commits incest against a child who is 13, 14, or 15 years old and the person is at least six years older than the child when the incest occurred.

(2) A person is guilty of a Class C felony if the person commits incest against a child who is 13, 14, or 15 and the person is more than four but less than six years older than the child when the incest occurred.

(3) In all other cases of incest, the parties are guilty of a Class F felony.

(c) No Liability for Children Under 16. - No child under the age of 16 is liable under this section if the other person is at least four years older when the incest occurred. (1879, c. 16, s. 1; Code, s. 1060; Rev., s. 3351; 1911, c. 16; C.S., s. 4337; 1965, c. 132; 1979, c. 760, s. 5; 1979, 2nd Sess., c. 1316, s. 47; 1981, c. 63, s. 1; c. 179, s. 14; 1993, c. 539, s. 1192; 1994, Ex. Sess., c. 24, s. 14(c); 2002-119, s. 1.)

§ 14-179: Repealed by Session Laws 2002-119, s. 2, effective December 1, 2002.

§ 14-180. Repealed by Session Laws 1975, c. 402.

§§ 14-181 through 14-182. Repealed by Session Laws 1973, c. 108, s. 4.

§ 14-183. Bigamy.

If any person, being married, shall marry any other person during the life of the former husband or wife, every such offender, and every person counseling, aiding or abetting such offender, shall be punished as a Class I felon. Any such offense may be dealt with, tried, determined and punished in the county where the offender shall be apprehended, or be in custody, as if the offense had been actually committed in that county. If any person, being married, shall contract a marriage with any other person outside of this State, which marriage would be punishable as bigamous if contracted within this State, and shall thereafter cohabit with such person in this State, he shall be guilty of a felony and shall be punished as in cases of bigamy. Nothing contained in this section shall extend to any person marrying a second time, whose husband or wife shall have been continually absent from such person for the space of seven years then last past, and shall not have been known by such person to have been living within that time; nor to any person who at the time of such second marriage shall have been lawfully divorced from the bond of the first marriage; nor to any person whose former marriage shall have been declared void by the sentence of any court of competent jurisdiction. (See 9 Geo. IV, c. 31, s. 22; 1790, c. 323, P.R.;

1809, c. 783, P.R.; 1829, c. 9; R.C., c. 34, s. 15; Code, s. 988; Rev., s. 3361; 1913, c. 26; C.S., s. 4342; 1979, c. 760, s. 5; 1979, 2nd Sess., c. 1316, s. 47; 1981, c. 63, s. 1, c. 179, s. 14; 1993, c. 539, s. 1193; 1994, Ex. Sess., c. 24, s. 14(c).)

§ 14-184. Fornication and adultery.

If any man and woman, not being married to each other, shall lewdly and lasciviously associate, bed and cohabit together, they shall be guilty of a Class 2 misdemeanor: Provided, that the admissions or confessions of one shall not be received in evidence against the other. (1805, c. 684, P.R.; R.C., c. 34, s. 45; Code, s. 1041; Rev., s. 3350; C.S., s. 4343; 1969, c. 1224, s. 9; 1993, c. 539, s. 119; 1994, Ex. Sess., c. 24, s. 14(c).)

§ 14-185. Repealed by Session Laws 1975, c. 402.

§ 14-186. Opposite sexes occupying same bedroom at hotel for immoral purposes; falsely registering as husband and wife.

Any man and woman found occupying the same bedroom in any hotel, public inn or boardinghouse for any immoral purpose, or any man and woman falsely registering as, or otherwise representing themselves to be, husband and wife in any hotel, public inn or boardinghouse, shall be deemed guilty of a Class 2 misdemeanor. (1917, c. 158, s. 2; C.S., s. 4345; 1969, c. 1224, s. 3; 1993, c. 539, s. 120; 1994, Ex. Sess., c. 24, s. 14(c).)

§ 14-187. Repealed by Session Laws 1975, c. 402.

§ 14-188. Certain evidence relative to keeping disorderly houses admissible; keepers of such houses defined; punishment.

(a) On a prosecution in any court for keeping a disorderly house or bawdy house, or permitting a house to be used as a bawdy house, or used in such a way as to make it disorderly, or a common nuisance, evidence of the general reputation or character of the house shall be admissible and competent; and evidence of the lewd, dissolute and boisterous conversation of the inmates and frequenters, while in and around such house, shall be prima facie evidence of the bad character of the inmates and frequenters, and of the disorderly character of the house. The manager or person having the care, superintendency or government of a disorderly house or bawdy house is the "keeper" thereof, and one who employs another to manage and conduct a disorderly house or bawdy house is also "keeper" thereof.

(b) On a prosecution in any court for keeping a disorderly house or a bawdy house, or permitting a house to be used as a bawdy house or used in such a way to make it disorderly or a common nuisance, the offense shall constitute a Class 2 misdemeanor. (1907, c. 779; C.S., s. 4347; 1969, c. 1224, s. 22; 1993, c. 539, s. 121; 1994, Ex. Sess., c. 24, s. 14(c).)

§§ 14-189 through 14-189.1. Repealed by Session Laws 1971, c. 405, s. 4.

§§ 14-189.2 through 14-190. Repealed by Session Laws 1971, c. 591, s. 4.

§ 14-190.1. Obscene literature and exhibitions.

(a) It shall be unlawful for any person, firm or corporation to intentionally disseminate obscenity. A person, firm or corporation disseminates obscenity within the meaning of this Article if he or it:

(1) Sells, delivers or provides or offers or agrees to sell, deliver or provide any obscene writing, picture, record or other representation or embodiment of the obscene; or

(2) Presents or directs an obscene play, dance or other performance or participates directly in that portion thereof which makes it obscene; or

(3) Publishes, exhibits or otherwise makes available anything obscene; or

(4) Exhibits, presents, rents, sells, delivers or provides; or offers or agrees to exhibit, present, rent or to provide: any obscene still or motion picture, film,

filmstrip, or projection slide, or sound recording, sound tape, or sound track, or any matter or material of whatever form which is a representation, embodiment, performance, or publication of the obscene.

(b) For purposes of this Article any material is obscene if:

(1) The material depicts or describes in a patently offensive way sexual conduct specifically defined by subsection (c) of this section; and

(2) The average person applying contemporary community standards relating to the depiction or description of sexual matters would find that the material taken as a whole appeals to the prurient interest in sex; and

(3) The material lacks serious literary, artistic, political, or scientific value; and

(4) The material as used is not protected or privileged under the Constitution of the United States or the Constitution of North Carolina.

(c) As used in this Article, "sexual conduct" means:

(1) Vaginal, anal, or oral intercourse, whether actual or simulated, normal or perverted; or

(2) Masturbation, excretory functions, or lewd exhibition of uncovered genitals; or

(3) An act or condition that depicts torture, physical restraint by being fettered or bound, or flagellation of or by a nude person or a person clad in undergarments or in revealing or bizarre costume.

(d) Obscenity shall be judged with reference to ordinary adults except that it shall be judged with reference to children or other especially susceptible audiences if it appears from the character of the material or the circumstances of its dissemination to be especially designed for or directed to such children or audiences.

(e) It shall be unlawful for any person, firm or corporation to knowingly and intentionally create, buy, procure or possess obscene material with the purpose and intent of disseminating it unlawfully.

(f)   It shall be unlawful for a person, firm or corporation to advertise or otherwise promote the sale of material represented or held out by said person, firm or corporation as obscene.

(g)   Violation of this section is a Class I felony.

(h)   Obscene material disseminated, procured, or promoted in violation of this section is contraband.

(i)   Nothing in this section shall be deemed to preempt local government regulation of the location or operation of sexually oriented businesses to the extent consistent with the constitutional protection afforded free speech. (1971, c. 405, s. 1; 1973, c. 1434, s. 1; 1985, c. 703, s. 1; 1993, c. 539, s. 1194; 1994, Ex. Sess., c. 24, s. 14(c); 1998-46, s. 2.)

§ 14-190.2. Repealed by Session Laws 1985, c. 703, s. 2.

§ 14-190.3. Repealed by Session Laws 1985, c. 703, s. 3.

§ 14-190.4. Coercing acceptance of obscene articles or publications.

No person, firm or corporation shall, as a condition to any sale, allocation, consignment or delivery for resale of any paper, magazine, book, periodical or publication require that the purchaser or consignee receive for resale any other article, book, or publication which is obscene within the meaning of G.S. 14-190.1; nor shall any person, firm or corporation deny or threaten to deny any franchise or impose or threaten to impose any penalty, financial or otherwise, by reason of the failure or refusal of any person to accept such articles, books, or publications, or by reason of the return thereof. Violation of this section is a Class 1 misdemeanor. (1971, c. 405, s. 1; 1985, c. 703, s. 4; 1993, c. 539, s. 122; 1994, Ex. Sess., c. 24, s. 14(c).)

§ 14-190.5. Preparation of obscene photographs, slides and motion pictures.

Every person who knowingly:

(1) Photographs himself or any other person, for purposes of preparing an obscene film, photograph, negative, slide or motion picture for the purpose of dissemination; or

(2) Models, poses, acts, or otherwise assists in the preparation of any obscene film, photograph, negative, slide or motion picture for the purpose of dissemination,

shall be guilty of a Class 1 misdemeanor. (1971, c. 405, s. 1; 1985, c. 703, s. 5; 1993, c. 539, s. 123; 1994, Ex. Sess., c. 24, s. 14(c).)

§ 14-190.6. Employing or permitting minor to assist in offense under Article.

Every person 18 years of age or older who intentionally, in any manner, hires, employs, uses or permits any minor under the age of 16 years to do or assist in doing any act or thing constituting an offense under this Article and involving any material, act or thing he knows or reasonably should know to be obscene within the meaning of G.S. 14-190.1, shall be guilty of a Class I felony. (1971, c. 405, s. 1; 1983, c. 916, s. 2; 1985, c. 703, s. 6.)

§ 14-190.7. Dissemination to minors under the age of 16 years.

Every person 18 years of age or older who knowingly disseminates to any minor under the age of 16 years any material which he knows or reasonably should know to be obscene within the meaning of G.S. 14-190.1 shall be guilty of a Class I felony. (1971, c. 405, s. 1; 1977, c. 440, s. 2; 1985, c. 703, s. 7.)

§ 14-190.8. Dissemination to minors under the age of 13 years.

Every person 18 years of age or older who knowingly disseminates to any minor under the age of 13 years any material which he knows or reasonably should know to be obscene within the meaning of G.S. 14-190.1 shall be punished as a Class I felon. (1971, c. 405, s. 1; 1977, c. 440, s. 3; 1979, c. 760, s. 5; 1983, c. 175, ss. 7, 10, c. 720, ss. 4, 10; 1985, c. 703, s. 8; 1993, c. 539, s. 1195; 1994, Ex. Sess., c. 24, s. 14(c).)

§ 14-190.9. Indecent exposure.

(a)   Unless the conduct is punishable under subsection (a1) of this section, any person who shall willfully expose the private parts of his or her person in any public place and in the presence of any other person or persons, except for those places designated for a public purpose where the same sex exposure is incidental to a permitted activity, or aids or abets in any such act, or who procures another to perform such act; or any person, who as owner, manager, lessee, director, promoter or agent, or in any other capacity knowingly hires, leases or permits the land, building, or premises of which he is owner, lessee or tenant, or over which he has control, to be used for purposes of any such act, shall be guilty of a Class 2 misdemeanor.

(a1)   Unless the conduct is prohibited by another law providing greater punishment, any person at least 18 years of age who shall willfully expose the private parts of his or her person in any public place in the presence of any other person less than 16 years of age for the purpose of arousing or gratifying sexual desire shall be guilty of a Class H felony. An offense committed under this subsection shall not be considered to be a lesser included offense under G.S. 14-202.1.

(b)   Notwithstanding any other provision of law, a woman may breast feed in any public or private location where she is otherwise authorized to be, irrespective of whether the nipple of the mother's breast is uncovered during or incidental to the breast feeding.

(c)   Notwithstanding any other provision of law, a local government may regulate the location and operation of sexually oriented businesses. Such local regulation may restrict or prohibit nude, seminude, or topless dancing to the extent consistent with the constitutional protection afforded free speech. (1971, c. 591, s. 1; 1993, c. 301, s. 1; c. 539, s. 124; 1994, Ex. Sess., c. 24, s. 14(c); 1998-46, s. 3; 2005-226, s. 1.)

§§ 14-190.10 through 14-190.12. Repealed by Session Laws 1985, c. 703, s. 9.

§ 14-190.13. Definitions for certain offenses concerning minors.

The following definitions apply to G.S. 14-190.14, displaying material harmful to minors; G.S. 14-190.15, disseminating or exhibiting to minors harmful material or performances; G.S. 14-190.16, first degree sexual exploitation of a minor; G.S. 14-190.17, second degree sexual exploitation of a minor; G.S. 14-190.17A, third degree sexual exploitation of a minor.

(1) Harmful to Minors. - That quality of any material or performance that depicts sexually explicit nudity or sexual activity and that, taken as a whole, has the following characteristics:

a. The average adult person applying contemporary community standards would find that the material or performance has a predominant tendency to appeal to a prurient interest of minors in sex; and

b. The average adult person applying contemporary community standards would find that the depiction of sexually explicit nudity or sexual activity in the material or performance is patently offensive to prevailing standards in the adult community concerning what is suitable for minors; and

c. The material or performance lacks serious literary, artistic, political, or scientific value for minors.

(2) Material. - Pictures, drawings, video recordings, films or other visual depictions or representations but not material consisting entirely of written words.

(3) Minor. - An individual who is less than 18 years old and is not married or judicially emancipated.

(4) Prostitution. - Engaging or offering to engage in sexual activity with or for another in exchange for anything of value.

(5) Sexual Activity. - Any of the following acts:

a. Masturbation, whether done alone or with another human or an animal.

b. Vaginal, anal, or oral intercourse, whether done with another human or with an animal.

c. Touching, in an act of apparent sexual stimulation or sexual abuse, of the clothed or unclothed genitals, pubic area, or buttocks of another person or the clothed or unclothed breasts of a human female.

d. An act or condition that depicts torture, physical restraint by being fettered or bound, or flagellation of or by a person clad in undergarments or in revealing or bizarre costume.

e. Excretory functions; provided, however, that this sub-subdivision shall not apply to G.S. 14-190.17A.

f. The insertion of any part of a person's body, other than the male sexual organ, or of any object into another person's anus or vagina, except when done as part of a recognized medical procedure.

g. The lascivious exhibition of the genitals or pubic area of any person.

(6) Sexually Explicit Nudity. - The showing of:

a. Uncovered, or less than opaquely covered, human genitals, pubic area, or buttocks, or the nipple or any portion of the areola of the human female breast, except as provided in G.S. 14-190.9(b); or

b. Covered human male genitals in a discernibly turgid state. (1985, c. 703, s. 9; 1989 (Reg. Sess., 1990), c. 1022, s. 2; 1993, c. 301, s. 2; 2008-218, s. 1; 2013-368, s. 18.)

§ 14-190.14. Displaying material harmful to minors.

(a) Offense. - A person commits the offense of displaying material that is harmful to minors if, having custody, control, or supervision of a commercial establishment and knowing the character or content of the material, he displays material that is harmful to minors at that establishment so that it is open to view by minors as part of the invited general public. Material is not considered displayed under this section if the material is placed behind "blinder racks" that cover the lower two thirds of the material, is wrapped, is placed behind the counter, or is otherwise covered or located so that the portion that is harmful to minors is not open to the view of minors.

(b) Punishment. - Violation of this section is a Class 2 misdemeanor. Each day's violation of this section is a separate offense. (1985, c. 703, s. 9; 1993, c. 539, s. 125; 1994, Ex. Sess., c. 24, s. 14(c).)

§ 14-190.15. Disseminating harmful material to minors; exhibiting harmful performances to minors.

(a) Disseminating Harmful Material. - A person commits the offense of disseminating harmful material to minors if, with or without consideration and knowing the character or content of the material, he:

(1) Sells, furnishes, presents, or distributes to a minor material that is harmful to minors; or

(2) Allows a minor to review or peruse material that is harmful to minors.

(b) Exhibiting Harmful Performance. - A person commits the offense of exhibiting a harmful performance to a minor if, with or without consideration and knowing the character or content of the performance, he allows a minor to view a live performance that is harmful to minors.

(c) Defenses. - Except as provided in subdivision (3), a mistake of age is not a defense to a prosecution under this section. It is an affirmative defense to a prosecution under this section that:

(1) The defendant was a parent or legal guardian of the minor.

(2) The defendant was a school, church, museum, public library, governmental agency, medical clinic, or hospital carrying out its legitimate function; or an employee or agent of such an organization acting in that capacity and carrying out a legitimate duty of his employment.

(3) Before disseminating or exhibiting the harmful material or performance, the defendant requested and received a driver's license, student identification card, or other official governmental or educational identification card or paper indicating that the minor to whom the material or performance was disseminated or exhibited was at least 18 years old, and the defendant reasonably believed the minor was at least 18 years old.

(4) The dissemination was made with the prior consent of a parent or guardian of the recipient.

(d) Punishment. - Violation of this section is a Class 1 misdemeanor. (1985, c. 703, s. 9; 1993, c. 539, s. 126; 1994, Ex. Sess., c. 24, s. 14(c).)

§ 14-190.16. First degree sexual exploitation of a minor.

(a) Offense. - A person commits the offense of first degree sexual exploitation of a minor if, knowing the character or content of the material or performance, he:

(1) Uses, employs, induces, coerces, encourages, or facilitates a minor to engage in or assist others to engage in sexual activity for a live performance or for the purpose of producing material that contains a visual representation depicting this activity; or

(2) Permits a minor under his custody or control to engage in sexual activity for a live performance or for the purpose of producing material that contains a visual representation depicting this activity; or

(3) Transports or finances the transportation of a minor through or across this State with the intent that the minor engage in sexual activity for a live performance or for the purpose of producing material that contains a visual representation depicting this activity; or

(4) Records, photographs, films, develops, or duplicates for sale or pecuniary gain material that contains a visual representation depicting a minor engaged in sexual activity.

(b) Inference. - In a prosecution under this section, the trier of fact may infer that a participant in sexual activity whom material through its title, text, visual representations, or otherwise represents or depicts as a minor is a minor.

(c) Mistake of Age. - Mistake of age is not a defense to a prosecution under this section.

(d) Punishment and Sentencing. - Violation of this section is a Class C felony. (1985, c. 703, s. 9; 1993, c. 539, s. 1196; 1994, Ex. Sess., c. 24, s. 14(c); 1995, c. 507, s. 19.5(o); 2008-117, s. 3; 2008-218, s. 2.)

§ 14-190.17. Second degree sexual exploitation of a minor.

(a) Offense. - A person commits the offense of second degree sexual exploitation of a minor if, knowing the character or content of the material, he:

(1) Records, photographs, films, develops, or duplicates material that contains a visual representation of a minor engaged in sexual activity; or

(2) Distributes, transports, exhibits, receives, sells, purchases, exchanges, or solicits material that contains a visual representation of a minor engaged in sexual activity.

(b) Inference. - In a prosecution under this section, the trier of fact may infer that a participant in sexual activity whom material through its title, text, visual representations or otherwise represents or depicts as a minor is a minor.

(c) Mistake of Age. - Mistake of age is not a defense to a prosecution under this section.

(d) Punishment and Sentencing. - Violation of this section is a Class E felony. (1985, c. 703, s. 9; 1993, c. 539, s. 1197; 1994, Ex. Sess., c. 24, s. 14(c); 2008-117, s. 4; 2008-218, s. 3.)

§ 14-190.17A. Third degree sexual exploitation of a minor.

(a) Offense. - A person commits the offense of third degree sexual exploitation of a minor if, knowing the character or content of the material, he possesses material that contains a visual representation of a minor engaging in sexual activity.

(b) Inference. - In a prosecution under this section, the trier of fact may infer that a participant in sexual activity whom material through its title, text, visual representations or otherwise represents or depicts as a minor is a minor.

(c) Mistake of Age. - Mistake of age is not a defense to a prosecution under this section.

(d) Punishment and Sentencing. - Violation of this section is a Class H felony. (1989 (Reg. Sess., 1990), c. 1022, s. 1; 1993, c. 539, s. 1198; 1994, Ex. Sess., c. 24, s. 14(c); 2008-117, s. 5; 2008-218, s. 4.)

§ 14-190.18: Repealed by Session Laws 2013-368, s. 4, effective October 1, 2013, and applicable to offenses committed on or after that date.

§ 14-190.19: Repealed by Session Laws 2013-368, s. 4, effective October 1, 2013, and applicable to offenses committed on or after that date.

§ 14-190.20. Warrants for obscenity offenses.

A search warrant or criminal process for a violation of G.S. 14-190.1 through 14-190.5 may be issued only upon the request of a prosecutor. (1985, c. 703, s. 9.1.)

§ 14-191. Repealed by Session Laws 1971, c. 591, s. 4.

§§ 14-192 through 14-193. Repealed by Session Laws 1971, c. 405, s. 4.

§ 14-194. Repealed by Session Laws 1971, c. 591, s. 4.

§ 14-195: Repealed by Session Laws 1993 (Reg. Sess., 1994), c. 767, s. 30(11).

§ 14-196. Using profane, indecent or threatening language to any person over telephone; annoying or harassing by repeated telephoning or making false statements over telephone.

(a) It shall be unlawful for any person:

(1) To use in telephonic communications any words or language of a profane, vulgar, lewd, lascivious or indecent character, nature or connotation;

(2) To use in telephonic communications any words or language threatening to inflict bodily harm to any person or to that person's child, sibling, spouse, or dependent or physical injury to the property of any person, or for the purpose of extorting money or other things of value from any person;

(3) To telephone another repeatedly, whether or not conversation ensues, for the purpose of abusing, annoying, threatening, terrifying, harassing or embarrassing any person at the called number;

(4) To make a telephone call and fail to hang up or disengage the connection with the intent to disrupt the service of another;

(5) To telephone another and to knowingly make any false statement concerning death, injury, illness, disfigurement, indecent conduct or criminal conduct of the person telephoned or of any member of his family or household with the intent to abuse, annoy, threaten, terrify, harass, or embarrass;

(6) To knowingly permit any telephone under his control to be used for any purpose prohibited by this section.

(b) Any of the above offenses may be deemed to have been committed at either the place at which the telephone call or calls were made or at the place where the telephone call or calls were received. For purposes of this section, the term "telephonic communications" shall include communications made or received by way of a telephone answering machine or recorder, telefacsimile machine, or computer modem.

(c) Anyone violating the provisions of this section shall be guilty of a Class 2 misdemeanor. (1913, c. 35; 1915, c. 41; C.S., s. 4351; 1967, c. 833, s. 1; 1989, c. 305; 1993, c. 539, s. 128; 1994, Ex. Sess., c. 24, s. 14(c); 1999-262, s. 1; 2000-125, s. 2.)

§§ 14-196.1 through 14-196.2. Repealed by Session Laws 1967, c. 833, s. 3.

§ 14-196.3. Cyberstalking.

(a) The following definitions apply in this section:

(1) Electronic communication. - Any transfer of signs, signals, writing, images, sounds, data, or intelligence of any nature, transmitted in whole or in part by a wire, radio, computer, electromagnetic, photoelectric, or photo-optical system.

(2) Electronic mail. - The transmission of information or communication by the use of the Internet, a computer, a facsimile machine, a pager, a cellular telephone, a video recorder, or other electronic means sent to a person identified by a unique address or address number and received by that person.

(b) It is unlawful for a person to:

(1) Use in electronic mail or electronic communication any words or language threatening to inflict bodily harm to any person or to that person's child, sibling, spouse, or dependent, or physical injury to the property of any person, or for the purpose of extorting money or other things of value from any person.

(2) Electronically mail or electronically communicate to another repeatedly, whether or not conversation ensues, for the purpose of abusing, annoying, threatening, terrifying, harassing, or embarrassing any person.

(3) Electronically mail or electronically communicate to another and to knowingly make any false statement concerning death, injury, illness, disfigurement, indecent conduct, or criminal conduct of the person electronically mailed or of any member of the person's family or household with the intent to abuse, annoy, threaten, terrify, harass, or embarrass.

(4) Knowingly permit an electronic communication device under the person's control to be used for any purpose prohibited by this section.

(c) Any offense under this section committed by the use of electronic mail or electronic communication may be deemed to have been committed where the electronic mail or electronic communication was originally sent, originally received in this State, or first viewed by any person in this State.

(d) Any person violating the provisions of this section shall be guilty of a Class 2 misdemeanor.

(e) This section does not apply to any peaceable, nonviolent, or nonthreatening activity intended to express political views or to provide lawful information to others. This section shall not be construed to impair any constitutionally protected activity, including speech, protest, or assembly. (2000-125, s. 1; 2000-140, s. 91.)

§ 14-197. Using profane or indecent language on public highways; counties exempt.

If any person shall, on any public road or highway and in the hearing of two or more persons, in a loud and boisterous manner, use indecent or profane language, he shall be guilty of a Class 3 misdemeanor. The following counties shall be exempt from the provisions of this section: Pitt and Swain. (1913, c. 40; C.S., s. 4352; Pub. Loc. Ex. Sess., 1924, c. 65; 1933, c. 309; 1937, c. 9; 1939, c. 73; 1945, c. 398; 1947, cc. 144, 959; 1949, c. 845; 1957, c. 348; 1959, c. 733; 1963, cc. 39, 123; 1969, c. 300; 1971, c. 718; 1973, cc. 120, 233; 1993, c. 539, s. 129; 1994, Ex. Sess., c. 24, s. 14(c).)

§ 14-198. Repealed by Session Laws 1975, c. 402.

§ 14-199. Obstructing way to places of public worship.

If any person shall maliciously stop up or obstruct the way leading to any place of public worship, or to any spring or well commonly used by the congregation, he shall be guilty of a Class 2 misdemeanor. (1785, c. 241, P.R.; R.C., c. 97, s. 5; Code, s. 3669; Rev., s. 3776; C.S., s. 4354; 1945, c. 635; 1969, c. 1224, s. 1; 1993, c. 539, s. 130; 1994, Ex. Sess., c. 24, s. 14(c).)

§§ 14-200 through 14-201: Repealed by Session Laws 1994, Ex. Sess., c. 14, s. 72(9), (10).

§ 14-202. Secretly peeping into room occupied by another person.

(a)   Any person who shall peep secretly into any room occupied by another person shall be guilty of a Class 1 misdemeanor.

(a1)   Unless covered by another provision of law providing greater punishment, any person who secretly or surreptitiously peeps underneath or through the clothing being worn by another person, through the use of a mirror or other device, for the purpose of viewing the body of, or the undergarments worn by, that other person without their consent shall be guilty of a Class 1 misdemeanor.

(b)   For purposes of this section:

(1)   The term "photographic image" means any photograph or photographic reproduction, still or moving, or any videotape, motion picture, or live television transmission, or any digital image of any individual.

(2)   The term "room" shall include, but is not limited to, a bedroom, a rest room, a bathroom, a shower, and a dressing room.

(c)   Unless covered by another provision of law providing greater punishment, any person who, while in possession of any device which may be used to create a photographic image, shall secretly peep into any room shall be guilty of a Class A1 misdemeanor.

(d)   Unless covered by another provision of law providing greater punishment, any person who, while secretly peeping into any room, uses any device to create a photographic image of another person in that room for the purpose of arousing or gratifying the sexual desire of any person shall be guilty of a Class I felony.

(e)   Any person who secretly or surreptitiously uses any device to create a photographic image of another person underneath or through the clothing being worn by that other person for the purpose of viewing the body of, or the undergarments worn by, that other person without their consent shall be guilty of a Class I felony.

(f)   Any person who, for the purpose of arousing or gratifying the sexual desire of any person, secretly or surreptitiously uses or installs in a room any device that can be used to create a photographic image with the intent to capture the image of another without their consent shall be guilty of a Class I felony.

(g)   Any person who knowingly possesses a photographic image that the person knows, or has reason to believe, was obtained in violation of this section shall be guilty of a Class I felony.

(h)   Any person who disseminates or allows to be disseminated images that the person knows, or should have known, were obtained as a result of the violation of this section shall be guilty of a Class H felony if the dissemination is without the consent of the person in the photographic image.

(i)   A second or subsequent felony conviction under this section shall be punished as though convicted of an offense one class higher. A second or subsequent conviction for a Class 1 misdemeanor shall be punished as a Class A1 misdemeanor. A second or subsequent conviction for a Class A1 misdemeanor shall be punished as a Class I felony.

(j)   If the defendant is placed on probation as a result of violation of this section:

(1)   For a first conviction under this section, the judge may impose a requirement that the defendant obtain a psychological evaluation and comply with any treatment recommended as a result of that evaluation.

(2)   For a second or subsequent conviction under this section, the judge shall impose a requirement that the defendant obtain a psychological evaluation and comply with any treatment recommended as a result of that evaluation.

(k)   Any person whose image is captured or disseminated in violation of this section has a civil cause of action against any person who captured or disseminated the image or procured any other person to capture or disseminate the image and is entitled to recover from those persons actual damages, punitive damages, reasonable attorneys' fees and other litigation costs reasonably incurred.

(l)   When a person violates subsection (d), (e), (f), (g), or (h) of this section, or is convicted of a second or subsequent violation of subsection (a), (a1), or (c) of this section, the sentencing court shall consider whether the person is a danger to the community and whether requiring the person to register as a sex offender pursuant to Article 27A of this Chapter would further the purposes of that Article as stated in G.S. 14-208.5. If the sentencing court rules that the person is a danger to the community and that the person shall register, then an order shall be entered requiring the person to register.

(m) The provisions of subsections (a), (a1), (c), (e), (g), (h), and (k) of this section do not apply to:

(1) Law enforcement officers while discharging or attempting to discharge their official duties; or

(2) Personnel of the Division of Adult Correction of the Department of Public Safety, the Division of Juvenile Justice of the Department of Public Safety, or of a local confinement facility for security purposes or during investigation of alleged misconduct by a person in the custody of the Division or the local confinement facility.

(n) This section does not affect the legal activities of those who are licensed pursuant to Chapter 74C, Private Protective Services, or Chapter 74D, Alarm Systems, of the General Statutes, who are legally engaged in the discharge of their official duties within their respective professions, and who are not engaging in activities for an improper purpose as described in this section. (1923, c. 78; C.S., s. 4356(a); 1957, c. 338; 1993, c. 539, s. 131; 1994, Ex. Sess., c. 24, s. 14(c); 2003-303, s. 1; 2004-109, s. 7; 2011-145, s. 19.1(h); 2012-83, s. 1.)

§ 14-202.1. Taking indecent liberties with children.

(a) A person is guilty of taking indecent liberties with children if, being 16 years of age or more and at least five years older than the child in question, he either:

(1) Willfully takes or attempts to take any immoral, improper, or indecent liberties with any child of either sex under the age of 16 years for the purpose of arousing or gratifying sexual desire; or

(2) Willfully commits or attempts to commit any lewd or lascivious act upon or with the body or any part or member of the body of any child of either sex under the age of 16 years.

(b) Taking indecent liberties with children is punishable as a Class F felony. (1955, c. 764; 1975, c. 779; 1979, c. 760, s. 5; 1979, 2nd Sess., c. 1316, s. 47; 1981, c. 63, s. 1, c. 179, s. 14; 1993, c. 539, s. 1201; 1994, Ex. Sess., c. 24, s. 14(c).)

§ 14-202.2. Indecent liberties between children.

(a) A person who is under the age of 16 years is guilty of taking indecent liberties with children if the person either:

(1) Willfully takes or attempts to take any immoral, improper, or indecent liberties with any child of either sex who is at least three years younger than the defendant for the purpose of arousing or gratifying sexual desire; or

(2) Willfully commits or attempts to commit any lewd or lascivious act upon or with the body or any part or member of the body of any child of either sex who is at least three years younger than the defendant for the purpose of arousing or gratifying sexual desire.

(b) A violation of this section is punishable as a Class 1 misdemeanor. (1995, c. 494, s. 1; 1995 (Reg. Sess., 1996), c. 742, s. 12.)

§ 14-202.3. Solicitation of child by computer or certain other electronic devices to commit an unlawful sex act.

(a) Offense. - A person is guilty of solicitation of a child by a computer if the person is 16 years of age or older and the person knowingly, with the intent to commit an unlawful sex act, entices, advises, coerces, orders, or commands, by means of a computer or any other device capable of electronic data storage or transmission, a child who is less than 16 years of age and at least five years younger than the defendant, or a person the defendant believes to be a child who is less than 16 years of age and who the defendant believes to be at least five years younger than the defendant, to meet with the defendant or any other person for the purpose of committing an unlawful sex act. Consent is not a defense to a charge under this section.

(b) Jurisdiction. - The offense is committed in the State for purposes of determining jurisdiction, if the transmission that constitutes the offense either originates in the State or is received in the State.

(c) Punishment. - A violation of this section is punishable as follows:

(1) A violation is a Class H felony except as provided by subdivision (2) of this subsection.

(2) If either the defendant, or any other person for whom the defendant was arranging the meeting in violation of this section, actually appears at the meeting location, then the violation is a Class G felony. (1995 (Reg. Sess., 1996), c. 632, s. 1; 2005-121, s. 1; 2008-218, s. 5; 2009-336, s. 1.)

§ 14-202.4. Taking indecent liberties with a student.

(a) If a defendant, who is a teacher, school administrator, student teacher, school safety officer, or coach, at any age, or who is other school personnel and is at least four years older than the victim, takes indecent liberties with a victim who is a student, at any time during or after the time the defendant and victim were present together in the same school but before the victim ceases to be a student, the defendant is guilty of a Class I felony, unless the conduct is covered under some other provision of law providing for greater punishment. A person is not guilty of taking indecent liberties with a student if the person is lawfully married to the student.

(b) If a defendant, who is school personnel, other than a teacher, school administrator, student teacher, school safety officer, or coach, and who is less than four years older than the victim, takes indecent liberties with a student as provided in subsection (a) of this section, the defendant is guilty of a Class A1 misdemeanor.

(c) Consent is not a defense to a charge under this section.

(d) For purposes of this section, the following definitions apply:

(1) "Indecent liberties" means:

a. Willfully taking or attempting to take any immoral, improper, or indecent liberties with a student for the purpose of arousing or gratifying sexual desire; or

b. Willfully committing or attempting to commit any lewd or lascivious act upon or with the body or any part or member of the body of a student.

For purposes of this section, the term indecent liberties does not include vaginal intercourse or a sexual act as defined by G.S. 14-27.1.

(1a) "Same school" means a school at which (i) the student is enrolled or is present for a school-sponsored or school-related activity and (ii) the school personnel is employed, volunteers, or is present for a school-sponsored or school-related activity.

(2) "School" means any public school, charter school, or nonpublic school under Parts 1 and 2 of Article 39 of Chapter 115C of the General Statutes.

(3) "School personnel" means any person included in the definition contained in G.S. 115C-332(a)(2), and any person who volunteers at a school or a school-sponsored activity.

(3a) "School safety officer" means any other person who is regularly present in a school for the purpose of promoting and maintaining safe and orderly schools and includes a school resource officer.

(4) "Student" means a person enrolled in kindergarten, or in grade one through grade 12 in any school. (1999-300, s. 1; 2003-98, s. 2; 2004-203, s. 19(a).)

§ 14-202.5. Ban use of commercial social networking Web sites by sex offenders.

(a) Offense. - It is unlawful for a sex offender who is registered in accordance with Article 27A of Chapter 14 of the General Statutes to access a commercial social networking Web site where the sex offender knows that the site permits minor children to become members or to create or maintain personal Web pages on the commercial social networking Web site.

(b) For the purposes of this section, a "commercial social networking Web site" is an Internet Web site that meets all of the following requirements:

(1) Is operated by a person who derives revenue from membership fees, advertising, or other sources related to the operation of the Web site.

(2) Facilitates the social introduction between two or more persons for the purposes of friendship, meeting other persons, or information exchanges.

(3) Allows users to create Web pages or personal profiles that contain information such as the name or nickname of the user, photographs placed on the personal Web page by the user, other personal information about the user, and links to other personal Web pages on the commercial social networking Web site of friends or associates of the user that may be accessed by other users or visitors to the Web site.

(4) Provides users or visitors to the commercial social networking Web site mechanisms to communicate with other users, such as a message board, chat room, electronic mail, or instant messenger.

(c) A commercial social networking Web site does not include an Internet Web site that either:

(1) Provides only one of the following discrete services: photo-sharing, electronic mail, instant messenger, or chat room or message board platform; or

(2) Has as its primary purpose the facilitation of commercial transactions involving goods or services between its members or visitors.

(d) Jurisdiction. - The offense is committed in the State for purposes of determining jurisdiction, if the transmission that constitutes the offense either originates in the State or is received in the State.

(e) Punishment. - A violation of this section is a Class I felony. (2008-218, s. 6; 2009-570, s. 4.)

§ 14-202.5A. Liability of commercial social networking sites.

(a) A commercial social networking site, as defined in G.S. 14-202.5, that complies with G.S. 14-208.15A or makes other reasonable efforts to prevent a sex offender who is registered in accordance with Article 27A of Chapter 14 of the General Statutes from accessing its Web site shall not be held civilly liable for damages arising out of a person's communications on the social networking site's system or network regardless of that person's status as a registered sex offender in North Carolina or any other jurisdiction.

(b) For the purposes of this section, "access" is defined as allowing the sex offender to do any of the activities or actions described in G.S. 14-202.5(b)(2) through G.S. 14-202.5(b)(4) by utilizing the Web site. (2008-218, s. 7; 2009-272, s. 1.)

§ 14-202.6. Ban on name changes by sex offenders.

It is unlawful for a sex offender who is registered in accordance with Article 27A of Chapter 14 of the General Statutes to obtain a change of name under Chapter 101 of the General Statutes. (2008-218, s. 8.)

§ 14-202.7. Reserved for future codification purposes.

§ 14-202.8. Reserved for future codification purposes.

§ 14-202.9. Reserved for future codification purposes.

Article 26A.

Adult Establishments.

§ 14-202.10. Definitions.

As used in this Article:

(1) "Adult bookstore" means a bookstore:

a. Which receives a majority of its gross income during any calendar month from the sale or rental of publications (including books, magazines, other periodicals, videotapes, compact discs, other photographic, electronic, magnetic, digital, or other imaging medium) which are distinguished or characterized by their emphasis on matter depicting, describing, or relating to specified sexual activities or specified anatomical areas, as defined in this section; or

b. Having as a preponderance (either in terms of the weight and importance of the material or in terms of greater volume of materials) of its publications (including books, magazines, other periodicals, videotapes, compact discs, other photographic, electronic, magnetic, digital, or other imaging medium) which are distinguished or characterized by their emphasis on matter depicting, describing, or relating to specified sexual activities or specified anatomical areas, as defined in this section.

(2) "Adult establishment" means an adult bookstore, adult motion picture theatre, adult mini motion picture theatre, adult live entertainment business, or massage business as defined in this section.

(3) "Adult live entertainment" means any performance of or involving the actual presence of real people which exhibits specified sexual activities or specified anatomical areas, as defined in this section.

(4) "Adult live entertainment business" means any establishment or business wherein adult live entertainment is shown for observation by patrons.

(5) "Adult motion picture theatre" means an enclosed building or premises used for presenting motion pictures, a preponderance of which are distinguished or characterized by an emphasis on matter depicting, describing, or relating to specified sexual activities or specified anatomical areas, as defined in this section, for observation by patrons therein. "Adult motion picture theatre" does not include any adult mini motion picture theatre as defined in this section.

(6) "Adult mini motion picture theatre" means an enclosed building with viewing booths designed to hold patrons which is used for presenting motion pictures, a preponderance of which are distinguished or characterized by an emphasis on matter depicting, describing or relating to specified sexual activities or specified anatomical areas as defined in this section, for observation by patrons therein.

(7) "Massage" means the manipulation of body muscle or tissue by rubbing, stroking, kneading, or tapping, by hand or mechanical device.

(8) "Massage business" means any establishment or business wherein massage is practiced, including establishments commonly known as health clubs, physical culture studios, massage studios, or massage parlors.

(9) "Sexually oriented devices" means without limitation any artificial or simulated specified anatomical area or other device or paraphernalia that is designed principally for specified sexual activities but shall not mean any contraceptive device.

(10) "Specified anatomical areas" means:

a. Less than completely and opaquely covered: (i) human genitals, pubic region, (ii) buttock, or (iii) female breast below a point immediately above the top of the areola; or

b. Human male genitals in a discernibly turgid state, even if completely and opaquely covered.

(11) "Specified sexual activities" means:

a. Human genitals in a state of sexual stimulation or arousal;

b. Acts of human masturbation, sexual intercourse or sodomy; or

c. Fondling or other erotic touchings of human genitals, pubic regions, buttocks or female breasts. (1977, c. 987, s. 1; 1985, c. 731, s. 1; 1998-46, s. 4.)

§ 14-202.11. Restrictions as to adult establishments.

(a) No person shall permit any building, premises, structure, or other facility that contains any adult establishment to contain any other kind of adult establishment. No person shall permit any building, premises, structure, or other facility in which sexually oriented devices are sold, distributed, exhibited, or contained to contain any adult establishment.

(b) No person shall permit any viewing booth in an adult mini motion picture theatre to be occupied by more than one person at any time.

(c) Nothing in this section shall be deemed to preempt local government regulation of the location or operation of adult establishments or other sexually oriented businesses to the extent consistent with the constitutional protection afforded free speech. (1977, c. 987, s. 1; 1985, c. 731, s. 2; 1998-46, s. 5.)

§ 14-202.12. Violations; penalties.

Any person who violates G.S. 14-202.11 shall be guilty of a Class 3 misdemeanor. Any person who has been previously convicted of a violation of G.S. 14-202.11, upon conviction for a second or subsequent violation of G.S. 14-202.11, shall be guilty of a Class 2 misdemeanor.

As used herein, "person" shall include:

(1) The agent in charge of the building, premises, structure or facility; or

(2) The owner of the building, premises, structure or facility when such owner knew or reasonably should have known the nature of the business located therein, and such owner refused to cooperate with the public officials in reasonable measures designed to terminate the proscribed use; provided, however, that if there is an agent in charge, and if the owner did not have actual knowledge, the owner shall not be prosecuted; or

(3) The owner of the business; or

(4) The manager of the business. (1977, c. 987, s. 1; 1985, c. 731, s. 3; 1993, c. 539, s. 132; 1994, Ex. Sess., c. 24, s. 14(c).)

Article 27.

Prostitution.

§ 14-203. Definition of terms.

The following definitions apply in this Article:

(1) Advance prostitution. - The term includes all of the following:

a. Soliciting for a prostitute by performing any of the following acts when acting as other than a prostitute or a patron of a prostitute:

1. Soliciting another for the purpose of prostitution.

2. Arranging or offering to arrange a meeting of persons for the purpose of prostitution.

3. Directing another to a place knowing the direction is for the purpose of prostitution.

4. Using the Internet, including any social media Web site, to solicit another for the purpose of prostitution.

b. Keeping a place of prostitution by controlling or exercising control over the use of any place that could offer seclusion or shelter for the practice of prostitution and performing any of the following acts when acting as other than a prostitute or a patron of a prostitute:

1. Knowingly granting or permitting the use of the place for the purpose of prostitution.

2. Granting or permitting the use of the place under circumstances from which the person should reasonably know that the place is used or is to be used for purposes of prostitution.

3. Permitting the continued use of the place after becoming aware of facts or circumstances from which the person should know that the place is being used for the purpose of prostitution.

(2) Minor. - Any person who is less than 18 years of age.

(3) Profit from prostitution. - When acting as other than a prostitute, to receive anything of value for personally rendered prostitution services or to receive anything of value from a prostitute, if the thing received is not for lawful consideration and the person knows it was earned in whole or in part from the practice of prostitution.

(4) Prostitute. - A person who engages in prostitution.

(5) Prostitution. - The performance of, offer of, or agreement to perform vaginal intercourse, any sexual act as defined in G.S. 14-27.1, or any sexual contact as defined in G.S. 14-27.1, for the purpose of sexual arousal or gratification for any money or other consideration. (1919, c. 215, s. 2; C.S., s. 4357; 2013-368, s. 5.)

§ 14-204. Prostitution.

(a) Offense. - Any person who willfully engages in prostitution is guilty of a Class 1 misdemeanor.

(b) First Offender; Conditional Discharge. -

(1) Whenever any person who has not previously been convicted of or placed on probation for a violation of this section pleads guilty to or is found guilty of a violation of this section, the court, without entering a judgment and with the consent of such person, shall place the person on probation pursuant to this subsection.

(2) When a person is placed on probation, the court shall enter an order specifying a period of probation of 12 months and shall defer further proceedings in the case until the conclusion of the period of probation or until the filing of a petition alleging violation of a term or condition of probation.

(3) The conditions of probation shall be that the person (i) not violate any criminal statute of any jurisdiction, (ii) refrain from possessing a firearm or other dangerous weapon, (iii) submit to periodic drug testing at a time and in a manner as ordered by the court, but no less than three times during the period of the probation, with the cost of the testing to be paid by the probationer, (iv) obtain a vocational assessment administered by a program approved by the court, and (v) attend no fewer than 10 counseling sessions administered by a program approved by the court.

(4) The court may, in addition to other conditions, require that the person do any of the following:

a. Make a report to and appear in person before or participate with the court or such courts, person, or social service agency as directed by the court in the order of probation.

b. Pay a fine and costs.

c. Attend or reside in a facility established for the instruction or residence of defendants on probation.

d. Support the person's dependents.

e. Refrain from having in the person's body the presence of any illicit drug prohibited by the North Carolina Controlled Substances Act, unless prescribed by a physician, and submit samples of the person's blood or urine or both for tests to determine the presence of any illicit drug.

(5) Upon violation of a term or condition of probation, the court may enter a judgment on its original finding of guilt and proceed as otherwise provided.

(6) Upon fulfillment of the terms and conditions of probation, the court shall discharge the person and dismiss the proceedings against the person. Upon the discharge of the person and dismissal of the proceedings against the person under this subsection, the person is eligible to apply for expunction of records pursuant to G.S. 15A-145.6.

(7) Discharge and dismissal under this subsection shall not be deemed a conviction for purposes of structured sentencing or for purposes of disqualifications or disabilities imposed by law upon conviction of a crime.

(8) There may be only one discharge and dismissal under this section.

(c) Immunity From Prosecution for Minors. - Notwithstanding any other provision of this section, if it is determined, after a reasonable detention for investigative purposes, that a person suspected of or charged with a violation of this section is a minor, that person shall be immune from prosecution under this section and instead shall be taken into temporary protective custody as an undisciplined juvenile pursuant to Article 19 of Chapter 7B of the General Statutes. Pursuant to the provisions of G.S. 7B-301, a law enforcement officer who takes a minor into custody under this section shall immediately report an allegation of a violation of G.S. 14-43.11 and G.S. 14-43.13 to the director of the department of social services in the county where the minor resides or is found, as appropriate, which shall commence an initial investigation into child abuse or child neglect within 24 hours pursuant to G.S. 7B-301 and G.S. 7B-302. (1919, c. 215, s. 1; C.S., s. 4358; 2013-368, s. 5.)

§ 14-204.1: Repealed by Session Laws 2013-368, s. 4, effective October 1, 2013, and applicable to offenses committed on or after that date.

§ 14-205: Repealed by Session Laws 2013-368, s. 4, effective October 1, 2013, and applicable to offenses committed on or after that date.

§ 14-205.1. Solicitation of prostitution.

Except as otherwise provided in this section, any person who solicits another for the purpose of prostitution is guilty of a Class 1 misdemeanor for a first offense and a Class H felony for a second or subsequent offense. Any person 18 years of age or older who willfully solicits a minor for the purpose of prostitution is guilty of a Class G felony. Any person who willfully solicits a person who is severely or profoundly mentally disabled for the purpose of prostitution is guilty of a Class E felony. Punishment under this section may include participation in a program devised for the education and prevention of sexual exploitation (i.e. "John School"), where available. A person who violates this subsection shall not be eligible for a disposition of prayer for judgment continued under any circumstances. (2013-368, s. 5.)

§ 14-205.2. Patronizing a prostitute.

(a) Any person who willfully performs any of the following acts with a person not his or her spouse commits the offense of patronizing a prostitute:

(1) Engages in vaginal intercourse, any sexual act as defined in G.S. 14-27.1, or any sexual contact as defined in G.S. 14-27.1, for the purpose of sexual arousal or gratification with a prostitute.

(2) Enters or remains in a place of prostitution with intent to engage in vaginal intercourse, any sexual act as defined in G.S. 14-27.1, or any sexual contact as defined in G.S. 14-27.1, for the purpose of sexual arousal or gratification.

(b) Except as provided in subsections (c) and (d) of this section, a first violation of this section is a Class A1 misdemeanor. Unless a higher penalty applies, a second or subsequent violation of this section is a Class G felony.

(c) A violation of this section is a Class F felony if the defendant is 18 years of age or older and the prostitute is a minor.

(d) A violation of this section is a Class D felony if the prostitute is a severely or profoundly mentally disabled person. (2013-368, s. 5.)

§ 14-205.3. Promoting prostitution.

(a) Any person who willfully performs any of the following acts commits promoting prostitution:

(1) Advances prostitution as defined in G.S. 14-203.

(2) Profits from prostitution by doing any of the following:

a. Compelling a person to become a prostitute.

b. Receiving a portion of the earnings from a prostitute for arranging or offering to arrange a situation in which the person may practice prostitution.

c. Any means other than those described in sub-subdivisions a. and b. of this subdivision, including from a person who patronizes a prostitute. This sub-subdivision does not apply to a person engaged in prostitution who is a minor. A person cannot be convicted of promoting prostitution under this sub-subdivision if the practice of prostitution underlying the offense consists exclusively of the accused's own acts of prostitution under G.S. 14-204.

(b) Any person who willfully performs any of the following acts commits the offense of promoting prostitution of a minor or mentally disabled person:

(1) Advances prostitution as defined in G.S. 14-203, where a minor or severely or profoundly mentally disabled person engaged in prostitution, or any person engaged in prostitution in the place of prostitution is a minor or is severely or profoundly mentally disabled at the time of the offense.

(2) Profits from prostitution by any means where the prostitute is a minor or is severely or profoundly mentally disabled at the time of the offense.

(3) Confines a minor or a severely or profoundly mentally disabled person against the person's will by the infliction or threat of imminent infliction of great bodily harm, permanent disability, or disfigurement or by administering to the minor or severely or profoundly mentally disabled person, without the person's consent or by threat or deception and for other than medical purposes, any alcoholic intoxicant or a drug as defined in Article 5 of Chapter 90 of the General Statutes (North Carolina Controlled Substances Act) and does any of the following:

a. Compels the minor or severely or profoundly mentally disabled person to engage in prostitution.

b. Arranges a situation in which the minor or severely or profoundly mentally disabled person may practice prostitution.

c. Profits from prostitution by the minor or severely or profoundly mentally disabled person.

For purposes of this subsection, administering drugs or an alcoholic intoxicant to a minor or a severely or profoundly mentally disabled person, as described in subdivision (3) of this subsection, shall be deemed to be without consent if the administering is done without the consent of the parents or legal guardian or if the administering is performed or permitted by the parents or legal guardian for other than medical purposes. Mistake of age is not a defense to a prosecution under this subsection.

(c) Unless a higher penalty applies, a violation of subsection (a) of this section is a Class F felony. A violation of subsection (a) of this section by a person with a prior conviction for a violation of this section or a violation of G.S. 14-204 (prostitution), G.S. 14-204.1 (solicitation of prostitution), or G.S. 14-204.2 (patronizing a prostitute) is a Class E felony.

(d) Unless a higher penalty applies, a violation of subdivision (1) or (2) of subsection (b) of this section is a Class D felony. A violation of subdivision (3) of subsection (b) of this section is a Class C felony. Any violation of subsection (b) of this section by a person with a prior conviction for a violation of this section or a violation of G.S. 14-204 (prostitution), G.S. 14-204.1 (solicitation of prostitution), G.S. 14-204.2 (patronizing a prostitute) is a Class C felony. (2013-368, s. 5.)

§ 14-205.4. Certain probation conditions.

(a)   The court may order any convicted defendant to be examined for sexually transmitted infections. If a person convicted of a crime under this Article receives a sentence which includes probation and that person is infected with a sexually transmitted infection, the period of probation may commence only upon such terms and conditions as shall ensure medical treatment and prevent the spread of the infection.

(b)   No female convicted under this Article shall be placed on probation in the care or charge of any person except a female probation officer. (2013-368, s. 5.)

§ 14-206. Reputation and prior conviction admissible as evidence.

In the trial of any person charged with a violation of any of the provisions of this Article, testimony of a prior conviction, or testimony concerning the reputation of any place, structure, or building, and of the person or persons who reside in or frequent the same, and of the defendant, shall be admissible in evidence in support of the charge. (1919, c. 215, s. 3; C.S., s. 4360.)

§ 14-207: Repealed by Session Laws 2013-368, s. 4, effective October 1, 2013, and applicable to offenses committed on or after that date.

§ 14-208: Repealed by Session Laws 2013-368, s. 4, effective October 1, 2013, and applicable to offenses committed on or after that date.

§ 14-208.1. Reserved for future codification purposes.

§ 14-208.2. Reserved for future codification purposes.

§ 14-208.3. Reserved for future codification purposes.

§ 14-208.4. Reserved for future codification purposes.

Article 27A.

Sex Offender and Public Protection Registration Programs.

Part 1. Registration Programs, Purpose and Definitions Generally.

§ 14-208.5. Purpose.

The General Assembly recognizes that sex offenders often pose a high risk of engaging in sex offenses even after being released from incarceration or commitment and that protection of the public from sex offenders is of paramount governmental interest.

The General Assembly also recognizes that persons who commit certain other types of offenses against minors, such as kidnapping, pose significant and unacceptable threats to the public safety and welfare of the children in this State and that the protection of those children is of great governmental interest. Further, the General Assembly recognizes that law enforcement officers' efforts to protect communities, conduct investigations, and quickly apprehend offenders who commit sex offenses or certain offenses against minors are impaired by the lack of information available to law enforcement agencies about convicted offenders who live within the agency's jurisdiction. Release of information about these offenders will further the governmental interests of public safety so long as the information released is rationally related to the furtherance of those goals.

Therefore, it is the purpose of this Article to assist law enforcement agencies' efforts to protect communities by requiring persons who are convicted of sex offenses or of certain other offenses committed against minors to register with law enforcement agencies, to require the exchange of relevant information about those offenders among law enforcement agencies, and to authorize the access to necessary and relevant information about those offenders to others as provided in this Article. (1995, c. 545, s. 1; 1997-516, s. 1.)

§ 14-208.6. Definitions.

The following definitions apply in this Article:

(1a)   "Aggravated offense" means any criminal offense that includes either of the following: (i) engaging in a sexual act involving vaginal, anal, or oral penetration with a victim of any age through the use of force or the threat of serious violence; or (ii) engaging in a sexual act involving vaginal, anal, or oral penetration with a victim who is less than 12 years old.

(1b)   "County registry" means the information compiled by the sheriff of a county in compliance with this Article.

(1c)   "Division" means the Division of Criminal Information of the Department of Justice.

(1d)   "Electronic mail" means the transmission of information or communication by the use of the Internet, a computer, a facsimile machine, a pager, a cellular telephone, a video recorder, or other electronic means sent to a person identified by a unique address or address number and received by that person.

(1e)   "Employed" includes employment that is full-time or part-time for a period of time exceeding 14 days or for an aggregate period of time exceeding 30 days during any calendar year, whether financially compensated, volunteered, or for the purpose of government or educational benefit.

(1f)   "Entity" means a business or organization that provides Internet service, electronic communications service, remote computing service, online service, electronic mail service, or electronic instant message or chat services whether the business or organization is within or outside the State.

(1g)   "Instant Message" means a form of real-time text communication between two or more people. The communication is conveyed via computers connected over a network such as the Internet.

(1h)   "Institution of higher education" means any postsecondary public or private educational institution, including any trade or professional institution, college, or university.

(1i)   "Internet" means the global information system that is logically linked together by a globally unique address space based on the Internet Protocol or its subsequent extensions; that is able to support communications using the Transmission Control Protocol/Internet Protocol suite, its subsequent extensions, or other Internet Protocol compatible protocols; and that provides, uses, or makes accessible, either publicly or privately, high-level services layered on the communications and related infrastructure described in this subdivision.

(1j) "Mental abnormality" means a congenital or acquired condition of a person that affects the emotional or volitional capacity of the person in a manner that predisposes that person to the commission of criminal sexual acts to a degree that makes the person a menace to the health and safety of others.

(1k) "Nonresident student" means a person who is not a resident of North Carolina but who is enrolled in any type of school in the State on a part-time or full-time basis.

(1l) "Nonresident worker" means a person who is not a resident of North Carolina but who has employment or carries on a vocation in the State, on a part-time or full-time basis, with or without compensation or government or educational benefit, for more than 14 days, or for an aggregate period exceeding 30 days in a calendar year.

(1m) "Offense against a minor" means any of the following offenses if the offense is committed against a minor, and the person committing the offense is not the minor's parent: G.S. 14-39 (kidnapping), G.S. 14-41 (abduction of children), and G.S. 14-43.3 (felonious restraint). The term also includes the following if the person convicted of the following is not the minor's parent: a solicitation or conspiracy to commit any of these offenses; aiding and abetting any of these offenses.

(1n) "Online identifier" means electronic mail address, instant message screen name, user ID, chat or other Internet communication name, but it does not mean social security number, date of birth, or pin number.

(2) "Penal institution" means:

a. A detention facility operated under the jurisdiction of the Section of Prisons of the Division of Adult Correction of the Department of Public Safety;

b. A detention facility operated under the jurisdiction of another state or the federal government; or

c. A detention facility operated by a local government in this State or another state.

(2a) "Personality disorder" means an enduring pattern of inner experience and behavior that deviates markedly from the expectations of the individual's culture, is pervasive and inflexible, has an onset in adolescence or early adulthood, is stable over time, and leads to distress or impairment.

(2b) "Recidivist" means a person who has a prior conviction for an offense that is described in G.S. 14-208.6(4).

(3) "Release" means discharged or paroled.

(4) "Reportable conviction" means:

a. A final conviction for an offense against a minor, a sexually violent offense, or an attempt to commit any of those offenses unless the conviction is for aiding and abetting. A final conviction for aiding and abetting is a reportable conviction only if the court sentencing the individual finds that the registration of that individual under this Article furthers the purposes of this Article as stated in G.S. 14-208.5.

b. A final conviction in another state of an offense, which if committed in this State, is substantially similar to an offense against a minor or a sexually violent offense as defined by this section, or a final conviction in another state of an offense that requires registration under the sex offender registration statutes of that state.

c. A final conviction in a federal jurisdiction (including a court martial) of an offense, which is substantially similar to an offense against a minor or a sexually violent offense as defined by this section.

d. A final conviction for a violation of G.S. 14-202(d), (e), (f), (g), or (h), or a second or subsequent conviction for a violation of G.S. 14-202(a), (a1), or (c), only if the court sentencing the individual issues an order pursuant to G.S. 14-202(l) requiring the individual to register.

e. A final conviction for a violation of G.S. 14-43.14, only if the court sentencing the individual issues an order pursuant to G.S. 14-43.14(e) requiring the individual to register.

(5) "Sexually violent offense" means a violation of G.S. 14-27.2 (first degree rape), G.S. 14-27.2A (rape of a child; adult offender), G.S. 14-27.3 (second degree rape), G.S. 14-27.4 (first degree sexual offense), G.S. 14-27.4A (sex

offense with a child; adult offender), G.S. 14-27.5 (second degree sexual offense), G.S. 14-27.5A (sexual battery), former G.S. 14-27.6 (attempted rape or sexual offense), G.S. 14-27.7 (intercourse and sexual offense with certain victims), G.S. 14-27.7A(a)(statutory rape or sexual offense of person who is 13-, 14-, or 15-years-old where the defendant is at least six years older), G.S. 14-43.11 (human trafficking) if (i) the offense is committed against a minor who is less than 18 years of age or (ii) the offense is committed against any person with the intent that they be held in sexual servitude, G.S. 14-43.13 (subjecting or maintaining a person for sexual servitude), G.S. 14-178 (incest between near relatives), G.S. 14-190.6 (employing or permitting minor to assist in offenses against public morality and decency), G.S. 14-190.9(a1)(felonious indecent exposure), G.S. 14-190.16 (first degree sexual exploitation of a minor), G.S. 14-190.17 (second degree sexual exploitation of a minor), G.S. 14-190.17A (third degree sexual exploitation of a minor), G.S. 14-202.1 (taking indecent liberties with children), G.S. 14-202.3 (Solicitation of child by computer or certain other electronic devices to commit an unlawful sex act), G.S. 14-202.4(a)(taking indecent liberties with a student), G.S. 14-205.2(c) or (d) (patronizing a prostitute who is a minor or a mentally disabled person), G.S. 14-205.3(b) (promoting prostitution of a minor or a mentally disabled person), G.S. 14-318.4(a1) (parent or caretaker commit or permit act of prostitution with or by a juvenile), or G.S. 14-318.4(a2) (commission or allowing of sexual act upon a juvenile by parent or guardian). The term also includes the following: a solicitation or conspiracy to commit any of these offenses; aiding and abetting any of these offenses.

(6) "Sexually violent predator" means a person who has been convicted of a sexually violent offense and who suffers from a mental abnormality or personality disorder that makes the person likely to engage in sexually violent offenses directed at strangers or at a person with whom a relationship has been established or promoted for the primary purpose of victimization.

(7) "Sheriff" means the sheriff of a county in this State.

(8) "Statewide registry" means the central registry compiled by the Division in accordance with G.S. 14-208.14.

(9) "Student" means a person who is enrolled on a full-time or part-time basis, in any postsecondary public or private educational institution, including any trade or professional institution, or other institution of higher education. (1995, c. 545, s. 1; 1997-15, ss. 1, 2; 1997-516, s. 1; 1999-363, s. 1; 2001-373, s. 1; 2002-147, s. 16; 2003-303, s. 2; 2004-109, s. 8; 2005-121, s. 2; 2005-130,

s. 1; 2005-226, s. 2; 2006-247, ss. 1(b), 19(a), 20(d); 2008-117, s. 6.1; 2008-220, s. 1; 2009-498, s. 1; 2010-174, s. 16(a); 2011-145, s. 19.1(h), (j); 2012-153, s. 3; 2012-194, s. 4(a); 2013-33, s. 1; 2013-368, s. 19.)

§ 14-208.6A. Lifetime registration requirements for criminal offenders.

It is the objective of the General Assembly to establish a 30-year registration requirement for persons convicted of certain offenses against minors or sexually violent offenses with an opportunity for those persons to petition in superior court to shorten their registration time period after 10 years of registration. It is the further objective of the General Assembly to establish a more stringent set of registration requirements for recidivists, persons who commit aggravated offenses, and for a subclass of highly dangerous sex offenders who are determined by a sentencing court with the assistance of a board of experts to be sexually violent predators.

To accomplish this objective, there are established two registration programs: the Sex Offender and Public Protection Registration Program and the Sexually Violent Predator Registration Program. Any person convicted of an offense against a minor or of a sexually violent offense as defined by this Article shall register in person as an offender in accordance with Part 2 of this Article. Any person who is a recidivist, who commits an aggravated offense, or who is determined to be a sexually violent predator shall register in person as such in accordance with Part 3 of this Article.

The information obtained under these programs shall be immediately shared with the appropriate local, State, federal, and out-of-state law enforcement officials and penal institutions. In addition, the information designated under G.S. 14-208.10(a) as public record shall be readily available to and accessible by the public. However, the identity of the victim is not public record and shall not be released as a public record. (1997-516, s. 1; 2001-373, s. 2; 2006-247, s. 2(a); 2008-117, s. 7.)

§ 14-208.6B. Registration requirements for juveniles transferred to and convicted in superior court.

A juvenile transferred to superior court pursuant to G.S. 7B-2200 who is convicted of a sexually violent offense or an offense against a minor as defined in G.S. 14-208.6 shall register in person in accordance with this Article just as an adult convicted of the same offense must register. (1997-516, s. 1; 1998-202, s. 13(e); 2006-247, s. 3(a).)

§ 14-208.6C. Discontinuation of registration requirement.

The period of registration required by any of the provisions of this Article shall be discontinued only if the conviction requiring registration is reversed, vacated, or set aside, or if the registrant has been granted an unconditional pardon of innocence for the offense requiring registration. (2001-373, s. 3.)

Part 2. Sex Offender and Public Protection Registration Program.

§ 14-208.7. Registration.

(a)   A person who is a State resident and who has a reportable conviction shall be required to maintain registration with the sheriff of the county where the person resides. If the person moves to North Carolina from outside this State, the person shall register within three business days of establishing residence in this State, or whenever the person has been present in the State for 15 days, whichever comes first. If the person is a current resident of North Carolina, the person shall register:

(1)   Within three business days of release from a penal institution or arrival in a county to live outside a penal institution; or

(2)   Immediately upon conviction for a reportable offense where an active term of imprisonment was not imposed.

Registration shall be maintained for a period of at least 30 years following the date of initial county registration unless the person, after 10 years of registration, successfully petitions the superior court to shorten his or her registration time period under G.S. 14-208.12A.

(a1)   A person who is a nonresident student or a nonresident worker and who has a reportable conviction, or is required to register in the person's state of residency, is required to maintain registration with the sheriff of the county where the person works or attends school. In addition to the information required under subsection (b) of this section, the person shall also provide information regarding the person's school or place of employment as appropriate and the person's address in his or her state of residence.

(b) The Division shall provide each sheriff with forms for registering persons as required by this Article. The registration form shall require all of the following:

(1) The person's full name, each alias, date of birth, sex, race, height, weight, eye color, hair color, drivers license number, and home address.

(1a) A statement indicating what the person's name was at the time of the conviction for the offense that requires registration; what alias, if any, the person was using at the time of the conviction of that offense; and the name of the person as it appears on the judgment imposing the sentence on the person for the conviction of the offense.

(2) The type of offense for which the person was convicted, the date of conviction, and the sentence imposed.

(3) A current photograph taken by the sheriff, without charge, at the time of registration.

(4) The person's fingerprints taken by the sheriff, without charge, at the time of registration.

(5) A statement indicating whether the person is a student or expects to enroll as a student within a year of registering. If the person is a student or expects to enroll as a student within a year of registration, then the registration form shall also require the name and address of the educational institution at which the person is a student or expects to enroll as a student.

(6) A statement indicating whether the person is employed or expects to be employed at an institution of higher education within a year of registering. If the person is employed or expects to be employed at an institution of higher education within a year of registration, then the registration form shall also require the name and address of the educational institution at which the person is or expects to be employed.

(7) Any online identifier that the person uses or intends to use.

(c) When a person registers, the sheriff with whom the person registered shall immediately send the registration information to the Division in a manner determined by the Division. The sheriff shall retain the original registration form and other information collected and shall compile the information that is a public record under this Part into a county registry.

(d) Any person required to register under this section shall report in person at the appropriate sheriff's office to comply with the registration requirements set out in this section. The sheriff shall provide the registrant with written proof of registration at the time of registration. (1995, c. 545, s. 1; 1997-516, s. 1; 2001-373, s. 4; 2002-147, s. 17; 2006-247, s. 5(a); 2008-117, s. 8; 2008-220, s. 2; 2011-61, s. 1.)

§ 14-208.8. Prerelease notification.

(a) At least 10 days, but not earlier than 30 days, before a person who will be subject to registration under this Article is due to be released from a penal institution, an official of the penal institution shall do all of the following:

(1) Inform the person of the person's duty to register under this Article and require the person to sign a written statement that the person was so informed or, if the person refuses to sign the statement, certify that the person was so informed.

(2) Obtain the registration information required under G.S. 14-208.7(b)(1), (2), (5), (6), and (7), as well as the address where the person expects to reside upon the person's release.

(3) Send the Division and the sheriff of the county in which the person expects to reside the information collected in accordance with subdivision (2) of this subsection.

(b) If a person who is subject to registration under this Article does not receive an active term of imprisonment, the court pronouncing sentence shall conduct, at the time of sentencing, the notification procedures specified in subsection (a) of this section. (1995, c. 545, s. 1; 1997-516, s. 1; 2002-147, s. 18; 2008-220, s. 3.)

§ 14-208.8A. Notification requirement for out-of-county employment if temporary residence established.

(a) Notice Required. - A person required to register under G.S. 14-208.7 shall notify the sheriff of the county with whom the person is registered of the person's place of employment and temporary residence, which includes a hotel, motel, or other transient lodging place, if the person meets both of the following conditions:

(1) Is employed or carries on a vocation in a county in the State other than the county in which the person is registered for more than 10 business days within a 30-day period, or for an aggregate period exceeding 30 days in a calendar year, on a part-time or full-time basis, with or without compensation or government or educational benefit.

(2) Maintains a temporary residence in that county for more than 10 business days within a 30-day period, or for an aggregate period exceeding 30 days in a calendar year.

(b) Time Period. - The notice required by subsection (a) of this section shall be provided within 72 hours after the person knows or should know that he or she will be working and maintaining a temporary residence in a county other than the county in which the person resides for more than 10 business days within a 30-day period, or within 10 days after the person knows or should know that he or she will be working and maintaining a temporary residence in a county other than the county in which the person resides for an aggregate period exceeding 30 days in a calendar year.

(c) Notice to Division. - Upon receiving the notice required under subsection (a) of this section, the sheriff shall immediately forward the information to the Division. The Division shall notify the sheriff of the county where the person is working and maintaining a temporary residence of the person's place of employment and temporary address in that county. (2006-247, s. 4(a); 2007-484, s. 2.)

§ 14-208.9. Change of address; change of academic status or educational employment status; change of online identifier; change of name.

(a) If a person required to register changes address, the person shall report in person and provide written notice of the new address not later than the third business day after the change to the sheriff of the county with whom the person had last registered. If the person moves to another county, the person shall also report in person to the sheriff of the new county and provide written notice of the person's address not later than the tenth day after the change of address. Upon receipt of the notice, the sheriff shall immediately forward this information to the Division. When the Division receives notice from a sheriff that a person required to register is moving to another county in the State, the Division shall inform the sheriff of the new county of the person's new residence.

(b) If a person required to register intends to move to another state, the person shall report in person to the sheriff of the county of current residence at least three business days before the date the person intends to leave this State to establish residence in another state or jurisdiction. The person shall provide to the sheriff a written notification that includes all of the following information: the address, municipality, county, and state of intended residence.

(1) If it appears to the sheriff that the record photograph of the sex offender no longer provides a true and accurate likeness of the sex offender, then the sheriff shall take a photograph of the offender to update the registration.

(2) The sheriff shall inform the person that the person must comply with the registration requirements in the new state of residence. The sheriff shall also immediately forward the information included in the notification to the Division, and the Division shall inform the appropriate state official in the state to which the registrant moves of the person's notification and new address.

(b1) A person who indicates his or her intent to reside in another state or jurisdiction and later decides to remain in this State shall, within three business days after the date upon which the person indicated he or she would leave this State, report in person to the sheriff's office to which the person reported the intended change of residence, of his or her intent to remain in this State. If the sheriff is notified by the sexual offender that he or she intends to remain in this State, the sheriff shall promptly report this information to the Division.

(c) If a person required to register changes his or her academic status either by enrolling as a student or by terminating enrollment as a student, then the person shall, within three business days, report in person to the sheriff of the county with whom the person registered and provide written notice of the person's new status. The written notice shall include the name and address of the institution of higher education at which the student is or was enrolled. The sheriff shall immediately forward this information to the Division.

(d) If a person required to register changes his or her employment status either by obtaining employment at an institution of higher education or by terminating employment at an institution of higher education, then the person shall, within three business days, report in person to the sheriff of the county with whom the person registered and provide written notice of the person's new status not later than the tenth day after the change to the sheriff of the county with whom the person registered. The written notice shall include the name and address of the institution of higher education at which the person is or was employed. The sheriff shall immediately forward this information to the Division.

(e) If a person required to register changes an online identifier, or obtains a new online identifier, then the person shall, within 10 days, report in person to the sheriff of the county with whom the person registered to provide the new or changed online identifier information to the sheriff. The sheriff shall immediately forward this information to the Division.

(f) If a person required to register changes his or her name pursuant to Chapter 101 of the General Statutes or by any other method, then the person shall, within three business days, report in person to the sheriff of the county with whom the person registered to provide the name change to the sheriff. The sheriff shall immediately forward this information to the Division. (1995, c. 545, s. 1; 1997-516, s. 1; 2001-373, s. 5; 2002-147, s. 19; 2006-247, s. 6(a); 2007-213, s. 9A; 2007-484, s. 42(b); 2008-117, s. 9; 2008-220, ss. 4, 5; 2011-61, ss. 2, 3.)

§ 14-208.9A. Verification of registration information.

(a) The information in the county registry shall be verified semiannually for each registrant as follows:

(1) Every year on the anniversary of a person's initial registration date, and again six months after that date, the Division shall mail a nonforwardable verification form to the last reported address of the person.

(2) The person shall return the verification form in person to the sheriff within three business days after the receipt of the form.

(3) The verification form shall be signed by the person and shall indicate the following:

a. Whether the person still resides at the address last reported to the sheriff. If the person has a different address, then the person shall indicate that fact and the new address.

b. Whether the person still uses or intends to use any online identifiers last reported to the sheriff. If the person has any new or different online identifiers, then the person shall provide those online identifiers to the sheriff.

c. Whether the person still uses or intends to use the name under which the person registered and last reported to the sheriff. If the person has any new or different name, then the person shall provide that name to the sheriff.

(3a) If it appears to the sheriff that the record photograph of the sex offender no longer provides a true and accurate likeness of the sex offender, then the sheriff shall take a photograph of the offender to include with the verification form.

(4) If the person fails to return the verification form in person to the sheriff within three business days after receipt of the form, the person is subject to the penalties provided in G.S. 14-208.11. If the person fails to report in person and provide the written verification as provided by this section, the sheriff shall make a reasonable attempt to verify that the person is residing at the registered address. If the person cannot be found at the registered address and has failed to report a change of address, the person is subject to the penalties provided in G.S. 14-208.11, unless the person reports in person to the sheriff and proves that the person has not changed his or her residential address.

(b) Additional Verification May Be Required. - During the period that an offender is required to be registered under this Article, the sheriff is authorized to attempt to verify that the offender continues to reside at the address last registered by the offender.

(c) Additional Photograph May Be Required. - If it appears to the sheriff that the current photograph of the sex offender no longer provides a true and accurate likeness of the sex offender, upon in-person notice from the sheriff, the sex offender shall allow the sheriff to take another photograph of the sex offender at the time of the sheriff's request. If requested by the sheriff, the sex offender shall appear in person at the sheriff's office during normal business hours within three business days of being requested to do so and shall allow the sheriff to take another photograph of the sex offender. A person who willfully fails to comply with this subsection is guilty of a Class 1 misdemeanor. (1997-516, s. 1; 2006-247, s. 7(a); 2008-117, s. 10; 2008-220, s. 6; 2011-61, s. 4.)

§ 14-208.10. Registration information is public record; access to registration information.

(a) The following information regarding a person required to register under this Article is public record and shall be available for public inspection: name, sex, address, physical description, picture, conviction date, offense for which registration was required, the sentence imposed as a result of the conviction, and registration status. The information obtained under G.S. 14-208.22 regarding a person's medical records or documentation of treatment for the person's mental abnormality or personality disorder shall not be a part of the public record.

The sheriff shall release any other relevant information that is necessary to protect the public concerning a specific person, but shall not release the identity of the victim of the offense that required registration under this Article.

(b) Any person may obtain a copy of an individual's registration form, a part of the county registry, or all of the county registry, by submitting a written request for the information to the sheriff. However, the identity of the victim of an offense that requires registration under this Article shall not be released. The sheriff may charge a reasonable fee for duplicating costs and for mailing costs when appropriate. (1995, c. 545, s. 1; 1997-516, s. 1.)

§ 14-208.11. Failure to register; falsification of verification notice; failure to return verification form; order for arrest.

(a) A person required by this Article to register who willfully does any of the following is guilty of a Class F felony:

(1) Fails to register as required by this Article, including failure to register with the sheriff in the county designated by the person, pursuant to G.S. 14-208.8, as their expected county of residence.

(2) Fails to notify the last registering sheriff of a change of address as required by this Article.

(3) Fails to return a verification notice as required under G.S. 14-208.9A.

(4) Forges or submits under false pretenses the information or verification notices required under this Article.

(5) Fails to inform the registering sheriff of enrollment or termination of enrollment as a student.

(6) Fails to inform the registering sheriff of employment at an institution of higher education or termination of employment at an institution of higher education.

(7) Fails to report in person to the sheriff's office as required by G.S. 14-208.7, 14-208.9, and 14-208.9A.

(8) Reports his or her intent to reside in another state or jurisdiction but remains in this State without reporting to the sheriff in the manner required by G.S. 14-208.9.

(9) Fails to notify the registering sheriff of out-of-county employment if temporary residence is established as required under G.S. 14-208.8A.

(10) Fails to inform the registering sheriff of any new or changes to existing online identifiers that the person uses or intends to use.

(a1) If a person commits a violation of subsection (a) of this section, the probation officer, parole officer, or any other law enforcement officer who is aware of the violation shall immediately arrest the person in accordance with G.S. 15A-401, or seek an order for the person's arrest in accordance with G.S. 15A-305.

(a2) A person arrested pursuant to subsection (a1) of this section shall be subject to the jurisdiction of the prosecutorial and judicial district that includes the sheriff's office in the county where the person failed to register, pursuant to this Article. If the arrest is made outside of the applicable prosecutorial district, the person shall be transferred to the custody of the sheriff of the county where the person failed to register and all further criminal and judicial proceedings shall be held in that county.

(b) Before a person convicted of a violation of this Article is due to be released from a penal institution, an official of the penal institution shall conduct the prerelease notification procedures specified under G.S. 14-208.8(a)(2) and (3). If upon a conviction for a violation of this Article, no active term of imprisonment is imposed, the court pronouncing sentence shall, at the time of sentencing, conduct the notification procedures specified under G.S. 14-208.8(a)(2) and (3).

(c) A person who is unable to meet the registration or verification requirements of this Article shall be deemed to have complied with its requirements if:

(1) The person is incarcerated in, or is in the custody of, a local, State, private, or federal correctional facility,

(2) The person notifies the official in charge of the facility of their status as a person with a legal obligation or requirement under this Article and

(3) The person meets the registration or verification requirements of this Article no later than 10 days after release from confinement or custody. (1995, c. 545, s. 1; 1997-516, s. 1; 2002-147, s. 20; 2006-247, ss. 8(a), 8(b); 2008-220, s. 7; 2013-205, s. 1.)

§ 14-208.11A. Duty to report noncompliance of a sex offender; penalty for failure to report in certain circumstances.

(a) It shall be unlawful and a Class H felony for any person who has reason to believe that an offender is in violation of the requirements of this Article, and who has the intent to assist the offender in eluding arrest, to do any of the following:

(1) Withhold information from, or fail to notify, a law enforcement agency about the offender's noncompliance with the requirements of this Article, and, if known, the whereabouts of the offender.

(2) Harbor, attempt to harbor, or assist another person in harboring or attempting to harbor, the offender.

(3)   Conceal, or attempt to conceal, or assist another person in concealing or attempting to conceal, the offender.

(4)   Provide information to a law enforcement agency regarding the offender that the person knows to be false information.

(b)   This section does not apply if the offender is incarcerated in or is in the custody of a local, State, private, or federal correctional facility. (2006-247, s. 9.1(a).)

§ 14-208.12: Repealed by Session Laws 1997-516, s. 1.

§ 14-208.12A. Request for termination of registration requirement.

(a)   Ten years from the date of initial county registration, a person required to register under this Part may petition the superior court to terminate the 30-year registration requirement if the person has not been convicted of a subsequent offense requiring registration under this Article.

If the reportable conviction is for an offense that occurred in North Carolina, the petition shall be filed in the district where the person was convicted of the offense.

If the reportable conviction is for an offense that occurred in another state, the petition shall be filed in the district where the person resides. A person who petitions to terminate the registration requirement for a reportable conviction that is an out-of-state offense shall also do the following: (i) provide written notice to the sheriff of the county where the person was convicted that the person is petitioning the court to terminate the registration requirement and (ii) include with the petition at the time of its filing, an affidavit, signed by the petitioner, that verifies that the petitioner has notified the sheriff of the county where the person was convicted of the petition and that provides the mailing address and contact information for that sheriff.

(a1)   The court may grant the relief if:

(1)   The petitioner demonstrates to the court that he or she has not been arrested for any crime that would require registration under this Article since completing the sentence,

(2)   The requested relief complies with the provisions of the federal Jacob Wetterling Act, as amended, and any other federal standards applicable to the termination of a registration requirement or required to be met as a condition for the receipt of federal funds by the State, and

(3)   The court is otherwise satisfied that the petitioner is not a current or potential threat to public safety.

(a2)   The district attorney in the district in which the petition is filed shall be given notice of the petition at least three weeks before the hearing on the matter. The petitioner may present evidence in support of the petition and the district attorney may present evidence in opposition to the requested relief or may otherwise demonstrate the reasons why the petition should be denied.

(a3)   If the court denies the petition, the person may again petition the court for relief in accordance with this section one year from the date of the denial of the original petition to terminate the registration requirement. If the court grants the petition to terminate the registration requirement, the clerk of court shall forward a certified copy of the order to the Division to have the person's name removed from the registry.

(b)   If there is a subsequent offense, the county registration records shall be retained until the registration requirement for the subsequent offense is terminated by the court under subsection (a1) of this section. (1997-516, s. 1; 2006-247, s. 10(a); 2008-117, s. 11; 2011-61, s. 5.)

§ 14-208.13. File with Police Information Network.

(a)   The Division shall include the registration information in the Police Information Network as set forth in G.S. 114-10.1.

(b)   The Division shall maintain the registration information permanently even after the registrant's reporting requirement expires. (1995, c. 545, s. 1; 1997-516, s. 1.)

§ 14-208.14. Statewide registry; Division of Criminal Statistics designated custodian of statewide registry.

(a) The Division of Criminal Statistics shall compile and keep current a central statewide sex offender registry. The Division is the State agency designated as the custodian of the statewide registry. As custodian the Division has the following responsibilities:

(1) To receive from the sheriff or any other law enforcement agency or penal institution all sex offender registrations, changes of address, changes of academic or educational employment status, and prerelease notifications required under this Article or under federal law. The Division shall also receive notices of any violation of this Article, including a failure to register or a failure to report a change of address.

(2) To provide all need-to-know law enforcement agencies (local, State, campus, federal, and those located in other states) immediately upon receipt by the Division of any of the following: registration information, a prerelease notification, a change of address, a change of academic or educational employment status, or notice of a violation of this Article.

(2a) To notify the appropriate law enforcement unit at an institution of higher education as soon as possible upon receipt by the Division of relevant information based on registration information or notice of a change of academic or educational employment status. If an institution of higher education does not have a law enforcement unit, then the Division shall provide the information to the local law enforcement agency that has jurisdiction for the campus.

(3) To coordinate efforts among law enforcement agencies and penal institutions to ensure that the registration information, changes of address, change of name, prerelease notifications, and notices of failure to register or to report a change of address are conveyed in an appropriate and timely manner.

(4) To provide public access to the statewide registry in accordance with this Article.

(4a) To maintain the system for public access so that a registrant's full name, any aliases, and any legal name changes are cross-referenced and a member of the public may conduct a search of the system for a registrant under any of those names.

(5) To maintain a system allowing an entity to access a list of online identifiers of persons in the central sex offender registry.

(b) The statewide registry shall include the following:

(1) Registration information obtained by a sheriff or penal institution under this Article or from any other local or State law enforcement agency.

(2) Registration information received from a state or local law enforcement agency or penal institution in another state.

(3) Registration information received from a federal law enforcement agency or penal institution. (1997-516, s. 1; 2002-147, s. 21; 2008-220, s. 8; 2011-61, ss. 6, 7.)

§ 14-208.15. Certain statewide registry information is public record: access to statewide registry.

(a) The information in the statewide registry that is public record is the same as in G.S. 14-208.10. The Division shall release any other relevant information that is necessary to protect the public concerning a specific person, but shall not release the identity of the victim of the offense that required registration under this Article.

(b) The Division shall provide free public access to automated data from the statewide registry, including photographs provided by the registering sheriffs, via the Internet. The public will be able to access the statewide registry to view an individual registration record, a part of the statewide registry, or all of the statewide registry. The Division may also provide copies of registry information to the public upon written request and may charge a reasonable fee for duplicating costs and mailings costs. (1997-516, s. 1.)

§ 14-208.15A. Release of online identifiers to entity; fee.

(a) The Division may release registry information regarding a registered offender's online identifier to an entity for the purpose of allowing the entity to prescreen users or to compare the online identifier information with information held by the entity as provided by this section.

(b)   An entity desiring to prescreen its users or compare its database of registered users to the list of online identifiers of persons in the statewide registry may apply to the Division to access the information. An entity that complies with the criteria developed by the Division regarding the release and use of the online identifier information and pays the fee may screen new users or compare its database of registered users to the list of online identifiers of persons in the statewide registry as frequently as the Division may allow for the purpose of identifying a registered user associated with an online identifier contained in the statewide registry.

(c)   The Division may charge an entity that submits a request for the online identifiers of persons in the statewide registry an annual fee of one hundred dollars ($100.00). Fees collected under this section shall be credited to the Department of Justice and applied to the cost of providing this service.

(d)   The Division shall develop standards regarding the release and use of online identifier information. The standards shall include a requirement that the information obtained from the statewide registry shall not be disclosed for any purpose other than for prescreening its users or comparing the database of registered users of the entity against the list of online identifiers of persons in the statewide registry.

(e)   An entity that receives:

(1)   A complaint from a user of the entity's services that a person uses its service to solicit a minor by computer to commit an unlawful sex act as defined in G.S. 14-202.3, or

(2)   A report that a user may be violating G.S. 14-190.17 or G.S. 14-190.17A by posting or transmitting material that contains a visual representation of a minor engaged in sexual activity,

shall report that information and the online identifier information of the person allegedly committing the offense, including whether that online identifier is included in the statewide registry, to the Cyber Tip Line at the National Center for Missing and Exploited Children, which shall forward that report to an appropriate law enforcement official in this State. The offense is committed in the State for purposes of determining jurisdiction, if the transmission that constitutes the offense either originates in the State or is received in the State.

(f) An entity that complies with this section in good faith is immune from civil or criminal liability resulting from either of the following:

(1) The entity's refusal to provide system service to a person on the basis that the entity reasonably believed that the person was subject to registration under State sex offender registry laws.

(2) A person's criminal or tortious acts against a minor with whom the person had communicated on the entity's system. (2008-220, s. 9; 2009-272, s. 2.)

§ 14-208.16. Residential restrictions.

(a) A registrant under this Article shall not knowingly reside within 1,000 feet of the property on which any public or nonpublic school or child care center is located. This subsection applies to any registrant who did not establish his or her residence, in accordance with subsection (d) of this section, prior to August 16, 2006.

(b) As used in this section, "school" does not include home schools as defined in G.S. 115C-563 or institutions of higher education, and the term "child care center" is defined by G.S. 110-86(3). The term "registrant" means a person who is registered, or is required to register, under this Article.

(c) This section does not apply to child care centers that are located on or within 1,000 feet of the property of an institution of higher education where the registrant is a student or is employed.

(d) Changes in the ownership of or use of property within 1,000 feet of a registrant's registered address that occur after a registrant establishes residency at the registered address shall not form the basis for finding that an offender is in violation of this section. For purposes of this subsection, a residence is established when the registrant does any of the following:

(1) Purchases the residence or enters into a specifically enforceable contract to purchase the residence.

(2) Enters into a written lease contract for the residence and for as long as the person is lawfully entitled to remain on the premises.

(3) Resides with an immediate family member who established residence in accordance with this subsection. For purposes of this subsection, "immediate family member" means a child or sibling who is 18 years of age or older, or a parent, grandparent, legal guardian, or spouse of the registrant.

(e) Nothing in this section shall be construed as creating a private cause of action against a real estate agent or landlord for any act or omission arising out of the residential restriction in this section.

(f) A violation of this section is a Class G felony. (2006-247, s. 11(a); 2007-213, s. 10; 2013-28, s. 1.)

§ 14-208.17. Sexual predator prohibited from working or volunteering for child-involved activities; limitation on residential use.

(a) It shall be unlawful for any person required to register under this Article to work for any person or as a sole proprietor, with or without compensation, at any place where a minor is present and the person's responsibilities or activities would include instruction, supervision, or care of a minor or minors.

(b) It shall be unlawful for any person to conduct any activity at his or her residence where the person:

(1) Accepts a minor or minors into his or her care or custody from another, and

(2) Knows that a person who resides at that same location is required to register under this Article.

(c) A violation of this section is a Class F felony. (2006-247, s. 11(b).)

§ 14-208.18. Sex offender unlawfully on premises.

(a) It shall be unlawful for any person required to register under this Article, if the offense requiring registration is described in subsection (c) of this section, to knowingly be at any of the following locations:

(1) On the premises of any place intended primarily for the use, care, or supervision of minors, including, but not limited to, schools, children's museums, child care centers, nurseries, and playgrounds.

(2) Within 300 feet of any location intended primarily for the use, care, or supervision of minors when the place is located on premises that are not intended primarily for the use, care, or supervision of minors, including, but not limited to, places described in subdivision (1) of this subsection that are located in malls, shopping centers, or other property open to the general public.

(3) At any place where minors gather for regularly scheduled educational, recreational, or social programs.

(b) Notwithstanding any provision of this section, a person subject to subsection (a) of this section who is the parent or guardian of a minor may take the minor to any location that can provide emergency medical care treatment if the minor is in need of emergency medical care.

(c) Subsection (a) of this section is applicable only to persons required to register under this Article who have committed any of the following offenses:

(1) Any offense in Article 7A of this Chapter.

(2) Any offense where the victim of the offense was under the age of 16 years at the time of the offense.

(d) A person subject to subsection (a) of this section who is a parent or guardian of a student enrolled in a school may be present on school property if all of the following conditions are met:

(1) The parent or guardian is on school property for the purpose for one of the following:

a. To attend a conference at the school with school personnel to discuss the academic or social progress of the parents' or guardians' child; or

b. The presence of the parent or guardian has been requested by the principal or his or her designee for any other reason relating to the welfare or transportation of the child.

(2) The parent or guardian complies with all of the following:

a. Notice: The parent or guardian shall notify the principal of the school of the parents' or guardians' registration under this Article and of his or her presence at the school unless the parent or guardian has permission to be present from the superintendent or the local board of education, or the principal has granted ongoing permission for regular visits of a routine nature. If permission is granted by the superintendent or the local board of education, the superintendent or chairman of the local board of education shall inform the principal of the school where the parents' or guardians' will be present. Notification includes the nature of the parents' or guardians' visit and the hours when the parent or guardian will be present at the school. The parent or guardian is responsible for notifying the principal's office upon arrival and upon departure. Any permission granted under this sub-subdivision shall be in writing.

b. Supervision: At all times that a parent or guardian is on school property, the parent or guardian shall remain under the direct supervision of school personnel. A parent or guardian shall not be on school property even if the parent or guardian has ongoing permission for regular visits of a routine nature if no school personnel are reasonably available to supervise the parent or guardian on that occasion.

(e) A person subject to subsection (a) of this section who is eligible to vote may be present at a location described in subsection (a) used as a voting place as defined by G.S. 163-165 only for the purposes of voting and shall not be outside the voting enclosure other than for the purpose of entering and exiting the voting place. If the voting place is a school, then the person subject to subsection (a) shall notify the principal of the school that he or she is registered under this Article.

(f) A person subject to subsection (a) of this section who is eligible under G.S. 115C-378 to attend public school may be present on school property if permitted by the local board of education pursuant to G.S. 115C-390.11(a)(2).

(g) A juvenile subject to subsection (a) of this section may be present at a location described in that subsection if the juvenile is at the location to receive medical treatment or mental health services and remains under the direct supervision of an employee of the treating institution at all times.

(g1) Notwithstanding any provision of this section, a person subject to subsection (a) of this section who is required to wear an electronic monitoring device shall wear an electronic monitoring device that provides exclusion zones around the premises of all elementary and secondary schools in North Carolina.

(h) A violation of this section is a Class H felony. (2008-117, s. 12; 2009-570, s. 5; 2011-245, s. 2(b); 2011-282, s. 14.)

§ 14-208.19. Community and public notification.

The licensee for each licensed day care center and the principal of each elementary school, middle school, and high school shall register with the North Carolina Sex Offender and Public Protection Registry to receive e-mail notification when a registered sex offender moves within a one-mile radius of the licensed day care center or school. (2008-117, s. 13.)

§ 14-208.19A. Commercial drivers license restrictions.

(a) The Division of Motor Vehicles, in compliance with G.S. 20-37.14A, shall not issue or renew a commercial drivers license with a P or S endorsement to any person required to register under this Article.

(b) The Division of Motor Vehicles, in compliance with G.S. 20-37.13(f) shall not issue a commercial driver learner's permit with a P or S endorsement to any person required to register under this Article.

(c) A person who is convicted of a violation that requires registration under Article 27A of Chapter 14 of the General Statutes is disqualified under G.S. 20-17.4 from driving a commercial motor vehicle that requires a commercial drivers license with a P or S endorsement for the period of time during which the person is required to maintain registration under Article 27A of Chapter 14 of the General Statutes.

(d) A person who drives a commercial passenger vehicle or a school bus and who does not have a commercial drivers license with a P or S endorsement because the person was convicted of a violation that requires registration under

Article 27A of Chapter 14 of the General Statutes shall be punished as provided by G.S. 20-27.1. (2009-491, s. 1.)

Part 3. Sexually Violent Predator Registration Program.

§ 14-208.20. Sexually violent predator determination; notice of intent; presentence investigation.

(a) When a person is charged by indictment or information with the commission of a sexually violent offense, the district attorney shall decide whether to seek classification of the offender as a sexually violent predator if the person is convicted. If the district attorney intends to seek the classification of a sexually violent predator, the district attorney shall within the time provided for the filing of pretrial motions under G.S. 15A-952 file a notice of the district attorney's intent. The court may for good cause shown allow late filing of the notice, grant additional time to the parties to prepare for trial, or make other appropriate orders.

(b) Prior to sentencing a person as a sexually violent predator, the court shall order a presentence investigation in accordance with G.S. 15A-1332(c). However, the study of the defendant and whether the defendant is a sexually violent predator shall be conducted by a board of experts selected by the Division of Adult Correction of the Department of Public Safety. The board of experts shall be composed of at least four people. Two of the board members shall be experts in the field of the behavior and treatment of sexual offenders, one of whom shall be selected from a panel of experts in those fields provided by the North Carolina Medical Society and not employed with the Division of Adult Correction of the Department of Public Safety or employed on a full-time basis with any other State agency. One of the board members shall be a victims' rights advocate, and one of the board members shall be a representative of law enforcement agencies.

(c) When the defendant is returned from the presentence commitment, the court shall hold a sentencing hearing in accordance with G.S. 15A-1334. At the sentencing hearing, the court shall, after taking the presentencing report under advisement, make written findings as to whether the defendant is classified as a sexually violent predator and the basis for the court's findings. (1997-516, s. 1; 2001-373, s. 6; 2011-145, s. 19.1(h).)

§ 14-208.21. Lifetime registration procedure; application of Part 2 of this Article.

Unless provided otherwise by this Part, the provisions of Part 2 of this Article apply to a person classified as a sexually violent predator, a person who is a recidivist, or a person who is convicted of an aggravated offense. The procedure for registering as a sexually violent predator, a recidivist, or a person convicted of an aggravated offense is the same as under Part 2 of this Article. (1997-516, s. 1; 2001-373, s. 7.)

§ 14-208.22. Additional registration information required.

(a) In addition to the information required by G.S. 14-208.7, the following information shall also be obtained in the same manner as set out in Part 2 of this Article from a person who is a recidivist, who is convicted of an aggravated offense, or who is classified as a sexually violent predator:

(1) Identifying factors.

(2) Offense history.

(3) Documentation of any treatment received by the person for the person's mental abnormality or personality disorder.

(b) The Division shall provide each sheriff with forms for registering persons as required by this Article.

(c) The Division of Adult Correction of the Department of Public Safety shall also obtain the additional information set out in subsection (a) of this section and shall include this information in the prerelease notice forwarded to the sheriff or other appropriate law enforcement agency. (1997-516, s. 1; 2001-373, s. 8; 2011-145, s. 19.1(h).)

§ 14-208.23. Length of registration.

A person who is a recidivist, who is convicted of an aggravated offense, or who is classified as a sexually violent predator shall maintain registration for the person's life. Except as provided under G.S. 14-208.6C, the requirement of registration shall not be terminated. (1997-516, s. 1; 2001-373, s. 9.)

§ 14-208.24. Verification of registration information.

(a) The information in the county registry shall be verified by the sheriff for each registrant who is a recidivist, who is convicted of an aggravated offense, or who is classified as a sexually violent predator every 90 days after the person's initial registration date.

(b) The procedure for verifying the information in the criminal offender registry is the same as under G.S. 14-208.9A, except that verification shall be every 90 days as provided by subsection (a) of this section. (1997-516, s. 1; 2001-373, s. 10.)

§ 14-208.25: Repealed by Session Laws 2001-373, s. 11.

Part 4. Registration of Certain Juveniles Adjudicated for Committing Certain Offenses.

§ 14-208.26. Registration of certain juveniles adjudicated delinquent for committing certain offenses.

(a) When a juvenile is adjudicated delinquent for a violation of G.S. 14-27.2 (first degree rape), G.S. 14-27.3 (second degree rape), G.S. 14-27.4 (first degree sexual offense), G.S. 14-27.5 (second degree sexual offense), or former G.S. 14-27.6 (attempted rape or sexual offense), and the juvenile was at least eleven years of age at the time of the commission of the offense, the court shall consider whether the juvenile is a danger to the community. If the court finds that the juvenile is a danger to the community, then the court shall consider whether the juvenile should be required to register with the county sheriff in accordance with this Part. The determination as to whether the juvenile is a danger to the community and whether the juvenile shall be ordered to register shall be made by the presiding judge at the dispositional hearing. If the judge rules that the juvenile is a danger to the community and that the juvenile shall register, then an order shall be entered requiring the juvenile to register. The court's findings regarding whether the juvenile is a danger to the community and whether the juvenile shall register shall be entered into the court record. No juvenile may be required to register under this Part unless the court first finds that the juvenile is a danger to the community.

A juvenile ordered to register under this Part shall register and maintain that registration as provided by this Part.

(a1)   For purposes of this section, a violation of any of the offenses listed in subsection (a) of this section includes all of the following: (i) the commission of any of those offenses, (ii) the attempt, conspiracy, or solicitation of another to commit any of those offenses, (iii) aiding and abetting any of those offenses.

(b)   If the court finds that the juvenile is a danger to the community and must register, the presiding judge shall conduct the notification procedures specified in G.S. 14-208.8. The chief court counselor of that district shall file the registration information for the juvenile with the appropriate sheriff. (1997-516, s. 1; 1999-363, s. 2; 2012-194, s. 4(b).)

§ 14-208.27. Change of address.

If a juvenile who is adjudicated delinquent and required to register changes address, the juvenile court counselor for the juvenile shall provide written notice of the new address not later than the third business day after the change to the sheriff of the county with whom the juvenile had last registered. Upon receipt of the notice, the sheriff shall immediately forward this information to the Division. If the juvenile moves to another county in this State, the Division shall inform the sheriff of the new county of the juvenile's new residence. (1997-516, s. 1; 2001-490, s. 2.36; 2008-117, s. 14.)

§ 14-208.28. Verification of registration information.

The information provided to the sheriff shall be verified semiannually for each juvenile registrant as follows:

(1)   Every year on the anniversary of a juvenile's initial registration date and six months after that date, the sheriff shall mail a verification form to the juvenile court counselor assigned to the juvenile.

(2) The juvenile court counselor for the juvenile shall return the verification form to the sheriff within three business days after the receipt of the form.

(3) The verification form shall be signed by the juvenile court counselor and the juvenile and shall indicate whether the juvenile still resides at the address last reported to the sheriff. If the juvenile has a different address, then that fact and the new address shall be indicated on the form. (1997-516, s. 1; 2001-490, s. 2.37; 2006-247, s. 13; 2008-117, s. 15.)

§ 14-208.29. Registration information is not public record; access to registration information available only to law enforcement agencies and local boards of education.

(a) Notwithstanding any other provision of law, the information regarding a juvenile required to register under this Part is not public record and is not available for public inspection.

(b) The registration information of a juvenile adjudicated delinquent and required to register under this Part shall be maintained separately by the sheriff and released only to law enforcement agencies and local boards of education. Registry information for any juvenile enrolled in the local school administrative unit shall be forwarded to the local board of education. Under no circumstances shall the registration of a juvenile adjudicated delinquent be included in the county or statewide registries, or be made available to the public via internet. (1997-516, s. 1; 2008-117, s. 12.2.)

§ 14-208.30. Termination of registration requirement.

The requirement that a juvenile adjudicated delinquent register under this Part automatically terminates on the juvenile's eighteenth birthday or when the jurisdiction of the juvenile court with regard to the juvenile ends, whichever occurs first. (1997-516, s. 1.)

§ 14-208.31. File with Police Information Network.

(a) The Division shall include the registration information in the Police Information Network as set forth in G.S. 114-10.1.

(b) The Division shall maintain the registration information permanently even after the registrant's reporting requirement expires; however, the records shall remain confidential in accordance with Article 32 of Chapter 7B of the General Statutes. (1997-516, s. 1; 1998-202, s. 14.)

§ 14-208.32. Application of Part.

This Part does not apply to a juvenile who is tried and convicted as an adult for committing or attempting to commit a sexually violent offense or an offense against a minor. A juvenile who is convicted of one of those offenses as an adult is subject to the registration requirements of Part 2 and Part 3 of this Article. (1997-516, s. 1.)

§ 14-208.33. Reserved for future codification purposes.

§ 14-208.34. Reserved for future codification purposes.

§ 14-208.35. Reserved for future codification purposes.

§ 14-208.36. Reserved for future codification purposes.

§ 14-208.37. Reserved for future codification purposes.

§ 14-208.38. Reserved for future codification purposes.

§ 14-208.39. Reserved for future codification purposes.

Part 5. Sex Offender Monitoring.

§ 14-208.40. Establishment of program; creation of guidelines; duties.

(a) The Division of Adult Correction of the Department of Public Safety shall establish a sex offender monitoring program that uses a continuous satellite-based monitoring system and shall create guidelines to govern the program. The program shall be designed to monitor three categories of offenders as follows:

(1) Any offender who is convicted of a reportable conviction as defined by G.S. 14-208.6(4) and who is required to register under Part 3 of Article 27A of Chapter 14 of the General Statutes because the defendant is classified as a sexually violent predator, is a recidivist, or was convicted of an aggravated offense as those terms are defined in G.S. 14-208.6.

(2) Any offender who satisfies all of the following criteria: (i) is convicted of a reportable conviction as defined by G.S. 14-208.6(4), (ii) is required to register under Part 2 of Article 27A of Chapter 14 of the General Statutes, (iii) has committed an offense involving the physical, mental, or sexual abuse of a minor, and (iv) based on the Division of Adult Correction's risk assessment program requires the highest possible level of supervision and monitoring.

(3) Any offender who is convicted of G.S. 14-27.2A or G.S. 14-27.4A, who shall be enrolled in the satellite-based monitoring program for the offender's natural life upon termination of the offender's active punishment.

(b) In developing the guidelines for the program, the Division of Adult Correction shall require that any offender who is enrolled in the satellite-based program submit to an active continuous satellite-based monitoring program, unless an active program will not work as provided by this section. If the Division of Adult Correction determines that an active program will not work as provided by this section, then the Division of Adult Correction shall require that the defendant submit to a passive continuous satellite-based program that works within the technological or geographical limitations.

(c) The satellite-based monitoring program shall use a system that provides all of the following:

(1) Time-correlated and continuous tracking of the geographic location of the subject using a global positioning system based on satellite and other location tracking technology.

(2) Reporting of subject's violations of prescriptive and proscriptive schedule or location requirements. Frequency of reporting may range from once a day (passive) to near real-time (active).

(d) The Division of Adult Correction may contract with a single vendor for the hardware services needed to monitor subject offenders and correlate their movements to reported crime incidents. The contract may provide for services necessary to implement or facilitate any of the provisions of this Part. (2006-

247, s. 15(a); 2007-213, s. 1; 2007-484, s. 42(b); 2008-117, s. 16; 2011-145, s. 19.1(h).)

§ 14-208.40A. Determination of satellite-based monitoring requirement by court.

(a) When an offender is convicted of a reportable conviction as defined by G.S. 14-208.6(4), during the sentencing phase, the district attorney shall present to the court any evidence that (i) the offender has been classified as a sexually violent predator pursuant to G.S. 14-208.20, (ii) the offender is a recidivist, (iii) the conviction offense was an aggravated offense, (iv) the conviction offense was a violation of G.S. 14-27.2A or G.S. 14-27.4A, or (v) the offense involved the physical, mental, or sexual abuse of a minor. The district attorney shall have no discretion to withhold any evidence required to be submitted to the court pursuant to this subsection.

The offender shall be allowed to present to the court any evidence that the district attorney's evidence is not correct.

(b) After receipt of the evidence from the parties, the court shall determine whether the offender's conviction places the offender in one of the categories described in G.S. 14-208.40(a), and if so, shall make a finding of fact of that determination, specifying whether (i) the offender has been classified as a sexually violent predator pursuant to G.S. 14-208.20, (ii) the offender is a recidivist, (iii) the conviction offense was an aggravated offense, (iv) the conviction offense was a violation of G.S. 14-27.2A or G.S. 14-27.4A, or (v) the offense involved the physical, mental, or sexual abuse of a minor.

(c) If the court finds that the offender has been classified as a sexually violent predator, is a recidivist, has committed an aggravated offense, or was convicted of G.S. 14-27.2A or G.S. 14-27.4A, the court shall order the offender to enroll in a satellite-based monitoring program for life.

(d) If the court finds that the offender committed an offense that involved the physical, mental, or sexual abuse of a minor, that the offense is not an aggravated offense or a violation of G.S. 14-27.2A or G.S. 14-27.4A and the offender is not a recidivist, the court shall order that the Division of Adult Correction do a risk assessment of the offender. The Division of Adult

Correction shall have a minimum of 30 days, but not more than 60 days, to complete the risk assessment of the offender and report the results to the court.

(e) Upon receipt of a risk assessment from the Division of Adult Correction pursuant to subsection (d) of this section, the court shall determine whether, based on the Division of Adult Correction's risk assessment, the offender requires the highest possible level of supervision and monitoring. If the court determines that the offender does require the highest possible level of supervision and monitoring, the court shall order the offender to enroll in a satellite-based monitoring program for a period of time to be specified by the court. (2007-213, s. 2; 2008-117, s. 16.1; 2011-145, s. 19.1(h).)

§ 14-208.40B. Determination of satellite-based monitoring requirement in certain circumstances.

(a) When an offender is convicted of a reportable conviction as defined by G.S. 14-208.6(4), and there has been no determination by a court on whether the offender shall be required to enroll in satellite-based monitoring, the Division of Adult Correction shall make an initial determination on whether the offender falls into one of the categories described in G.S. 14-208.40(a).

(b) If the Division of Adult Correction determines that the offender falls into one of the categories described in G.S. 14-208.40(a), the district attorney, representing the Division of Adult Correction, shall schedule a hearing in superior court for the county in which the offender resides. The Division of Adult Correction shall notify the offender of the Division of Adult Correction's determination and the date of the scheduled hearing by certified mail sent to the address provided by the offender pursuant to G.S. 14-208.7. The hearing shall be scheduled no sooner than 15 days from the date the notification is mailed. Receipt of notification shall be presumed to be the date indicated by the certified mail receipt. Upon the court's determination that the offender is indigent and entitled to counsel, the court shall assign counsel to represent the offender at the hearing pursuant to rules adopted by the Office of Indigent Defense Services.

(c) At the hearing, the court shall determine if the offender falls into one of the categories described in G.S. 14-208.40(a). The court shall hold the hearing and make findings of fact pursuant to G.S. 14-208.40A.

If the court finds that (i) the offender has been classified as a sexually violent predator pursuant to G.S. 14-208.20, (ii) the offender is a recidivist, (iii) the conviction offense was an aggravated offense, or (iv) the conviction offense was a violation of G.S. 14-27.2A or G.S. 14-27.4A, the court shall order the offender to enroll in satellite-based monitoring for life.

If the court finds that the offender committed an offense that involved the physical, mental, or sexual abuse of a minor, that the offense is not an aggravated offense or a violation of G.S. 14-27.2A or G.S. 14-27.4A, and the offender is not a recidivist, the court shall order that the Division of Adult Correction do a risk assessment of the offender. The Division of Adult Correction shall have a minimum of 30 days, but not more than 60 days, to complete the risk assessment of the offender and report the results to the court. The Division of Adult Correction may use a risk assessment of the offender done within six months of the date of the hearing.

Upon receipt of a risk assessment from the Division of Adult Correction, the court shall determine whether, based on the Division of Adult Correction's risk assessment, the offender requires the highest possible level of supervision and monitoring. If the court determines that the offender does require the highest possible level of supervision and monitoring, the court shall order the offender to enroll in a satellite-based monitoring program for a period of time to be specified by the court. (2007-213, s. 3; 2007-484, s. 42(b); 2008-117, s. 16.2; 2009-387, s. 4; 2011-145, s. 19.1(h).)

§ 14-208.40C. Requirements of enrollment.

(a) Any offender required to enroll in satellite-based monitoring pursuant to G.S. 14-208.40A or G.S. 14-208.40B who receives an active sentence shall be enrolled and receive the appropriate equipment immediately upon the offender's release from the Section of Prisons of the Division of Adult Correction.

(b) Any offender required to enroll in satellite-based monitoring pursuant to G.S. 14-208.40A or G.S. 14-208.40B who receives an intermediate punishment shall, immediately upon sentencing, report to the Section of Community Corrections of the Division of Adult Correction for enrollment in the satellite-based monitoring program, and, if necessary, shall return at any time designated by that Division to receive the appropriate equipment. If the intermediate sentence includes a required period of imprisonment, the offender shall not be required to be enrolled in the satellite-based monitoring program during the period of imprisonment.

(c) Any offender required to enroll in satellite-based monitoring pursuant to G.S. 14-208.40A or G.S. 14-208.40B who receives a community punishment shall, immediately upon sentencing, report to the Section of Community Corrections of the Division of Adult Correction for enrollment in the satellite-based monitoring program, and, if necessary, shall return at any time designated by that Section to receive the appropriate equipment. (2007-213, s. 4; 2007-484, s. 42(b); 2011-145, s. 19.1(j), (k).)

§ 14-208.41. Enrollment in satellite-based monitoring programs mandatory; length of enrollment.

(a) Any person described by G.S. 14-208.40(a)(1) shall enroll in a satellite-based monitoring program with the Section of Community Corrections of the Division of Adult Correction office in the county where the person resides. The person shall remain enrolled in the satellite-based monitoring program for the registration period imposed under G.S. 14-208.23 which is the person's life, unless the requirement to enroll in the satellite-based monitoring program is terminated pursuant to G.S. 14-208.43.

(b) Any person described by G.S. 14-208.40(a)(2) who is ordered by the court pursuant to G.S. 14-208.40A or G.S. 14-208.40B to enroll in a satellite-based monitoring program shall do so with the Section of Community Corrections of the Division of Adult Correction office in the county where the person resides. The person shall remain enrolled in the satellite-based monitoring program for the period of time ordered by the court.

(c) Any person described by G.S. 14-208.40(a)(3), upon completion of active punishment, shall enroll in a satellite-based monitoring program with the Section of Community Corrections of the Division of Adult Correction office in the county where the person resides. The person shall enroll in the satellite-based monitoring program for the entire period of post-release supervision and shall remain enrolled in the satellite-based monitoring program for the person's life, unless the requirement to enroll in the satellite-based monitoring program is terminated pursuant to G.S. 14-208.43. (2006-247, s. 15(a); 2007-213, s. 13; 2007-484, s. 42(b); 2008-117, s. 17; 2008-187, s. 5; 2011-145, s. 19.1(k).)

§ 14-208.42. Offenders required to submit to satellite-based monitoring required to cooperate with Division of Adult Correction upon completion of sentence.

Notwithstanding any other provision of law, when an offender is required to enroll in satellite-based monitoring pursuant to G.S. 14-208.40A or G.S. 14-208.40B, upon completion of the offender's sentence and any term of parole, post-release supervision, intermediate punishment, or supervised probation that follows the sentence, the offender shall continue to be enrolled in the satellite-based monitoring program for the period required by G.S. 14-208.40A or G.S. 14-208.40B unless the requirement that the person enroll in a satellite-based monitoring program is terminated pursuant to G.S. 14-208.43.

The Division of Adult Correction shall have the authority to have contact with the offender at the offender's residence or to require the offender to appear at a specific location as needed for the purpose of enrollment, to receive monitoring equipment, to have equipment examined or maintained, and for any other purpose necessary to complete the requirements of the satellite-based monitoring program. The offender shall cooperate with the Division of Adult Correction and the requirements of the satellite-based monitoring program until the offender's requirement to enroll is terminated and the offender has returned all monitoring equipment to the Division of Adult Correction. (2006-247, s. 15(a); 2007-213, s. 5; 2007-484, s. 42(b); 2011-145, s. 19.1(h).)

§ 14-208.43. Request for termination of satellite-based monitoring requirement.

(a) An offender described by G.S. 14-208.40(a)(1) or G.S. 14-208.40(a)(3) who is required to submit to satellite-based monitoring for the offender's life may file a request for termination of monitoring requirement with the Post-Release Supervision and Parole Commission. The request to terminate the satellite-based monitoring requirement and to terminate the accompanying requirement of unsupervised probation may not be submitted until at least one year after the offender: (i) has served his or her sentence for the offense for which the satellite-based monitoring requirement was imposed, and (ii) has also completed any period of probation, parole, or post-release supervision imposed as part of the sentence.

(b) Upon receipt of the request for termination, the Commission shall review documentation contained in the offender's file and the statewide registry to determine whether the person has complied with the provisions of this Article. In addition, the Commission shall conduct fingerprint-based state and federal criminal history record checks to determine whether the person has been convicted of any additional reportable convictions.

(c) If it is determined that the person has not received any additional reportable convictions during the period of satellite-based monitoring and the person has substantially complied with the provisions of this Article, the Commission may terminate the monitoring requirement if the Commission finds that the person is not likely to pose a threat to the safety of others.

(d) If it is determined that the person has received any additional reportable convictions during the period of satellite-based monitoring or has not substantially complied with the provisions of this Article, the Commission shall not order the termination of the monitoring requirement.

(d1) Notwithstanding the provisions of this section, if the Commission is notified by the Division of Adult Correction of the Department of Public Safety that the offender has been released, pursuant to G.S. 14-208.12A, from the requirement to register under Part 2 of Article 27A of this Chapter, upon request of the offender, the Commission shall order the termination of the monitoring requirement.

(e) The Commission shall not consider any request to terminate a monitoring requirement except as provided by this section. The Commission has no authority to consider or terminate a monitoring requirement for an offender described in G.S. 14-208.40(a)(2). (2006-247, s. 15(a); 2007-213, s. 11; 2007-484, s. 42(b); 2008-117, s. 18; 2011-145, s. 19.1(h).)

§ 14-208.44. Failure to enroll; tampering with device.

(a) Any person required to enroll in a satellite-based monitoring program who fails to enroll shall be guilty of a Class F felony.

(b) Any person who intentionally tampers with, removes, vandalizes, or otherwise interferes with the proper functioning of a device issued pursuant to a satellite-based monitoring program to a person duly enrolled in the program shall be guilty of a Class E felony.

(c) Any person required to enroll in a satellite-based monitoring program who fails to provide necessary information to the Division of Adult Correction, or fails to cooperate with the Division of Adult Correction's guidelines and regulations for the program shall be guilty of a Class 1 misdemeanor.

(d) For purposes of this section, "enroll" shall include appearing, as directed by the Division of Adult Correction, to receive the necessary equipment. (2006-247, s. 15(a); 2007-213, s. 6; 2011-145, s. 19.1(h).)

§ 14-208.45. Fees.

(a) Except as provided in subsections (b) and (b1) of this section, each person required to enroll pursuant to this Part shall pay a one-time fee of ninety dollars ($90.00). The fee shall be payable to the clerk of superior court, and the fees shall be remitted quarterly to the Division of Adult Correction of the Department of Public Safety. This fee is intended to offset only the costs associated with the time-correlated tracking of the geographic location of subjects using the location tracking crime correlation system.

(b) When a court determines a person is required to enroll pursuant to G.S. 14-208.40A or G.S. 14-208.40B, the court may exempt a person from paying the fee required by subsection (a) of this section only for good cause and upon motion of the person required to enroll in satellite-based monitoring. The court may require that the fee be paid in advance or in a lump sum or sums, and a probation officer may require payment by those methods.

(c) When a person is required to enroll based on a determination by the Division of Adult Correction pursuant to G.S. 14-208.40B, the Division of Adult Correction shall have the authority to exempt the person from paying the fee only for good cause and upon request of the person required to enroll in satellite-based monitoring. The Division of Adult Correction may require that the fee be paid in advance or in a lump sum or sums, and a probation officer may require payment by those methods. (2006-247, s. 15(a); 2007-213, s. 12; 2007-484, ss. 42(a), (b); 2011-145, s. 19.1(h).)

SUBCHAPTER VIII. OFFENSES AGAINST PUBLIC JUSTICE.

Article 28.

Perjury.

§ 14-209. Punishment for perjury.

If any person shall willfully and corruptly commit perjury, on his oath or affirmation, in any suit, controversy, matter or cause, depending in any of the courts of the State, or in any deposition or affidavit taken pursuant to law, or in any oath or affirmation duly administered of or concerning any matter or thing whereof such person is lawfully required to be sworn or affirmed, every person so offending shall be punished as a Class F felon. (1791, c. 338, s. 1, P.R.; R.C., c. 34, s. 49; Code, s. 1092; Rev., s. 3615; C.S., s. 4364; 1979, c. 760, s. 5; 1979, 2nd Sess., c. 1316, s. 47; 1981, c. 63, s.1, c. 179, s. 14; 1993, c. 539, s. 1202; 1994, Ex. Sess., c. 24, s. 14(c).)

§ 14-210. Subornation of perjury.

If any person shall, by any means, procure another person to commit such willful and corrupt perjury as is mentioned in G.S. 14-209, the person so offending shall be punished as a Class I felon. (1791, c. 338, s. 2, P.R.; R.C., c. 34, s. 50; Code, s. 1093; Rev., s. 3616; C.S., s. 4365; 1993, c. 539, s. 1203; 1994, Ex. Sess., c. 24, s. 14(c).)

§ 14-211. Perjury before legislative committees.

If any person shall willfully and corruptly swear falsely to any fact material to the investigation of any matter before any committee or commission of either house of the General Assembly, he shall be subject to all the pains and penalties of willful and corrupt perjury, and, on conviction in the Superior Court of Wake County, shall be punished as a Class I felon. (1869-70, c. 5, s. 4; Code, s. 2857; Rev., s. 3611; C.S., s. 4366; 1977, c. 344, s. 4; 1979, c. 760, s. 5; 1979, 2nd Sess., c. 1316, s. 47; 1981, c. 63, s. 1, c. 179, s. 14; 1993, c. 539, s. 1204; 1994, Ex. Sess., c. 24, s. 14(c).)

§ 14-212: Repealed by Session Laws 1994, Extra Session, c. 14, s. 71(7).

§§ 14-213 through 14-216: Repealed by Session Laws 1989 (Reg. Sess., 1990), c. 1054, s. 6.

Article 29.

Bribery.

§ 14-217. Bribery of officials.

(a) If any person holding office, or who has filed a notice of candidacy for or been nominated for such office, under the laws of this State who, except in payment of his legal salary, fees or perquisites, shall receive, or consent to receive, directly or indirectly, anything of value or personal advantage, or the promise thereof, for performing or omitting to perform any official act, which lay within the scope of his official authority and was connected with the discharge of his official and legal duties, or with the express or implied understanding that his official action, or omission to act, is to be in any degree influenced thereby, he shall be punished as a Class F felon.

(b) Indictments issued under these provisions shall specify:

(1) The thing of value or personal advantage sought to be obtained; and

(2) The specific act or omission sought to be obtained; and

(3) That the act or omission sought to be obtained lay within the scope of the defendant's official authority and was connected with the discharge of his official and legal duties.

(c) Repealed by Session Laws 1993 (Reg. Sess., 1994), c. 539, s. 1207.

(d) For purposes of this section, a thing of value or personal advantage shall include a campaign contribution made or received under Article 22A of Chapter 163 of the General Statutes. (1868-9, c. 176, s. 2; Code, s. 991; Rev., s. 3568; C.S., s. 4372; 1979, c. 760, s. 5; 1979, 2nd Sess., c. 1316, s. 47; 1981, c. 63, s. 1; c. 179, s. 14; 1983 (Reg. Sess., 1984), c. 1050, s. 1; 1993, c. 539, ss. 1206, 1207; 1994, Ex. Sess., c. 24, s. 14(c); 2010-169, s. 3(a).)

§ 14-218. Offering bribes.

If any person shall offer a bribe, whether it be accepted or not, he shall be punished as a Class F felon. (1870-1, c. 232; Code, s. 992; Rev., s. 3569; C.S., s. 4373; 1979, c. 760, s. 5; 1979, 2nd Sess., c. 1316, s. 47; 1981, c. 63, s. 1, c. 179, s. 14; 1993, c. 539, s. 1208; 1994, Ex. Sess., c. 24, s. 14(c).)

§ 14-219. Repealed by Session Laws 1983, c. 780, s. 1.

§ 14-220. Bribery of jurors.

If any juror, either directly or indirectly, shall take anything from the plaintiff or defendant in a civil suit, or from any defendant in a State prosecution, or from any other person, to give his verdict, every such juror, and the person who shall give such juror any fee or reward to influence his verdict, or induce or procure him to make any gain or profit by his verdict, shall be punished as a Class F felon. (5 Edw. III, c. 10; 34 Edw. III, c. 8; 38 Edw. III, c. 12; R.C., c. 34, s. 34; Code, s. 990; Rev., s. 3697; C.S., s. 4375; 1979, c. 760, s. 5; 1979, 2nd Sess., c. 1316, s. 47; 1981, c. 63, s. 1, c. 179, s. 14; 1993, c. 539, s. 1209; 1994, Ex. Sess., c. 24, s. 14(c).)

Article 30.

Obstructing Justice.

§ 14-221. Breaking or entering jails with intent to injure prisoners.

If any person shall conspire to break or enter any jail or other place of confinement of prisoners charged with crime or under sentence, for the purpose of killing or otherwise injuring any prisoner confined therein; or if any person shall engage in breaking or entering any such jail or other place of confinement of such prisoners with intent to kill or injure any prisoner, he shall be punished as a Class F felon. (1893, c. 461, s. 1; Rev., s. 3698; C.S., s. 4376; 1979, c. 760, s. 5; 1979, 2nd Sess., c. 1316, s. 47; 1981, c. 63, s. 1, c. 179, s. 14; 1993, c. 539, s. 1210; 1994, Ex. Sess., c. 24, s. 14(c).)

§ 14-221.1. Altering, destroying, or stealing evidence of criminal conduct.

Any person who breaks or enters any building, structure, compartment, vehicle, file, cabinet, drawer, or any other enclosure wherein evidence relevant to any criminal offense or court proceeding is kept or stored with the purpose of altering, destroying or stealing such evidence; or any person who alters, destroys, or steals any evidence relevant to any criminal offense or court proceeding shall be punished as a Class I felon.

As used in this section, the word evidence shall mean any article or document in the possession of a law-enforcement officer or officer of the General Court of Justice being retained for the purpose of being introduced in evidence or having been introduced in evidence or being preserved as evidence. (1975, c. 806, ss. 1, 2; 1979, c. 760, s. 5; 1979, 2nd Sess., c. 1316, s. 47; 1981, c. 63, s. 1; c. 179, s. 14.)

§ 14-221.2. Altering court documents or entering unauthorized judgments.

Any person who without lawful authority intentionally enters a judgment upon or materially alters or changes any criminal or civil process, criminal or civil pleading, or other official case record is guilty of a Class H felony. (1979, c. 526; 1979, 2nd Sess., c. 1316, s. 14; 1981, c. 63, s. 1; c. 179, s. 14.)

§ 14-222: Repealed by Session Laws 1993 (Reg. Sess., 1994), c. 767, s. 30(12).

§ 14-223. Resisting officers.

If any person shall willfully and unlawfully resist, delay or obstruct a public officer in discharging or attempting to discharge a duty of his office, he shall be guilty of a Class 2 misdemeanor. (1889, c. 51, s. 1; Rev., s. 3700; C.S., s. 4378; 1969, c. 1224, s. 1; 1993, c. 539, s. 136; 1994, Ex. Sess., c. 24, s. 14(c).)

§ 14-224. Repealed by Session Laws 1973, c. 1286, s. 26.

§ 14-225. False reports to law enforcement agencies or officers.

(a)   Except as provided in subsection (b) of this section, any person who shall willfully make or cause to be made to a law enforcement agency or officer any false, deliberately misleading or unfounded report, for the purpose of interfering with the operation of a law enforcement agency, or to hinder or obstruct any law enforcement officer in the performance of his duty, shall be guilty of a Class 2 misdemeanor.

(b) A violation of subsection (a) of this section is punishable as a Class H felony if the false, deliberately misleading, or unfounded report relates to a law enforcement investigation involving the disappearance of a child as that term is defined in G.S. 14-318.5 or child victim of a Class A, B1, B2, or C felony offense. For purposes of this subsection, a child is any person who is less than 16 years of age. (1941, c. 363; 1969, c. 1224, s. 3; 1993, c. 539, s. 137; 1994, Ex. Sess., c. 23, ss. 1-3; c. 24, s. 14(c); 2013-52, s. 6.)

§ 14-225.1. Picketing or parading.

Any person who, with intent to interfere with, obstruct, or impede the administration of justice, or with intent to influence any justice or judge of the General Court of Justice, juror, witness, district attorney, assistant district attorney, or court officer, in the discharge of his duty, pickets, parades, or uses any sound truck or similar device within 300 feet of an exit from any building housing any court of the General Court of Justice, or within 300 feet of any building or residence occupied or used by such justice, judge, juror, witness, district attorney, assistant district attorney, or court officer, shall upon plea or conviction be guilty of a Class 1 misdemeanor. (1977, c. 266, s. 1; 1993, c. 539, s. 138; 1994, Ex. Sess., c. 24, s. 14(c).)

Vision Books Order Form

Fax Orders: 1-980-299-5965

Phone Orders: 1-704-898-0770

E-mail Orders: www.visionbooks.org

Mail Orders: Vision Books, LLC
P.O. Box 42406
Charlotte, NC 28215

Shipp To:
Name_____
Address_____
City_____State_____Zip_____
Phone_____Fax_____
Email_____@_____

Bill To: We can bill a third party on your behalf.
Name_____
Address_____
City_____State_____Zip_____
Phone____(_____)_____Fax_____
Email_____@_____

Pamphlet Number ($15.00 Each)	Qty	Total Cost
_____	_____	_____
_____	_____	_____
_____	_____	_____
_____	_____	_____
_____	_____	_____
_____	_____	_____
_____	_____	_____
_____	_____	_____
Full Volume Set 1-92	92 Pamphlets	1,380.00

Free Shipping Shipping & Handling on Full Volume Orders
Add $1.00 Shipping & Handling per pamphlet $_____

Total Cost $_____

Thank You for Your Support. Management!

DID YOU ENJOY THIS BOOK?

Vision Books, LLC would like to hear from you! If you or someone you know has been fasely imprisoned, we would like to hear your story. If the 'North Carolina Criminal Law and Procedure' has had an effect in your life or if you have suggestions, we would like to hear from you. Send your letters to:

Vision Books, LLC
Attn: Staff Writers
P.O. Box 42406
Charlotte, NC 28215
Email: staff@visionbooks.org

Order Additional Copies:

Fax Orders:	1-980-299-5965
Phone Orders:	1-704-898-0770
E-mail Orders:	www.visionbooks.org
Mail Orders:	Vision Books, LLC P.O. Box 42406 Charlotte, NC 28215

www.ingramcontent.com/pod-product-compliance
Lightning Source LLC
Chambersburg PA
CBHW071357170526
45165CB00001B/89